Encountering China

Aperçus: Histories Texts Cultures

a Bucknell series

Series Editor: Greg Clingham

Aperçu (apersü). 1882 [Fr.] *A summary exposition, a conspectus.*

Relations among historiography, culture and textual representation are presently complex and rich in possibilities. Aperçus is a series of books exploring the connections between these crucial terms. Revisionist in intention, Aperçus seeks to open up new possibilities for humanistic knowledge and study, and thus deepen and extend our understanding of what history, culture, and texts have been and are, as these terms are made to bear on each other by new thinking and writing.

Titles in the Series

Encountering China

Early Modern European
Responses

Edited by
Rachana Sachdev and
Qingjun Li

Lewisburg: Bucknell University Press

Published by Bucknell University Press

Co-published with The Rowman & Littlefield Publishing Group, Inc.

4501 Forbes Boulevard, Suite 200, Lanham, Maryland 20706

www.rowman.com

10 Thornbury Road, Plymouth PL6 7PP, United Kingdom

British Library Cataloguing in Publication Information Available

Library of Congress Cataloging-in-Publication Data

Encountering China : early modern European responses / edited by Rachana Sachdev and Qingjun Li.
  p. cm.
 Includes bibliographical references and index.
  ISBN 978-1-61148-438-0 (cloth : alk. paper) -- ISBN 978-1-61148-482-3 (pbk. : alk. paper) -- ISBN 978-1-61148-439-7 (electronic)
 1. China--Description and travel--Early works to 1800. 2. Europeans--China--History. 3. Travelers' writings, European. 4. China--Foreign public opinion, European. 5. European literature--Chinese influences. 6. Chinese literature--European influences. I. Sachdev, Rachana. II. Li, Qingjun.

 DS708.E63 2012
 303.48'2405109031--dc23

2012024133

This book is dedicated with love and gratitude
to our parents and to the next generation:
Wentao, Miranda, and Rohan

Contents

Acknowledgments

WE WOULD LIKE TO THANK THE ASIAN STUDIES
Development Program (ASDP) at the East West Center for fostering
the growth of our individual essays at its various conferences. It was at
an ASDP conference that we met and the book project was born.

Without Ronnie Littlejohn's encouragement, active involvement,
and help through all the stages of this project, it would have been a
much harder process. As the Chinese saying expresses, "when eating
bamboo sprouts, remember the man who planted them." Thank you,
Ronnie, friend and mentor *par excellence*, for your caring and generosity.

We acknowledge our debt to Greg Clingham, director of Bucknell University Press, for his support of this endeavor, and to the
anonymous reader whose careful and detailed suggestions have vastly
improved this manuscript.

Rachana Sachdev: I am grateful to Susquehanna University for the
sabbatical that allowed me to write my chapter and edit the manuscript.
Patricia Akhimie and other members of Mary Fuller's "Reading Voyages and Travels" seminar at the Shakespeare Association of America
Annual Conference in 2009 enriched the essay through their comments
on an early version, as did participants at ASDP and ASIANetwork
conferences. I thank Crystal VanHorn for her technological assistance.
I'd also like to express my gratitude to Peter Hershock who offered
invaluable suggestions on my essay and whose support was essential
for seeing this project through. Puja Paul deserves a special mention for
being there for me through all my emergencies, however minor, and for
various bits of practical help. My sisters, Shabnam and Vandana, have
been the best friends and the most supportive family one could ever
hope for. Finally and most importantly, I thank my children, Miranda
and Rohan, for filling my life with joy.

Qingjun Li: I owe enormous gratitude to Ronnie Littlejohn, who
has been my mentor, colleague, and friend over the years of my graduate study and teaching in the United States. It is he who introduced
me to the ASDP conference and encouraged me to present my papers
there. I am also indebted to Dr. Marion Hollings, who guided me in

generating a paper in one of my graduate seminars. That paper was an early version of the current form of my paper in this collection. Last but not least, I want to thank sincerely each of our contributors for this book. They have worked untiringly in revising their essays numerous times. My son, Wentao, has also given me consistent encouragement and support in the whole process of the project. My appreciation and affection for him are beyond words.

For both of us, editing this book has been about discovering a new and vital friendship. This book is a testament to our great affection and admiration for each other.

Rachana Sachdev and Qingjun Li

Rachana Sachdev, Susquehanna University

*I*ntroduction

OVER THE LAST FEW DECADES, THE WESTERN WORLD has had to contend with China's undoubted economic might and its growing ascendancy in political and military power. Books are published with increasing frequency with titles such as *When China Rules the World: The End of the Western World and the Birth of a New Global Order*, and *China Shakes the World: A Titan's Rise and Troubled Future*. These studies have begun to contemplate a future dominated by China.[1] News reports emphasize the Chinese ability to keep the economic growth rate poised around an astounding 10 percent, its status as the world's second-largest economy, and its 1.3 billion plus people which comprise the largest market in the world. Propelled possibly by this monetary resurgence in China, economic historians over the last couple of decades have begun to analyze the patterns of trade and commerce in the beginning of the early modern era, and assert with confidence that the current dominance of China in the global economy is matched by its past glories. Andre Gunder Frank even boldly asserts that, in the early modern era, "if any economy had a 'central' position and role in the world economy and its possible hierarchy of 'centers,' it was China."[2] In consonance with his views, Frank terms the early modern era the "Asian Age," with China as its principal player. This new perspective is obviously vastly different from a Eurocentric worldview which saw the early modern era as the dawning of European supremacy and emphasized European civilization and its control of resources, based primarily on an Enlightenment and Industrialization model. In many ways, the Western response to China is about to come full circle—though tonally much more celebratory, the first European encounters with China, which are the focus of the essays in this collection, resulted in glowing reports about the country's fabled wealth, its economic successes, and its cultured civilization.

Understandably, given the centrality of trade and commerce to the cross-cultural contact between Asia and Europe after the discovery of the route around the Cape of Good Hope, the focus of the recent revisionist histories of the early modern European encounters with China has so far been on the economic.[3] These studies supplement the valuable analyses of the missionary activity in Asia offered by earlier sinologists[4] and the more recent interdisciplinary examinations of gender and family relations by cultural historians.[5] Lately, though, reflection on early contact has filtered down to literary critics who, in their examination of works from the early modern canon, have begun to claim with increasing frequency that the early European interactions with the East cannot be characterized as fully colonialist or Orientalist. In his work *Ideographia* (2001), David Porter argues that the interest in linguistic and cultural universalism exhibited in the work of early modern thinkers who both constructed and drew upon the travel-genre narratives devoted to China demonstrated how that culture was used as a cipher for many types of European problems. *Sinographies: Writing China*, edited by Eric Hayot, Haun Saussy, and Steven G. Yao, has taken up the challenge of rewriting China for the twenty-first-century scholars, with essays that range in their reassessment from the early modern period to the present. Robert Markley in his excellent study, *The Far East and the English Imagination, 1600–1730*, has used the insights of the economic historians to think through early modern English trade relations with China, Japan, and the Spice Islands and their literary representations.[6]

Our intervention in this scholarly evaluation takes the form of examining the early modern European encounters with just one country, China. Essays by Sachdev, Li, Littlejohn, and Mazurak focus on narratives presenting themselves as based on travelogue testimonies from the

2

early sixteenth century to the late eighteenth. The authors of the essays analyze sources such as those by Galeote Pereira (1565), Gaspar da Cruz (1569/70), the early Jesuits (1580s), and Mendes Pinto (written in the 1570s and published in 1614); as well as Juan Gonzalez de Mendoza's *The Historie of the Great and Mightie Kingdom of China* (1585) and Matteo Ricci's *Journals* (1615). These authors also set their interpretations of early modern works in the context of the earliest European writings available on China and the East, including those by Marco Polo (1298), Odoric of Pordenone (1340), and Sir John Mandeville (circa 1360), although no author considers pre-sixteenth century sources as "early modern." In addition, the essays by Dooghan and Ma focus most directly on novels in China and early modern Europe as forms of literature which can reveal much about these two great cultures in the historical period demarcated. In its concentration on China from the early sixteenth to the late eighteenth centuries, its expansive understanding of the travel-genre, and its coverage of the emergence of the novel in China and Europe, our collection of essays is closest to the approach employed in Adrian Hsia's *The Vision of China in the English Literature of the Seventeenth and Eighteenth Centuries* though it ranges outside the textual, chronological, and disciplinary boundaries established by Hsia's study.

3

The situation for the Europeans in their early contacts with China was different in several ways than even in India and Japan. While they were able to get strong footholds in Goa and Kyushu fairly quickly after their arrival in each country, the Portuguese were unsuccessful with their first embassy to Peking in 1517 and only managed to locate a tentative base in Macau in 1557. As Donald Lach documents, it took the Portuguese "most of a century" to get answers to the basic questions about China.[7] In the early years, contact with China was minimal and was limited to trading in Canton or certain ports in Kwangtung (modern Guangdong) and Fukien (Fujian) provinces. The Europeans got some rudimentary reports about the country from Tomé Pires, the leader of the 1517 Portuguese embassy, and from the letters sent by two of the embassy who were held captive in China along with Pires. Subsequent information about China was mostly obtained from visitors who stayed in China for a few months during trade or missionary trips. As Alessandro Valignano, who was sent by the Jesuits to East Asia in

1573, understood, the strategies adopted by the missionaries in all other places were ineffective in China. He recommended the policy of cultural accommodation to adjust to the high level of civilization found in China. Matteo Ricci, the main adopter of Valignano's vision in China, was finally able to make significant sustained contact in his twenty-seven years (1583–1610) of living in the country. In the meanwhile, however, Europe remained thirsty for news about this mighty kingdom, as is evident from the fact that Mendoza's history of China, which was commissioned by Pope Gregory XIII in 1583, was translated into all major European languages within a few years of its publication and is believed to have been read by all the educated people in Europe. The laudatory tone about China remained predominant in most early accounts of the country, even when religious differences could have and did sometimes lead to easy dismissal and denigration. The positive portrayal continued in the seventeenth and eighteenth centuries, though with some different permutations and combinations, as the vogue for all things Chinese, Chinoiserie, became a major cultural determinant all over Europe by the eighteenth century.

In focusing on the constructions of China available to early modern Europeans, the authors in this collection provide glimpses of Ming and early-Qing China both from within and without. While their primary focus remains the external gaze obtained through the European sources about China, the essays are also centrally concerned with grounding the analysis in an understanding of the Chinese worldview from the period. The collection brings together scholars of literature, religion, and Chinese language to focus on source material in the early modern period which offered itself as providing information on China based on travel and eyewitness reports. Accordingly, the authors make use of histories, journals, and reports written as travel recollections. Some essays are directly comparative, working with Chinese and European texts simultaneously; others engage Chinese history or Chinese primary texts from the time period to think through the European representations of China. In addition, the contributors reproduce the moment of contact by setting Chinese literary and historical texts in dialogue with European ones of the same period or on similar subjects. In this respect, this volume of essays differs significantly even from other collections that combine perspectives from different disciplines, such as Daniel Carey's *Asian Travel in the Renaissance*.

In addition, the authors have deliberately chosen to work with narratives from various early modern European nations, published originally in several languages including Latin, Spanish, Portuguese, Italian, and Dutch. Recognizing that most of these narratives were translated into English and other European languages almost immediately upon publication, the essays are based on the premise that national boundaries are not a useful limiting category for an analysis of the early European contact with China. As Kate Teltscher points out, until the mid-eighteenth century, it is probably more accurate to speak of a European discourse of the East, rather than a construction of China demarcated by the national identity of the author or editor, because of the rapid translations of all accounts into various European languages.[8] It is also important to understand that both collaboration and competition defined the early modern national travel to the East. For example, Macao was a Portuguese stronghold and the Portuguese tried to keep the Spanish away from it; however, while national tensions surfaced most clearly in the political sphere, the demands of evangelism could not be supplied by one nation alone. There were Spanish Jesuits as well as Portuguese during the early years of eastern travel. In addition, the first missionaries to China differed not only in their national origins, but also in their religious affiliations: there were twenty-five Jesuits, twenty-two Franciscans, one Dominican, and one Augustinian who visited China between 1552 and 1583.[9] Both Spanish friars and Portuguese Jesuits wrote early accounts of China; Michele Ruggieri and Matteo Ricci, the two Jesuit pioneers of the China mission in the 1580s, were both Italian, as was the architect of the policy of accommodation in China, Alessandro Valignano. The most famous history of China in the sixteenth century was composed by the Spanish writer, Juan González de Mendoza, at the behest of the Pope, even though China was in the Portuguese missionary zone according to the Treaty of Tordesillas. While we may recognize the necessity of distinguishing between various European nations and the problem of collapsing together the rivals for the East, the Portuguese and the Spanish, as European, it is also true that in the early years of travel, the Jesuits recruited missionaries to China from various European nations, and that the Portuguese and the Spanish were forced to work together. The essays in this collection are based on the recognition of these necessities of early modern travel in China.

Rachana Sachdev's essay deals with this recognition head on and makes use of a rich diversity of European sources on Ming China, incorporating analyses of letters, diaries, narratives by both laymen and missionaries, and larger compilations or histories undertaken by writers both with and no direct knowledge of the country. Such variety in source materials fits the plan of the collection because the authors are concerned with all those kinds of texts that presented themselves to early modern Europeans as based on actual travel encounter with China. Sachdev's project focuses on an area of knowledge generally not accessible to casual, external scrutiny that we might assume to be the major source of knowledge for the linguistically challenged Europeans in China—the position of children. However, the early modern maritime travelers were cognizant of the extensive social welfare policies adopted by the rulers of China for the protection of the children as well as the persistent problems with poverty within the culture. The Europeans observed an interesting social dilemma—many poor Chinese sold their children for money or abandoned them despite the fact that the society as a whole seemed wealthy and had many well-planned and well-executed welfare policies in place. In her essay, Sachdev maps out the moments of European recognition of the customs of child abandonment and selling of children, and analyzes what impact, if any, these discoveries have on their understanding of Ming China. She concludes that it is exactly the presence of the public support system that keeps the image of a wealthy China untarnished despite the presence of the more visible poor in late Ming China. The common European contention that there were no beggars in Ming China excused the fact that some Chinese families abandoned their unwanted infants at birth or sold their children.

As China prepares to enjoy its hard-won economic power in the twenty-first century, it is instructive to note that in earlier eras, reports of Chinese wealth were contextualized by reports of its intricate sociopolitical organization and its extensive public welfare policies. China existed almost as a synonym for utopia for early modern Europeans both because it contained large quantities of goods for trade and because it was able to care successfully for its large population containing more than 150 million people. Report after report testified to the many hospitals for the poor and the sick established in each city and to China's streets being free of beggars at a time when the reality of socioeconomic hardships was evident everywhere in Europe.

China had a surplus of goods, and an extensive infrastructure for flow of trade and people; in addition, it had a society which, at least to external scrutiny, seemed well controlled and orderly. Travelogues commented on the quiet, almost invisible Chinese women and added to the portrait of a perfectly governed society in which everyone followed a rational, hierarchical order and contributed equally and without dissension for the common good. Unlike England, where in the early seventeenth century, patriarchal social order was being challenged by rebellious women often cross-dressed as men and widows who controlled young men's access to property, upper-class Chinese women were reportedly perfectly docile and obedient. They bound their feet, kept themselves busy weaving and spinning, and only went out, when necessary, in close chairs, inaccessible even by sight to all men. Their chastity and social containment were lauded as exemplary by European travelers hoping to find transcultural truths that would help them solve some of the crises riddling the societies back home.

Qingjun Li's analysis of narratives functioning as early modern travelogues about China sets these sources in dialogue with the English conduct books for women. In "Of Golden Lilies and Gentlewomen: Constructions of Chinese Women in Early Modern European Travel Narratives," she argues that the demands for greater gender equality by English women were presented as deviations from the perceived universal pattern of women's conduct found in other advanced cultures, of which China was considered a prime example. Her essay includes an appraisal of the ways in which views of Chinese women and their roles were turned into ideals that mirrored those vigorously defended by dozens of male writers in early modern England. Attempts to move outside of the accepted gender models met with what can only be called misogynistic reactions. These reactions were based on several foundations, one of which was an appeal to the belief that the place of women in society was supported by transcultural gender truths. European travel narratives played an important role in providing supporting evidence for those who wished to defend restrictions on women's conduct and roles in English society because from the sixteenth to the mid-eighteenth centuries, they constituted the principal source genre providing information about women and gender in China. Li's essay offers an overview of the substance of the most important of these European travel reports about women and then provides an analytical study of how these writings were actually applied in the gender struggles of England by English writers. For the English writers, reports about China conveniently provided the model of docility for women needed to sustain their views on gender relations. In their travels to China, the Europeans had found a society that not only matched but also exceeded the wealth, technological sophistication, and social organization that they had proudly vaunted in their experiences with other non-European nations. They were forced to yield their notions of cultural superiority, fostered as a consequence of recent colonization of the Americas, and instead hope to emulate the example of orderliness and wealth found in China.

8

This image of China as a quasi-utopia was supplemented by discussions of its ancient and large-scale printing industry and of the excellence of its literary products. If the Europeans hoped to emulate China's financial and social successes, they also drew inspiration from Chinese literature. In Johann Wolfgang Goethe's famous words, "the Chinese think, act, and feel almost exactly like us; and we soon find that we are perfectly like them, except that all they do is more clear, pure, and decorous, than with us."[10] Part of the background for such an appraisal lies in the discovery of the similarity of themes and ideas, styles and forms, between Chinese and European literatures. The novel developed as a nascent form in both China and Europe at about the same time, suggesting that similar philosophical and ideological changes were happening across the seas, further propelling the search for transcultural truths.

In his essay, "Earlier Moderns: The Novel Form as National Development in China and Europe," Daniel Dooghan argues that the development of China's polyphonic literary tradition through the late Ming anticipates the European cultural modernization during the Renaissance. Early European visitors to China encountered not only a politically and economically advanced state, but also an intellectual climate that recognized its own modernity. Dooghan's comparative analysis of seminal works from the Chinese and European vernaculars, *Journey to the West* and *Don Quixote*, respectively, reveals similar concerns with nascent national identity and the status of tradition that mark the emergence of a modern, national culture. Chinese vernacular fiction, over the course of its centuries-long development, appropriated the formal elements of many other literary genres. When the novel emerges in its extant form during the Ming, it does so as an archive of historically marked forms subordinated to an overarching narrative. Although the formal evolution of the European novel differs significantly from that of its Chinese counterpart, it exhibits many of the same qualities when it appears in the early seventeenth century. The way in which vernacular fiction in both contexts deploys similar literary forms in the same period historically indicates an awareness of all preceding periods as qualitatively similar—past—in contrast to the distinction of the present—modern. Furthermore, this consciously modern genre contains within it recognition of "civilizational others," suggesting a conception of the state as nation.

The continuities and resemblances between literary works in China and Europe that existed in the sixteenth century can also be traced into the eighteenth, as Ning Ma undertakes to do in her essay. The desire for socially constrained women remained strong enough in English literature of the eighteenth century to become an important ideological goal in the developing genre of the novel. As the late seventeenth century in England imposed its literal domestication of women in the household through a stricter moral code, chastity became defined as the preeminent female virtue. In many ways, novelistic representations of English women began to resemble the portraits of Chinese women drawn by European travel writers and by Chinese fiction writers as well. Sociopolitical and economic changes propelled the convergence of these traditions on gender and led to a similar emphasis on female virtue in China as well as in Europe.

In "'A Strong Resemblance': Samuel Richardson, Chinese Talent-Beauty Novels, and a Secret Origin of 'World Literature,'" Ning Ma asserts that a rarely discussed aspect of Goethe's groundbreaking notion of "World Literature" is that it was in fact inspired by a "strong resemblance" he observed between the works of Samuel Richardson and a few Chinese "talent-beauty" novels then translated into European languages. Her essay explores this curious cross-cultural convergence by arguing that the "resemblance" in question concerns a similar emphasis on the virtue of female chastity, a literary trend that points to a larger shift in both cultures when private conduct and inner sentiment began to take precedence over sociopolitical roles as the foundation of moral identity. Still more intriguingly, these parallel developments on both ends of the Eurasian continent can be traced to a common sociological grounding: that is, the weakening of traditional cultural values and social relationships in the face of a rapidly rising monetary economy—a widespread phenomenon in the early modern world inseparable from the emergence of a global trading network. These underlying global parallels and interconnections constitute a secret "origin" of the notion of "World Literature," which registers not just the birth of a concept, but also the contour of a world-historical moment shared by what seems to be the most distant places.

No matter how strong the resemblances were between their European cultures and the China they encountered in their travels, the missionaries in particular were unable to respond positively to the different practices and doctrines espoused by the Buddhists and Daoists in Ming and early-Qing China. As Ronnie Littlejohn discusses, the bias the missionaries supposedly demonstrated against the Chinese religions, in particular, Daoism and Buddhism, led Adam Smith in his *An Inquiry into the Nature and Causes of the Wealth of Nations* (1776) to appraise the travel writings of the Jesuits as the reports of "stupid and lying missionaries," and this evaluation has continued as a virtually unchallenged assumption down to the present. Indeed, T. H. Barrett writes in his "Chinese Religion in English Guise," that the English-language world sustained a description of China in its early depictions that was "at very considerable variance with the facts." In his essay, Littlejohn reconstructs the Jesuit portrayal of Daoism during the early modern period by focusing on the most significant contributions to the travel corpus during the time period from Matteo Ricci's *Journals* (1615) to the publication of Jean Baptiste Du Halde's *General History of China* (1736).

Littlejohn, as Terry Mazurak also does in his essay, makes use of the widely known English translation of the version of Ricci's *Journals* edited by Nicolas Trigault, a China Jesuit. Both authors are aware that Trigault may have omitted relevant happenings during Ricci's work in China in the interest of promoting the Jesuit mission. Moreover, Trigault embellished other matters in a descriptive style with a heavily pietistic reading of devotion both to Ricci and to Chrisitianity. Neither Mazurak nor Littlejohn compare Trigault's version to Ricci's original manuscript; instead, they regard Trigault's version as of interest in itself as part of the reconstruction of early modern accounts of Chinese Daoism and Buddhism respectively. Both commend to readers the three-volume Italian edition of Ricci's original *Journals* by Pasquale M. d'Elia and acknowledge that important extensions of their essays, for scholarship on Ricci particularly, could be forthcoming by those interested in a comparison of the materials from Trigault's version and the original as edited by d'Elia.

As Littlejohn works his way through the Jesuit materials on Daoism, he explains briefly but substantively what the most relevant beliefs and practices of Daoism in the Ming and Qing looked like as we can reconstruct them now. He brings this new knowledge into conversation with the reports of the most important Jesuits writing on China in the early modern period and poses the following questions. Is it the case, based on what the Jesuits reported and what we now know about Ming and Qing dynasty Daoism, that these descriptions were only the testimonies of "stupid and lying missionaries"? Did they, in fact, pass to Europe a lens for viewing Chinese Daoism that could only yield "variance with the facts"? His conclusion is that if we separate our current knowledge of Daoist activities and practices in the Jesuit narratives from the accounts offered by the missionaries, then the journals and letters of the Jesuits are, on the whole, largely accurate and revealing with respect to Daoist practices during the early modern period, although the spiritualized and Christian interpretations of their value and efficacy must be separated out.

If the missionaries rejected Daoism, despite their policy of cultural accommodation, their indictments against Buddhist "idolatry" were especially virulent, given that they had to disentangle themselves from the early associations they themselves had fostered between Christianity and Buddhism. Terry Mazurak, in "Buddhism and Idolatry," argues that in assessing the influence Chinese Buddhism had upon early modern Europe, it is instructive to bear in mind a point that apparently has been nearly universally overlooked: in all his years in China, Trigault's version of Ricci's *Journals* never presented him as knowingly encountering a Buddhist. The same may be said of those Europeans who visited China before him and those early modern Europeans who were so influenced by his reports. What the early modern Europeans were aware of in China was called simply "idolatry," a concept with an entirely different range of meaning, set of background assumptions, and functions than "Buddhism." However, "idolatry" in this context was supplanted in the mid-nineteenth century by "Buddhism," a specific interpretation of Asian reality offered by certain European academics which rapidly spread to the cultural elite and, later, the wider population.

Mazurak's essay revives, at least partially, the relevant early modern conception of idolatry in China in three steps. First, he offers a summary of the construction of "Buddhism" focusing upon the work of Eugene Burnouf. Then, he explores the contrasting meanings and functions of "idolatry" in the early modern European imagination by examining Juan Gonzales de Mendoza's and Matteo Ricci's accounts of what they called "the cult of Sciequa." Mazurak carefully makes the reader aware of the previously mentioned concerns that might arise from a use of Trigault's version of Ricci's *Journals* by consistentily referencing "Ricci-Trigault." Like Littlejohn, he stays with this version of Ricci from the early modern period because of its widespread usage. In the seventeenth century alone, it had five Latin editions, three French ones, and editions in German, Spanish, and Italian. Finally, he asks, "What have we lost in refusing to consider the possibility that idolatry is a legitimate human response to the world and that the belief that a god or a demon could animate a material representation of itself is not *a priori* primitive and irrational?" It is with this provocative question that this collection comes to a close.

We have omitted an analysis of the Christian response to Confucianism in the seventeenth and eighteenth centuries, even though the missionaries did successfully incorporate some Confucian ideas into their proselytizing efforts in the early years, because it has already been studied extensively. The Jesuits realized the necessity for a policy of cultural accommodation, of building bridges at least between Christianity and Confucianism; this policy was suggested by St. Francis Xavier in the mid-sixteenth century, orchestrated in China by Alessandro Valignano in the late 1570s, and exemplified preeminently by Ricci after he arrived in Macao in the 1580s. In their policies and actions, especially under Ricci's leadership, the Jesuits demonstrated the possibility of transculturalism.[11] Ricci realized that in order to reach the *literati*, those associated with the Jesuit mission had to make connections, translate texts from Chinese into Latin and vice versa, and share scientific and religious knowledge. However, the Christian missionaries also had to give up the Buddhist robes they had adopted as their dress on their arrival in China if they had to appeal successfully to the more refined cultural sensibilities of the Confucian scholar-officials. To succeed in their conversion efforts, they later chose to criticize both Buddhism and Daoism strenuously, portraying both as superstitious and as deliberately misleading the general population. However, in the early years at least, even this rejection of Buddhism and Daoism was still based on accommodations to other ideas, lifestyles, and practices within China. The missionaries dressed in the robes of the *literati*, allowed themselves to be carried in sedan chairs like them, and generally adopted a Chinese lifestyle while they lived in China.

The essays in this volume address the emerging motif of transcultural or universal truths appearing frequently in the travel-based genre writings of early moderns who, awed by the wealth and sophistication of the society they encountered, attempted primarily to build bridges, to explore similarities, and to emulate, though they were also selectively critical of some local traditions and practices. It was only much later, after the rejection of the policy of accommodation, after a host of political and economic changes both in Europe and in China during two centuries of contact, in the late-eighteenth century, that Goethe's sense of the superiority of the Chinese was finally lost from the European worldview. Our collection deals with the earlier period of vital contact when exchange of knowledge went hand in hand with trade, and when China led Europe because of its economic and organizational successes. What further distinguishes this collection is the attempt to engage directly with a wide range of source material which presented itself as providing information on China based on travel and eyewitness reports, including journals, reports, histories, travel fictions, and travelogues. These narratives are not treated merely as occasional sources of relevant information for understanding the early views of China spawned by them but as primary materials for analysis. We hope that in delving deep into the words and ideas of the early travelers to China, in exploring the European constructions of this "glorious" nation, and in pitting them against the Chinese self-constructions during the period, we have allowed the observations to retain their complexities and dissonances. We also hope to demonstrate that in this early period of contact, transculturalism was regarded as a real possibility, based on an exchange between advanced cultures.

Notes

1. See Joseph Kahn, "Waking Dragon," review of *When China Rules the World: The End of the Western World and the Birth of a New Global Order*, by Martin Jacques, *New York Times*, December 31, 2009, Sunday Book Review, www.nytimes.com/2010/01/03/books/review/Kahn-t.html.

2. Andre Gunder Frank, *ReOrient: Global Economy in the Asian Age* (Berkeley: University of California Press, 1998), 5.

3. Even the titles of the most prominent works on the topic show this. K. N. Chaudhuri, who led the movement, reassessed global relations in his 1990 publication, *Asia before Europe: Economy and Civilization of the Indian Ocean from the Rise of Islam to 1750* (Cambridge: Cambridge University Press, 1990). Other prominent works include Paul Bairoch, *Economics and World History: Myths and Paradoxes* (Hemel Hempstead: Harvester, 1993); R. Bin Wong, *China Transformed: Historical Change and the Limits of European Experience* (Ithaca, NY: Cornell University Press, 1997); Andre Gunder Frank, *ReOrient: Global Economy in the Asian Age* (Berkeley: University of California Press, 1997); Kenneth Pomeranz, *The Great Divergence: China, Europe, and the Making of the Modern World Economy* (Princeton, NJ: Princeton University Press, 2000). A large number of these books rely on data from the early Qing period, a period of prosperity and extensive trade relations.

4. There are too many excellent scholarly works, both recent and from the past, to be listed here. Prominent among them are studies by Jonathan Spence and David Mungello. See, in particular, David E. Mungello, *Curious Land: Jesuit Accommodation and the Origins of Sinology* (Honolulu: University of Hawai'i Press, 1989), and Liam Matthew Brockey, *Journey to the East: The Jesuit Mission to China, 1579–1724* (Cambridge, MA: Harvard University Press, 2008).

5. See, for example, Dorothy Ko, *Teachers of the Inner Chambers: Women and Culture in Seventeenth-Century China* (Stanford, CA: Stanford University Press, 1994); Susan Mann, *Precious Records: Women in China's Long Eighteenth Century* (Stanford, CA: Stanford University Press, 1997); Patricia Buckley Ebrey, *Women and the Family in Chinese History* (London: Routledge, 2003).

6. Significantly more attention has been paid to early modern relations with India. See, for instance, Joan-Pau Rubiés, *Travel and Ethnology in the Renaissance: South India through European Eyes, 1250–1625* (Cambridge: Cambridge University Press, 2000); Richmond Barbour, *Before Orien-*

talism: London's Theatre of the East, 1576–1626 (Cambridge: Cambridge University Press, 2003); and Pompa Banerjee, *Burning Women: Widows, Witches, and Early Modern European Travelers in India* (New York: Palgrave, 2003).

7. Donald Lach, *Asia in the Making of Europe* (Chicago: University of Chicago Press, 1965), Vol. 1, Bk. 2, 731.

8. Kate Teltscher, "India/Calcutta: City of Palaces and Dreadful Night," *The Cambridge Companion to Travel Writing*, eds. Peter Hulme and Tim Youngs (Cambridge: Cambridge University Press, 2002), 191.

9. See Joseph Sebes, S. J.'s important analysis of the early visitors in "The Precursors of Ricci," in *East Meets West: The Jesuits in China, 1582–1773*, eds. Charles E. Ronan, S. J., and Bonnie B. C. Oh (Chicago: Loyola University Press, 1988), 27–30.

10. Johann Peter Eckermann, *Conversations of Goethe*, trans. John Oxenford (New York: Da Capo Press, 1998), 164.

11. See Virginia H. Milhouse, Molefi Kete Asante, and Peter O. Nwosu, eds. *Transcultural Realities: Inter-Disciplinary Perspectives on Cross-Cultural Relations* (Thousand Oaks, CA: Sage, 2001), 2.

Part 1

Rachana Sachdev, Susquehanna University

'European Responses to Child Abandonment, Sale of Children, and Social Welfare Policies in Ming China

THE LAST COUPLE OF DECADES HAVE SEEN A SERIOUS shift in academic responses to pre-modern Asia; starting with K. N. Chaudhuri, a number of economic and demographic historians have pointed out that neither colonialism nor Orientalism provides an adequate paradigm to think through early modern European interactions with China or India.[1] As Robert Markley reports, "until 1800 an integrated world economy was dominated by China and to a lesser extent Japan and Moghul India."[2] Andre Gunder Frank claims categorically that China was the center of the world economy in the early modern era.[3] The finely crafted merchandise available in China was the major draw for the Europeans who could sell Indian cloth and Southeast Asian spices to the Chinese in return for porcelain, silk, as well as many other manufactured goods. The trade imbalance remained favorable to China, however, in spite of the many Asian goods transported by the Europeans to Chinese shores—most of the Chinese goods were paid for by the Europeans in American or Japanese silver, contributing even further to the image of China as a fabulously wealthy nation. The Europeans were awed enough by the wealth of Ming China (1368–1644) to recognize that this society matched, if not surpassed, theirs in many ways. They were impressed as well by the intricate sociopolitical system in place in China and continued to portray China as the "most Glorious Kingdom" in the world, as Macro Polo had done. Their admiration for China also led them to the desire to emulate many of its policies, particularly the practice of the examination system for magistrates, as we can see in Robert Burton's proposal for his utopia, in which the Judges and "all other inferiour Magistrates [are] to bee chosen as the Literati in China."[4]

Laudatory though the reports were about the riches and social organization of China, they reflect as well the early modern European understanding of China as a haven for the poor and the sick. I argue in this essay that an important component of the European eulogization of China was its social welfare system which was seen to offer opportunities for survival and growth to all its citizens, and which ensured, in particular, the welfare of the children. China was considered to be rich not simply because it had large quantities of merchandise and a wealthy aristocracy but also because it was able to take care of its poorest and the neediest. Most of the early European observers of China, starting with Polo, include significant detail about the ways in which the Chinese provided for the well-being of its indigent population, especially its children; many even claim that there was no poverty in China because of the extensive policies related to public welfare. In particular, the Europeans noted repeatedly that the conditions for children in China were vastly superior to those present in Europe, even though some of the Chinese sold their children or abandoned them due to poverty.[5] My goal in this essay is to work through the reports of the early travelers to China to figure out why they repeatedly claimed lack of poverty in China despite their observations of the economic necessities surrounding what they themselves claimed were large-scale abandonment and selling of children.[6]

There is arguably no better index for the wealth and social conscience of a culture than the way in which it takes care of the most helpless of its citizens: the children, especially the infants. The Europeans who visited China from the twelfth century onwards were observant of the ways in which the society provided for its young and destitute. These observations might not appear in the forefront of their discussions of the Chinese society, but almost all the writers are cognizant of the ways in which the response of this society to its powerless and marginalized members provided an index for its success as a functional state. In this essay, my major intent is to chart the ways in which the early modern European travelers responded to the position of children within China in order to understand their constructions of this nation as a welfare state.

Theoretical Considerations

I am restricting my analysis to the early phase of European contact with China, from the beginning of the sixteenth century to the mid-seventeenth century prior to the Manchu rule, because some of the traditional support structures were still intact at that time; the growing capitalism as well as the disintegration attendant upon the end of the Ming dynasty left a very different China in place during the 1630s and 1640s. The depletion of resources caused by the need to defend Korea from Japanese attacks had started the downfall as early as the beginning of the seventeenth century, with royal eunuchs beginning a regime of oppression to fund the imperial household.[7] However, as Atwell documents, changes in farming policies, along with natural disasters and political fighting, resulted in the 1640s being a decade of crisis. As a native of Soochow, a once prosperous city, wrote in 1642: "in the streets there are numerous beggars, very thin and worn. . . . The people are dying in great numbers through lack of food. I have seen with my own eyes several tens of [starved] corpses being buried daily in the property of the price."[8] Jonathan Spence suggests that political uprisings and epidemics combined "caused many communities to suffer losses of half or more of their inhabitants."[9] Father Alvarez Semedo, who wrote his account of China in the 1640s based on twenty-two years of experience in the country, must have suffered through enough of the breakdown of social structures, testified to in the Ming sources, that he did not claim lack of poverty in China. On the other hand, he condemned the contemporary Chinese for their inability to follow worthy traditional wisdoms and practices.[10] The focus on the era prior to the 1630s allows us to recuperate some of the optimism evident in sixteenth and early seventeenth-century European readings of China.[11]

In this essay, I am not making any claims about the veracity of the early modern European statements or about the power dynamics or profit motives involved in the external scrutiny.[12] Since so few of the early missionaries and traders had extensive contact with the Chinese (because of the language barrier and because of the Chinese law about foreigners not being welcome in their land), all discussions of early modern European travel narratives have to take into account the fact that recirculation of information and the authors' personal and political stances characterize their constructions of China. Galeote Pereira spent at least three years in China, having been captured as an illegal trader, but he was a prisoner being transported across the country. His perspective about China has to be limited by these factors,[13] but is it likelier to be more "true" than that of Juan González de Mendoza, who wrote the most popular history of China in 1585 without ever having visited the country?[14] What do we do with the detailed and careful descriptions of China provided by Friar Gaspar da Cruz who had only visited one part of China, Canton (with possibly some brief stops along the Chinese coast), for only a few weeks, and who based his treatise on Pereira's limited eyewitness account?[15] The cases of Macro Polo and Mendez Pinto are even more troublesome, since Polo's narrative leaves out so many of the details about China easily observable by visitors,[16] and Pinto was, according to scholarly consensus, given to exaggeration and imaginative building on the information he received.[17] Even the published letters of the Jesuit missionaries in China are problematic since they were seriously edited, before publication, to fit the agenda of the Jesuit mission;[18] this is true as well of Matteo Ricci's journals.[19] These critical problems of historical veracity notwithstanding, I have chosen to include all these sources in my study because, in their own significant ways, they helped shape the discourse about China available in early modern Europe. Polo, though he wrote well before the main time span of my inquiry, is crucial to my analysis because his reports about the supposed Chinese wealth and welfare policies created the forum for the discussions that followed on this topic, and many early modern European writers obviously copied and were influenced by his accounts.

The separation of the "true" from the fabricated is difficult in any travel document, but it is particularly thorny in the case of the travelogue genre about Ming China. The repetition of the same information in various sources might prove corroboration of the veracity of the statements, were it not for the fact that most authors were simply re-circulating the information they had found elsewhere. Contradictions between various accounts might help us to think through the existing conditions in China—for example, while most travelers testify to a benevolent government and assert that there were no beggars in China, one of the earliest eyewitness reports on China by Christovão Vieira talked about the oppression faced by the general populace because of the scholar-officials; he claims that the magistrates do "nothing but rob, kill, beat and torture the people."[20] Martín de Rada, the Span-ish friar who visited China on a brief mission from the Philippines in 1575, believed that most of the people in China were poor because of the large population, and he claimed that he "saw poor people who went begging through the streets, especially blind."[21] The supposedly eyewitness accounts of the exploited poor and beggars, resisting the dominant interpretations, must make us pause, even though they are less numerous than the reports about the prosperity of the nation. In the essay, I have teased out both the repetitions and the contradic-tions in order to provide a more nuanced reading of the constructions of China. Checking the information against Ming historical sources provides us with some additional insight into the existing conditions or actual policies adopted. However, as the historical information is limited by its own political agenda and official status, it only partially helps us in understanding the Europeans' portraits of China. Hence, my policy in this essay has been to treat all narratives about China presenting themselves as travelogues as constructions based on some level of either direct or reported observation, that serve a variety of ideological and personal agendas, and to treat the information available in them about the welfare policies adopted by China on the same level because of their role in shaping European consciousness throughout the period of my study. I have attempted to garner as complete a picture of the early modern European response to the conditions of children in China as possible, using a multitude of sources from authors of various nationalities, occupations, and agendas.

In addition, my discussion is framed by an attempt to place the narratives within a broader look at some of the material and cultural practices related to children within Europe. One of the basic premises of this essay is that the Europeans' recognition of China as a prosperous and well-organized society that could not easily be condemned as savage led to their willingness to pay closer attention to the details of life there. They were more comparative in their outlook as a consequence, but they also hoped to find transcultural truths that could help them solve some of the economic, social, or cultural crises back in their own nations. The travelers carried in their heads a picture of their own limited exposure to their homelands and supplemented this with a limited understanding of China; the result was a portrait that was part observation/analysis and part dream/fantasy *on both ends.* Hence, I have tried to bolster my analysis of the early modern travelers' response to conditions for children in China by looking at the situation within Europe, especially within Portugal, Spain, Italy, and Holland, where most of the early travelers came from.

Pre-Early Modern Travel Genre Sources

Marco Polo's late thirteenth-century account developed a portrait of China that reported it to be far wealthier and more efficiently run than any country in Europe. However, even in this land of plenty, there were significant markers of poverty, as Polo is forced to note, though he glosses over the social issues involved: "In the province of Mangi almost all the poor and needy people—who cannot bring up their children—sell sons and daughters to others who are rich and noble that for the price of them they may be able to sustain themselves and that the children may be better brought up and may have a more comfortable living with those persons."[22] The selling of children is made to appear beneficial for everyone concerned and is practiced almost like a redistribution of social and economic wealth. There are no questions asked about the status of children in their new homes; it is assumed that they are adopted into the new households as children of the family and not as virtual slaves. In this portrait of the efficiently managed, wealthy paradise, even the selling of children has no trauma associated with it.[23]

Polo's admiration for the kingdom is also partly based on the social welfare policies, which included making provisions for the sustenance of needy children. In his travels through Mangi province (southern

China), Polo noted that "in that province they cast (them) out the child as soon as he is born and the poor women who cannot feed them nor bring them up for poverty do this"[24] The babies thus abandoned at birth became state responsibility. The state found wet nurses for them and housed them. Even though there were supposedly twenty thousand male and female children yearly who needed this level of care,[25] abandoned children received not only the basics of survival, but were also socially reintegrated, with possibilities of adoption into families, education, gainful employment at adulthood, and suitable marriage partners all provided as part of the social response for their welfare.[26] They even had their horoscopes made up. The potential horrors that could be suffered by helpless children are averted through timely interventions by the state or prosperous citizens. China appears that much wealthier because it is able to solve easily and well the social crises that plague Europe.

Early Modern Materials on Children and Social Welfare in China

Our account may begin with Galeote Pereira who comments that hordes of poor children in China live in trees for want of better housing, especially outside the "abundantly provided" cities and towns. The large population of China, which was its glory for most Europeans, could also be a source of poverty especially in the well populated, coastal areas,[27] though Pereira commends the state for its ability to take care of the people. His praise for the welfare system in China is open and direct: "they have moreover one thing very good and that which made us all to marvel at them being gentiles: namely, that there be hospitals in all their cities."[28] These hospitals took care of the sick and the poor, providing mostly shelter, food, and some medical care. Foresight appears to be the key concept in the early modern Chinese management of the needy. Pereira notes that "in every city there is a great circuit, wherein be many houses for poor people, for blind, lame, old folk, not able to travel for age, nor having any other means to live. . . . When one is sick, blind, or lame, he maketh a supplication to the *Ponchassi* and proving that to be true he writeth, he remaineth in the aforesaid great lodging as long as he liveth. Besides this they keep in these places swine and Hens, whereby the poore be relieved without going a begging."[29] The government makes available the organization and the officials, ensuring both that the rules exist and are enforced, to make the lives of the poor easier. In addition, each charitable institution is provided with the means to make it as self-sufficient as possible. The existence of well run hospitals in every city testifies to China's ability to take care of its needy.

Pereira's conclusion is borne out by João de Barros who similarly claims an absence of beggars in China[30] and by Father Gaspar da Cruz, a Dominican Friar, who directly compares the indigent in Portugal and in China and comments that the "these poor people notwithstanding do not live so poorly and beggarly in their apparel as do those who live poorly in Portugal."[31] Cruz ascribes the relative ease of living in China to the light tax load[32] and lack of tyranny in the government[33]; since people are able to keep most of what they earn or grow, the incentive to work hard and save is strong. According to Cruz, the Chinese do work hard and laugh at anyone who supports beggars. The only form of charity they practice is providing shoes for the poor; only those with long-term, incurable diseases or serious disability are maintained by the state in hospitals.[34]

Cruz understands that this comfortable lifestyle is only available to men and their families—poor widows have a different fate assigned to them. Especially if their offspring are too young to work and earn a living, the widows, who are bound by custom not to work outside the home, are forced to sell some of their children in order to survive. However, they are forbidden to sell them to the Portuguese. The boys thus sold live a life of relative ease, for the masters are bound by law to teach them a profession and provide them with a wife and a house when they reach the right age, in exchange for a yearly sum to be paid to them for their investment. The girls are forced to become prostitutes and remain in this profession until they are too old to work; they, too, pay a yearly sum to their benefactors. Cruz takes seriously the pos-sibility of the masters sexually assaulting the young women or selling them and considers there to be "no greater servitude than that of these wenches" in China.[35] Despite this concern for the young women sold into prostitution, Cruz emphasizes the fairness of the system in that "the laws of China give authority to the women for to sell their children and not to the men, for as the men are bound to seek a living for themselves and their children, if the man lacks a livelihood, they hold that he is in the fault for that."[36] Most narratives about China from the early modern period stress that the sale of children was a last option resorted to by indigent widows with very young, dependent children and without an obvious familial support system.

Bernadine of Escalante, the Spanish writer who popularized Cruz's and Barros's narratives in the 1570s (the English translation by Frampton appeared in 1579), also emphasizes the gendered twist to the story told by Cruz about poor widows selling their children—mostly young girls are sold and they are raised by the wealthy patrons as future prostitutes or concubines, having been taught the arts of entertainment in their youth. To ensure that the girls are not totally exploited, an officer of the king is put in charge of overseeing that only a certain agreed-upon sum is paid to the master each year, with the rest available to the woman for her own upkeep, present, and future. Old age brings freedom from sexual servitude: "when they are olde and of no more profit, they remaine free without any longer bondage unto their maisters, or any else, mainteyning themselves of that which they have gotten in their youth."[37] There is enough left from their incomes for the women to sustain themselves and to build some savings for their future, especially if they are good at singing or playing musical instruments, as Escalante points out. What is missing from Escalante's narrative is Cruz's awareness of the potential disasters attendant upon the sale of the young women and his sympathy for the women. As far as Escalante is concerned, even the children who are sold in China have rights and social protection provided for them by the government.[38]

The care of the state in ensuring the welfare of even the most destitute results in a society where there are no poor people begging on the streets, as exploitation-free means of livelihood are found for all. Escalante, following Cruz, builds a portrait of Chinese society in which everyone contributes to the general social welfare through their labor, and in which every indigent or disabled person has either an occupation or some other means of recourse, obviating the necessity for begging.[39] The government attempted to place poor, handicapped children first within their extended families; since familial structures were tight and filial duty an important aspect of one's social and personal existence, this would be the case for most children after their fathers' death, in any case. Escalante maintains that if they have no one who can comfortably take care of them, the children can petition the state for protection and live in the many local hospitals that are built for this purpose, where the officers "doo minister and give to every one what they have need of aboundantly."[40] The state maintains the needy well, taking care to give generously.

Mendes Pinto's representation of the welfare system in China builds on this portrait of state munificence and emphasizes the way in which all eventualities are anticipated and a whole bulwark of familial or state support is available to all individuals.[41] Pinto asserts that in Peking alone, there are over two hundred orphanages where "fatherless youngsters are taught doctrine, as well as reading, writing and all the mechanical trades, until they are ready to earn a living for themselves."[42] There are a similar number of foundling homes for unwanted babies who, he informs us, are taken care of by state-sponsored wet nurses. Extensive as the charity is, it is built upon the labor of all concerned. Even the disabled have their work assigned to them based on their capabilities, and the government ensures that they are hired for the right jobs when the merchants apply for their licenses: the blind are employed in mills, the crippled are employed making ropes, and the ones who cannot work with their hands carry baskets on their backs. The employers are required to provide all necessities for these handicapped children. Pinto isolates the influence of Buddhism[43] in keeping the general population charitable—even if the government doesn't force them, the merchants are ready to employ the disabled children because of the spiritual benefits they accrue. In addition, Pinto points to a system of social justice that oversees that the fines paid by the wrong-doers are used for the support of the destitute according to their crimes: the "loud-mouthed and shameless women who dishonor themselves in public"[44] fund the welfare of deaf and dumb children; young prostitutes pay for the upkeep of older and diseased prostitutes; and adulterous women are fined to benefit orphaned girls.[45] The state provides opportunities for education and employment to all and ensures that a regular system is in place to take care of the needy from within the society.

The same efficiency and orderliness characterize as well the distribution of food within the country. Pinto guesses that there are fourteen thousand granaries that keep an adequate supply of grain for all citizens. In good harvest years, the citizens pay back the food loans they receive, but in years of famine, the "wheat is still distributed among the general population, free of interest, at no profit to anyone."[46] Part of the munificence is funded by the large amounts of state revenue, fully a third of which is reserved for charitable purposes, and not even the king is allowed to touch those funds. All these details of governance lead Pinto to conclude that "in this as well in all other matters, this kingdom is so well governed, with such a high degree of excellence and with such prompt execution in all its affairs"[47] that if St. Frances Xavier had not died in Asia, he would have tried to persuade the king of Portugal to follow the Chinese model.

Juan González de Mendoza's "best-seller" amalgamated history of China published in 1585 is similarly interested enough in social welfare policies to devote a whole chapter to it. He starts the discussion with reference to a harsh law against begging: "for the auoyding therof the king hath set downe an order, vpon great and gréeuous penaltie to be executed vpon the saide poore, if they do begge or craue in the stréetes and a greater penaltie vpon the citizens or townes men, if they do giue vnto any such that beggeth."[48] Even though the initial tone suggests a punitive system in which the destitute are punished or put to death for begging, Mendoza gradually builds a portrait of China as a haven for the disabled, sick, or indigent.[49] He credits the state for the well-being of the population as it provides a Judge for the Poor whose only responsibility is to make decisions regarding the welfare of the needy. Mendoza lists the various procedures the Judge undertakes to find adequate economic and social support for the poor or the handicapped, including training the children in professions they can handle, or the possibility of recourse to extended families. However, in the absence of other means of support, the children are still well taken care of: "But if it hath no parents, or they be so poore that they cannot contribute nor supply any part thereof; then doth the king maintaine them in verie ample manner of his owne costes in hospitalles, verie sumptuous, that he hath in everie citie throughout his kingdome for the same effect and purpose."[50] The state acts almost as an extended family for the children because it provides sustenance, Mendoza claims, even when the parents are alive. He builds the portrait of state generosity even further and sees the king maintaining all poor children in "verie sumptuous" condition.[51]

In addition, his discussions of the blind prostitutes or the young women sold into prostitution emphasize the social control required to guarantee the possibility of a decent life for the women; the women are protected from the possibility of abuse and are well cared for in their houses. Indeed, he stresses that the women "passe away the time maruellous pleasantly by reason of their singing and playing, which they doo with great cunning."[52] Even though the young women are forced to be courtesans or prostitutes, the acquisition of musical skills provides pleasure in their own lives and not just their customers'. The state also ensures that though these young women are well provided for, they do not corrupt the morals of the rest of the women, by limiting their residences to the suburbs. Orderliness and efficiency produce happiness for all in Mendoza's Chinese utopia.

30

Pierre D'Avity's discussion of the Chinese society published in his *Discourse of the Estate of the King of China* (French edition, 1614) and translated into English in 1615 by Edward Grimstone, highlights as well the organizational structure behind the charity.[53] For D'Avity, like Mendoza, sees the "Judge of the Poor" assigned by the state as responsible for ensuring that the handicapped and poor have some means of sustenance, whether they come from a rich relative, contributions from various extended family members, or from the government. Efficiency is guaranteed by the provision of multiple levels of oversight: "The Judge doth often visit the Administrator or Overseer and is also visited by another which comes expresly from court to visit the hospitalls of the prouince."[54] The state ensures that the venality or inefficiency of one official does not result in the mismanagement of the entire system.

Judges were also appointed to safeguard the welfare of the children who were sold by poverty-stricken mothers. Like Cruz, Escalante, and Mendoza, D'Avity notes that the masters are not allowed to benefit directly from the sexual labors of their wards; instead, when the children come of age and are ready to be employed, the masters bring them to a Judge who assigns the prostitutes a home and who is responsible for paying the masters a monthly sum to offset the costs of raising the wards. This state intervention prevents direct or indirect exploitation of the poor and also ensures, as much as possible, that the prostitutes do not end up on state rolls after their working years. To maintain justice and help the needy, the judges are sometimes also called upon to handle the finances directly, especially of blind prostitutes: "There are blind women and others which give all that remaines (whenas their foster father is paid) unto their Judge, & he keeps it faithfully and gives an account yearely unto the Visitors; then when they grow old he delivers it unto them with his owne hand, measuring it in such sort as they may haue no necessitie."[55] The responsibility and morality of the officials provide the basis for a good life for the hard-working prostitutes. A good welfare state is one, it appears, which invests continually in the legal and social infrastructure for taking care of the indigent, rather than one which relies on the charity of the rich or which simply builds hospitals and lets them be overrun by corruption and greed. According to D'Avity, the Chinese government provides realistic and exploitation-free opportunities for growth and work for all, incorporating everyone into the social fabric, requiring of each member of society that he contributes to the general welfare.

However, the social reality in China was much more complex than most short-term foreign travelers realized.[56] Matteo Ricci, who spent over two decades in China and who was fluent in conversational and written Chinese, provides evidence both of the efficient public administrative structure bolstering the welfare of the poor and strong, and irrefutable evidence of the continuing poverty in spite of it. Ricci discusses at length the various checks and balances provided to offset corruption, ensure efficiency and reliability, and forestall tyranny. He admires the leading role that philosophers, highly learned and morally motivated men, play in the administration of the land; he thinks highly of the various levels of oversight of administrative responsibilities, mentioning in particular the important role played by the royal investigator, the *Ciayuen*; he is in favor of the rotation system that ensured that all officials moved at least every three years; and he is particularly impressed by the inspection that every ranking official underwent every third year. Ricci mentions that "not even the King would dare to change a decision settled upon by the judges of this public investigation."[57] However, he remains aware that some officials amass vast fortunes despite their low salaries,[58] and there is widespread fear of the power of the magistrates,[59] though he also understands that public investigation might result in the dismissal of a large number of these officials. Apparently, in 1607, after the investigation, four thousand magistrates were handed a sentence, testifying both to the widespread corruption and the system of surveillance that tried to curb venality.[60]

All these admirable administrative decisions cannot, however, get rid of the most persistent problem all societies face—poverty. Despite its fabled wealth and organizational structure, China faced poverty serious enough for people to sell or kill their children. Ricci states that acting troupes buy children from the poor and force them to perform almost from their infancy.[61] In addition, the poor sell their children into perpetual servitude in order to feed their sexual appetites or when the family becomes too large, with the consequence that "the whole country is virtually filled with slaves. . . . Many of them are also taken out of the country as slaves by the Portuguese and the Spaniards."[62] According to the Chinese, the sale of children to the Portuguese was a problem not only because of the conversions to Christianity but also because slavery in China was very different from that practiced by the Europeans; it was "less exacting than among any other people in the world," but the fact of the forced servitude of children continues to sully Ricci's portrait of a wealthy China. Ricci also mentions that people sometimes castrated their children and sold them to be brought up as eunuchs in hopes of their preferment, since the country was almost ruled by the many eunuchs in the royal household. Ricci's account differs from Cruz's in highlighting that men sell their children into slavery at least as often, if not more so, than poor widows. The reality of poverty was such that traditional social norms could no longer function to protect the children.

Despite this awareness of the realities of socioeconomic deprivation in China and even when there is some evidence of a pre-colonialist attitude on the part of the author,[63] the portrait of China retains its contours as a well-ordered state. The description of the natural wealth of China and the industry of the people leads Botero, "the accomplished Italian political theorist and social thinker,"[64] to conclude that it is because everyone is forced to contribute to the general welfare of the society that China prospers: "That none may excuse themselves, in saying hee can doe nothing, every one is bound to learne his fathers occupation, which is the reason that the children (borne as it were tradesmen) learne their fathers occupations before they perceive it, by continuall practice becoming in time most artificiall mechanickes."[65] Botero adds to Pinto's description about the disabled children being put to work by referring to the children learning their father's work at home—the family structure and the social fabric sustain the work potential and contribution of each member of society. The Chinese distaste for begging was so well known among the Europeans that Richard Cocks, the cape-merchant in the English factory in Japan, surmised that the Chinese would not admit any missionaries because the Jesuits were "always begging without shame."[66] Despite the admissions about some continuing issues with poverty, the Europeans construct a portrait of China that is able to take care of its young and provide the foresight, organizational structure, and means for the survival of all.

Children and Social Welfare in Early Modern Europe

The European travelers' portrait of China's welfare system for children resembles in some part the specialized foundling homes or orphanages that were started during the Renaissance all over Europe, though it adds a much greater level of state involvement within the project. Richard Trexler found that "the basic public institutions of Florentine child welfare developed between the thirteenth and early sixteenth century. First to surface were receptacles for unwanted children."[67] Tuscany and northern Italy saw the establishment of small hospitals for children by the *Scoule Grandi* in the early fifteenth century. The Ospedale degli Innocenti, a hospital for foundlings and orphans, was established in Florence in 1445 by the Silk Guild. Seville established homes for boys in the fifteenth and for girls in the sixteenth century, both under municipal care.[68] As Philip Gavitt discusses, the impetus for the establishment of these institutions was both economic and social: "Both population pressures and endemic plague combined in the fourteenth and fifteenth centuries to motivate urban laymen and municipal authorities to establish orphanages and foundling hospitals."[69] The charitable establishments focused on the need to take care of the many children, destitute, orphaned, or unwanted for other social reasons, who were increasingly found within early modern European cities. Since a number of these foundling homes and orphanages had been established before the European sea travel to China began in the early sixteenth century, the merchants and missionaries who went to China could be assumed to have a rudimentary familiarity with the European charitable institutions for children. Their assessment of the ways in which the Chinese took care of the needs of unwanted children had to have been influenced at least partly by the systems that had been in place in the Europe they had left behind. In addition, their responses to the system of social welfare in China reflect their hopes and desires about their own homelands. The European travelers observed well the ways in which the Chinese society handled the thorny issue of poverty and the solutions they arrived at to deal with unwanted children, both infants and older children.

It is important, as Brian Pullan does, to distinguish between the abandoned and the orphans in Europe—the foundlings had no known social identity and were usually considered to be illegitimate, whereas the orphans often had an established social network, with known and respected parents and neighbors.[70] In early modern Seville, Bologna, and Florence, that distinction had important consequences for the children, with the foundlings and orphans housed separately. The orphanages generally took in older children with known parentage and offered better living conditions. In addition, Gavitt asserts that "in many cases motives other than poverty compelled parents to abandon children."[71] Death of a father, the fear of social ostracism in cases of unmarried mothers, an economic downturn in the family, and the social consequences of a child born to a slave mother all led to temporary or permanent abandonment of young children and infants. Interestingly, there is contradictory evidence about the familial status of the unwanted children. Viazzo et al. claim that "a sizeable proportion of children abandoned in the fifteenth (and sixteenth) century were not born out of wedlock."[72] In Amsterdam, at the Municipal Orphanage, there was even a requirement that the children could enter the institution only if "their parents had been members of the city corporation for a minimum of seven years,"[73] ensuring that children born out of wedlock or the children of the poor did not unduly hamper the survival of middle class children with proven parentage. Valentina Tikoff's analysis of Seville's orphanages also points to the use of these institutions by the poor parents who were unable to maintain their children. She claims that "orphanages accommodated large numbers of children who were only half-orphans (children with one deceased parent) and some who were not orphans at all."[74] Based on these findings, it would seem reasonable to draw the conclusion that children in Europe as well as in China came mostly from intact families with at least one parent still alive.

However, Nicholas Terpstra and Gavitt both contend that in Florence and Bologna at least, "most of these [unwanted] children were girls and most were illegitimate."[75] The establishment of orphanages might have made it easier for some parents to avoid destitution and/or personal responsibility by sending their children to institutions that could provide for them better, but the orphanages and foundling homes were still necessary for the one population that had no choice: illegitimate children. Indeed, as Pullan explains, based on the Italian novelist Cinthio's sixteenth-century description of them, foundling homes were established for the sole purpose of housing illegitimate children.[76] Trexler's statistical analysis shows only one of the first hundred admissions to the Innocenti as definitely being legitimate. A large number of these children were the result of forced or consensual sexual unions between slaves or servants and their masters—thirty-four out of the original hundred admissions to the Innocenti were the offspring of slave mothers.[77] Even though only some charitable institutions admitted these children, the necessity for the homes was an indisputable fact for most European cities where increasing number of young maids worked to earn their dowries and where, outside the parental jurisdiction, they could be either cajoled or forced into giving up their virginity. Hence, however useful a corrective the recent studies of the records of the class-based and gentrified admissions of the orphanages are, they do not supplant the conclusion that abandoned infants were often and were also widely considered to be illegitimate children of unmarried women and in this,

35

the situation regarding unwanted children in Europe was much different from that found in China.

Thinking Comparatively about Children in Early Modern Europe and China

In China, there was a significant majority of girls in the numbers of exposed or killed infants. In rapidly growing areas, like Fukien (modern Fujian), apparently even the "wealthiest families killed baby girls after the second one."[78] Even though most Western observers thought that all brides received a dowry rather than the other way around, Chinese sources from the Ming period show that women were indeed expected to bring a dowry and increasingly so, a more sizeable dowry, if they wanted to marry well.[79] Similarly, in Europe, girls were discarded more often—most of the hospitals and foundling homes housed around 61 percent girls. The charitable organizations helped in the reintegration of these girls into society by providing them small dowries in addition to training them in the household arts. Orphanages dedicated especially to the care of girls could be found by the 1530s in Bologna and "about three hundred girls could find shelter in one of three homes that was now dedicated to their care."[80] In Portugal, the *misericórdia* established orphanages and took on as their regular responsibility the providing of dowries for the orphan girls to prevent them from having to work as prostitutes,[81] testifying to the urgent necessity for dowries in the social rehabilitation of foundling girls. If there were more cases of female abandonment in China, the European travelers would not have been surprised by the trend, as the southern European countries faced similar pressures.

The exposed babies in China as well as those in Europe drew a common response from the European authorities—the first item on the agenda was making sure that the babies were baptized so at least their souls could be saved, if not their bodies. In Europe, if the child was healthy but did not have proof of having been baptized, the baptism would take place within the first two days, but it was performed immediately if there was a possibility of the child dying.[82] In China, since all exposed babies were unbaptized, the missionaries could undertake to save their souls and their lives if the parents permitted the baptism. The first Chinese baptism in 1583 was of a "poore diseased man cast foorth by his parents" who died shortly after this momentous event.[83] David Mungello documents that "the earliest reference to Christians baptizing abandoned children in China dates to 1612 in Nanjing. In 1622 Fr. Pierre Van Spiere (de Spira) divided the Nanjing Christians into eight congregations and assigned them to perform works of mercy that included baptizing abandoned children. In Fujian in 1633 the Dominican Juan de Morales baptized moribund (dying) infants whose parents had abandoned them because of poverty and thrown them into the trash or rivers."[84] The emphasis on the spiritual also permitted the authorities as well as the public to focus their attention away from the fact that by the mid-seventeenth century, most of the foundling homes in Europe had become sites of mass destruction for the children left there. At this late date, even though parents continued to leave their children at the homes and hospitals in the hope that they might have better chances of survival there than on the street or on a storefront, this was no longer true.

In Europe, despite evidence of a couple of isolated cases and some rhetoric about infants being abandoned in rivers and ditches, most infants were abandoned at door steps or upon an altar until the *ruota* (turntable), first introduced at the Innocenti, obviated the necessity for even such open abandonment. Trexler discusses that "desertion to fortune, by a ditch or a river, was most uncommon."[85] By contrast, in China, Chen Longzheng, a magistrate, found "parents tossing their infants over the Bridge of Scattered Stars into the rapids below"[86] during a great famine. The famine also caused others to abandon their children under trees or by the river.[87] The hero of the famous novel, *Journey to the West*, by Wu Chengen (ca. 1500–1582) was abandoned by his mother on a floating plank down the river. Drowning was the most common method of disposing of unwanted babies in China, and this was undertaken inside the house by the midwives, or the babies were thrown into the river.[88] If the child was going to be exposed, there was very little shielding the parents from the unpleasantness of their decision.

In China, for those children who survived the first three days and who were initiated into the family,[89] there was traditionally a support system available, as the European travelers to China pointed out. The conclusions of these travelers can be substantiated by an analysis of the

Ming Chinese sources. Ping-Chen Hsiung outlines the extensive steps taken by the Chinese government to ensure neonatal well-being in premodern China: "promoting medicine, publishing medical books and dispensing remedies were legitimate state functions and indispensable public duties."[90] Advances in pediatric care were widely disseminated by the state, resulting in more hygienic procedures for cutting the umbilical cord, treatment of infections, and better emergency care. The state of pediatric medicine and the widespread knowledge about newborn care in China assured that young children survived the trials of early life relatively well in China. Low infant mortality resulted in larger numbers of children surviving to adulthood, raising the population to record levels, and ironically causing the abandonment of later children in financially challenged families.[91]

In addition, as Jonna Smith states in her groundbreaking study of late Ming charity, the Chinese had traditionally adopted various methods to deal with their socioeconomic crises before the advent of widespread notions of personal charity: "Emperors extended their governance to sponsor poorhouses (*yangyi yuan*) and dispensaries for the 'poor, sick, disabled, and lonely,' thereby expressing their paternalistic care for the people."[92] Influenced by Confucian doctrine, both the emperor and the district magistrates saw the welfare of the residents within their jurisdiction as their own moral and familial duty and cast themselves in the role of parents to all the residents, exemplifying the phrase, "father-and-mother officials" (*fumu guan*). Smith includes the example of one such magistrate who, "facing an outbreak of disease in his district," commissioned the setting up of medical clinics where doctors worked around the clock to "reduce the number of untimely deaths among the destitute poor."[93] In addition, inspired by the success of one such endeavor in the early sixteenth century, the emperor established community covenants throughout the country in 1567 which were responsible for overseeing welfare of residents at the local level.[94]

The tradition of state welfare had been present in China since at least the Song dynasty. Ebrey demonstrates that from the Song dynasty on, there were laws on the books protecting the claims of orphan girls to their share of the property for their dowries.[95] As Mungello discusses, Song orphanages were state run institutions. Later on, Zhu Xi (1130–

1200), the famous Neo-Confucian scholar-official, "developed the idea of communal granaries (*shecang*), conceived of [as] 'granaries for bearing children' (*juzicang*). The purpose of these granaries was to distribute food to parents too poor to feed their children."[96] In the thirteenth century, the Bureau of Childhood Mercy was established in several Chinese cities to oversee the welfare of unwanted babies, though there is no evidence of these institutions having survived into the sixteenth century. From an external perspective at least, the Chinese government seemed to provide both the means as well as the structure to provide sustenance to needy children.

On the other hand, most of the charitable organizations in Europe were the fruit of collaboration between the pious lay people and the confraternities and "grew out of some combination of private charitable initiative, government fiat and clerical encouragement."[97] Nicholas Terpstra's study of these institutions in Florence and Bologna demonstrates that these specialized orphanages had better success rates, at least in their early years, in preserving the abandoned children than the hospitals which had formerly cared for them. Pinto's assignment of this joint European enterprise to the Chinese government reflects the desire for a fully functional welfare state, especially as the number of the unwanted children increased to 37.3 percent of all baptismal children in the economically difficult year of 1552.[98] His own poverty during his childhood years possibly made him more sensitive to the plight of the poor and to the need for reliable solutions[99]; one potential solution to the problems of Europe's needy lay in the model provided by China.

39

Concluding Remarks

The Europeans who traveled to China in the sixteenth and early seventeenth centuries had some likelihood of being aware of the charitable institutions for children in their own countries—Ricci had studied in Rome, and had to have known about the hospitals there. Rome had started rescuing exposed infants and housing them in hospitals as early as 1220, and in the 1470s, "Pope Sixtus IV expanded the Hospital of the Holy Spirit in Rome to take in many more children."[100] They were also very likely to be aware of the rarity of these institutions and were thus impressed by the Chinese ability to provide them in every city, and to provide every citizen with a way to earn a decent living. They soon realized that the children abandoned by their parents in Ming China were either incorporated into the economy by appropriate magistrates and a Judge for the Poor or housed in the hospitals if they were unable to work at all; the children sold by the parents also had rights and protection provided by the state to prevent exploitation. These seemingly long-term solutions appealed to the visitors enough that they could contextualize their understanding of the practices of child abandonment and selling. If they could focus on the long-term organizational and economic solutions undertaken by the Chinese, they could temporarily dismiss the unease caused by the increasing numbers of abandoned children found on the roadside or in the rivers in late-Ming China or the fact that they observed children being sold by the poor for income.

By the late Ming era, as Brook demonstrates, the gap between the poor and the rich was widening and the growing population put "a mounting pressure on resources."[101] There were famines caused by droughts in the Peking area in 1584, 1585, and 1587; however, even though the situation for the poor was dire, the emperor himself got involved in several measures to attempt to solve the crisis in 1585.[102] Despite the setbacks, China still had recourse to an ideology of paternalistic government and an inherited organizational structure that worked to minimize hardships. Challenged though it was by its own internal breakdowns and the growing political instability, the Ming Chinese government was better able to provide for and structurally devise solutions for the welfare of the children, and that the Europeans found laudatory and worth emulating. The missionaries and traders who visited China after 1550 saw a crumbling social welfare system, but there was still enough of it left intact to prop up the sense of relative well-being at least until the 1630s. The missionaries themselves provided an alternative solution by baptizing and bringing up some abandoned children as Christians. Though they were thus able to insert themselves in an appropriate way into this utopia, the Europeans appreciated the fact that the Chinese government did not leave long-term solutions for the welfare of the citizens to chance or the generosity of the rich. China remains in the early modern European representations as a utopia—the well planned care and long-term sustenance available to the abandoned young allows this "civill commonwealth"[103] to be the land of wish-fulfillment. Through their detailing of the public welfare system that provided for the indigent, the European travelers expressed their desire for a strong government in their own homelands that provided a similar infrastructure and support system. Pinto had hoped that St. Francis Xavier would be the catalyst of such a transformation in Portugal.

It is ironic (and possibly educational for the twenty-first century China as it is commercializing and privatizing its welfare institutions) that the extensive state-mandated social welfare policies were exactly the reason that Ming China continued to exist in the minds of the Europeans as wealthy even when the poor were becoming more visible. The recognition of the poor and their problems did not dispel the impression of the general well-being of Chinese citizens; the provisions traditionally made for the poor heightened instead the sense of the wealth of the country. The welfare policies adopted by the state also resulted in greater acceptance of Chinese customs by all visitors. That most Europeans could contend that there were no beggars in Ming China, based on the extensive system provided for the sustenance of the needy, excused the fact that some Chinese families abandoned their young or sold their children. That even the sold and abandoned children had rights and privileges made China "the most Glorious Kingdom."

41

Notes

1. Some prominent names include Jack Goldstone, J. M. Blaunt, R. Bin Wong, Andre Gunder Frank, and Kenneth Pomeranz.

2. Robert Markley, *The Far East and the English Imagination, 1600–1730* (Cambridge: Cambridge University Press, 2006), 2.

3. Andre Gunder Frank, *ReOrient: Global Economy in the Asian Age* (Berkeley: University of California Press, 1998), 5.

4. Robert Burton, *The Anatomy of Melancholy*, ed. Thomas C. Faulkner, Nicholas K. Kiessling, and Rhonda L Blair (Oxford: Clarendon Press, 1989), 91. I am indebted to Zhongsu Qian's analysis of China in seventeenth-century English literature for this reference. See Zhongsu Qian, "China in the English Literature of the Seventeenth Century," in *The Vision of China in the English Literature of the Seventeenth and Eighteenth Centuries*, ed. Adrian Hsia (Hong Kong: Chinese University Press, 1998), 29–68.

5. As Anne Behnke Kinney explains, poverty was not the only motive for the parents to abandon their children, even though it was a significant factor, at least in Han China (206 BC–220 AD). Unlucky omens, astrological considerations, and the unusual appearance of a child could all lead to the child being abandoned. Kinney mentions the cultural belief that "children born on

the fifth day of the fifth month would grow up to harm their parents." See Anne Behnke Kinney, *Representations of Childhood and Youth in Early China* (Stanford, CA: Stanford University Press, 2004), 110. Even though the late Ming society the Europeans observed was very different, child abandonment as a cultural practice had existed in China from the Han times.

6. The Europeans first heard of infanticide being practiced in China from Matteo Ricci whose journals were published in 1615. Ricci partially attributed the practice to poverty. For an analysis of the European understanding of the killing of infants in China, see my essay, "Contextualizing Female Infanticide: Ming China in Early Modern European Travelogues," *ASIANetwork Exchange*, 18, 1 (Fall 2010): 24–39.

7. As the letters from the Jesuits described, the eunuchs "imposed new tributes," tried to dig up silver despite a law against it, and found new ways to oppress the people, causing increasing tensions between the magistrates and the eunuchs. The people also started to revolt openly in the seventeenth century. See "The Jesuits in the Far East" in Samuel Purchas, *Purchas His Pilgrimes*, Vol. 12, 329. For an analysis of this era, see Albert Chan, S. J. "Late Ming Society and the Jesuit Missionaries," In *East Meets West: The Jesuits in China, 1582–1773*, eds. Charles E. Ronan, S. J., and Bonnie B. C. Oh (Chicago: Loyola University Press, 1988), 153–72.

8. Quoted in William Atwell, "Ming China and the Emerging World Economy," *The Cambridge History of China*, Vol. 8, Part 2, eds. Denis Twitchett and Frederick W. Mote (Cambridge: Cambridge University Press, 1998), 413.

9. Jonathan D. Spence, *The Search for Modern China* (New York: Norton, 1990), 22. See also Lynn A. Struve, ed. and trans. *Voices from the Ming-Qing Cataclysm: China in Tigers' Jaws* (New Haven, CI: Yale University Press, 1993) which uses contemporary Chinese accounts to document that "no locale in China escaped some sort of 'soldier calamity' (*hingbuo*) during the middle decades of the seventeenth century" (Page 2).

10. See Friar Alvarez Semedo, *The History of that Great and Renowned Monarchy of China Wherein All the particular Provinces Are Accurately Described, as Also the Dispositions, Manners, Learning, Lawes, Militia, Government and Religion of the People : Together with the Traffick and Commodities of that Countrey* (1642; London, 1655), 23.

11. The peaceful early Qing era saw a rise in the standard of living and in the public welfare system but both were the result of new policies and a more capitalistic outlook, and hence this era was very different from the late Ming period I examine in my essay.

12. The profitable trade was, of course, a draw and the possibility of saving the souls of China's almost 150 million a missionary's dream. The Europeans were soon aware of the fact that China had more merchandise and traffic of goods than any other Eastern nation. See "An Excellent Treatise of the Kingdome of China and of the Estate and Government Thereof," in Richard Hakluyt, ed. *The Principal Navigations, Voyages, Traffiques and Discoveries of the English Nation* (London: J. M. Dent, 1927), 213. The traders and the missionaries also paid specific attention to China because it resisted any easy conclusions.

13. Galeote Pereira, "Certain Reports of China, Learned through the Portugals There Imprisoned," in C. R. Boxer, ed. *South China in the Sixteenth Century*, Second series, No. CVI (London: Hakluyt Society, 1953).

14. This history was commissioned by Pope Gregory XIII and was first published in 1585. It was so popular that in the fifteen years after it was published, it was reprinted forty-six times in seven European languages, Spanish, German, Dutch, Italian, French, English, and Latin. Mendoza's book had been "read by the majority of well-educated Europeans at the beginning of the sev-

enteenth century." See Donald Lach, *Asia in the Making of Europe*, Vol. 1 (Chicago: University of Chicago Press, 1965), xvii.

15. The full title of Cruz's work is *Tractado em que se cotam muito por esteso as cousas da China* (1569) (*Treatise in which the Things of China Are Related at Great Length*). Boxer claims that Cruz had access to some of the translations of Chinese state documents and private letters but he provides no evidence. I have not been able to find any substantiation for this claim. See Boxer, *South China in the Sixteenth Century*, lxi.

16. Stephen Haw has recently argued that Polo provides enough contemporary information about events in the country to make his claim to having lived in China credible. See Stephen G. Haw, *Marco Polo's China: A Venetian in the Realm of Khubilai Khan* (London: Routledge, 2006). The case is not fully rested, however.

17. Rebecca Catz, who has edited the authoritative edition of Pinto's work in English, concludes that "modern investigation has disclosed that Pinto's *Travels* is indeed based, in large part, on historical fact, though some disagreement still exists as to the exact proportion of fact to fancy." See Rebecca Catz, ed. and trans., *The Travels of Mendez Pinto* (Chicago: University of Chicago Press, 1989), xxviii.

18. See the discussion of the published letter collections in M. Howard Rienstra, ed. and trans., *Jesuit Letters from China, 1583–84* (Minneapolis: University of Minnesota Press, 1986), esp. 6–7.

19. As pointed out in the Introduction to this collection and in the contributions by Littlejohn and Mazurak, the widely used edition of Ricci's journals made by Nicolas Trigault, although based on Ricci's original journal recording his twenty-seven years of continuous living in China and his fluent use of Chinese language, was heavily and pietistically edited and not published until five years after Ricci's death. Nonetheless, Spence holds that Trigault's version "provided a new benchmark for the study and description of China." See Jonathan Spence, *The Chan's Great Continent: China in Western Minds* (New York: Norton, 1998), 33. Mackerras notes that a decade after its publication in 1615, the journals were "reprinted four times in Latin and translated into German, Spanish, French, and Italian, and excerpts were translated into English. Like Mendoza's work, Ricci's was widely read and popular." Colin Mackerras, *Western Images of China* (New York: Oxford University Press, 1989), 31.

20. Vieria, in Boxer, ed. *South China in the Sixteenth Century*, xxx.

21. Martín de Rada, "Relation of the Things of China which Is Properly Called Taybin," in Boxer, ed. *South China in the Sixteenth Century*, 294.

22. Marco Polo, *The Description of the World*, ed. A. C. Moule and Paul Pelliot (London: George Routledge, 1938), 340.

23. Even though the selling had different economic consequences for the families, in some ways it was no different than the circulation of children in medieval or early modern Europe with the various apprentice networks.

24. Polo, *Description of the World*, 312.

25. Ibid, 312.

26. Friar Odoric of Pordenone, who visited China in the fourteenth century, attributes the well-being of the people more to their industry than to the social welfare system, though he also mentions that "no man ever seeketh alms. . . . But those who are fallen into indigence and infirmity are well looked after and provided with necessaries." See "The Travels of Friar Odoric of Pordenone," in *Cathay and the Way Thither*, ed. Sir Henry Yule (London: Hakluyt Society, 1913),

179. Odoric's observations were copied, almost word for word, by Sir John Mandeville in his wildly popular travelogue.

27. Galeote Pereira, in Boxer, *South China in the Sixteenth Century*, 7. As Boxer documents, Pereira's account of China was widely circulated in his time; the first English translation appeared in 1577 and was reprinted both in Hakluyt and Purchas.

28. Pereira in Boxer, *South China in the Sixteenth Century*, 30.

29. Ibid., 31.

30. Barros was in India from 1533 to 1567 and had "in his possession at Lisbon a collection of Chinese books and an intelligent Chinese slave to read and abstract them for him." See Boxer, Vol.1, Bk. 2, 738. The third book of Barros's *Décades* (1563) includes his longest account of China.

31. Gaspar da Cruz, "Treatise in which the Things of China Are Related at Great Length, with Their Particularities, as Likewise of the Kingdom of Ormuz," in Boxer, *South China in the Sixteenth Century*, 115.

32. Huang corroborates, based on his study of Ming sources: "Taxes were low. Land was taxed at about 3 percent of the total yield." See Ray Huang, "The Ming Fiscal Administration," *Cambridge History of China*, 107.

33. Here he differs from Vieria who had pointed to the constant oppression of the poor by the magistrates. See pg. 23 above.

44

34. Cruz, "Treatise," in Boxer, *South China in the Sixteenth Century*, 118–21.

35. Ibid., 151.

36. Ibid., 152.

37. Bernadine of Escalante, *A Discourse of the Navigation which the Portugales Make to the Realms and Provinces of the East Partes of the World and of the Knowledge that Growes by Them of the Great Thinges, Which Are in the Dominions of China* (London, 1579), 22v.

38. Writing in 1602, Father Diego de Pantoia, a Spanish priest who accompanied Matteo Ricci in his travels from Nanking to Beijing, castigates the sale of children as "vile"; because of the large population, children are "the cheapest thing in China" according to him, though he does recognize, like Escalante, that the children are not exploited and that they are married off when the right time comes. Despite his much more negative portrayal of China, Father de Pantoia still commended the industry of the poor which led to better social conditions. See "A Letter of father Diego De Pantoia, one of the Company of Jesus, to father Luys de Guzman, Provinciall in the Province of Toledo; written in Paquin, which is the Court of the King of China, the ninth of March, the yeare 1602" in Purchas, *Hakluytus Posthumus, or Purchas His Pilgrimes: Containing a History of the World in Sea Voyages and Lande Travells by Englishmen and Others* (1625; London: Glasgow: James MacLehose, 1906), Vol. 12, 377.

39. Escalante, *Discourse of the Navigation*, 24r.

40. Ibid., 24v.

41. Pinto traveled in Asia from 1537 to 1558 but his memoirs, *The Travels of Mendes Pinto*, were written between the years 1569 and 1578 and not published until 1614. Once they were published, however, during the seventeenth century, they "rivaled in popularity . . . Cervantes' famous classic." See Catz, xv.

42. Fernão Mendez Pinto, *The Travels of Mendes Pinto*, 230.

43. Even though he rues the spread of Buddhism, equating it with the "poison of herpes" (231), Pinto is able to appreciate the social benefits of the doctrines of charity taught by the Buddha. Marco Polo had similarly credited Buddhism with inspiring the Mongols to charity; his description includes references to grain stored in granaries for poor relief as well. See Polo, *Description of the World*, 250–51. Unlike Pinto, the Jesuits, with their policy of accommodation, were in fact able to draw parallels between the charitable deeds encouraged by Buddhism and Christianity. A letter from Father Longobard written in October 1598 discusses the "Many things in which the Jesuits and Chinois concurre," chiefly their "workes of Piety and Charity, Almes, Hospitals for Poore." Niccolo Longobard's essay is included in "A Generall Collection and Historical Representation of the Jesuites Entrance into Japon and China, until Their Admission in the Royall Citie of Nanquin," in Samuel Purchas, *Purchas His Pilgrimes*, Vol. 12, 317.

44. Pinto, *The Travels of Mendes Pinto*, 231.

45. The perfectly balanced social justice system seems to be the imaginative product of Pinto's own desires, and interestingly, most of the culpable are women. Spence detects a keen note of satire in the passage detailing Pinto's vision of social justice. See Jonathan Spence, *The Chan's Great Continent*, 30.

46. Pinto, *The Travels of Mendes Pinto*, 233. Pinto's observations about the granaries can be corroborated by Ming records. In 1368, Zhu Yuanzhang, the founder of the Ming dynasty, had ordered every county magistrate to set up four granaries. Most of the granaries functioned as Pinto describes, though by the mid-sixteenth century when Pinto would have visited China, some were no longer hoarding grain for emergency relief in the same ways. Instead, a capitalist system was emerging in which the magistrates bought grain from surrounding areas in times of crop failure. See Timothy Brook, *The Confusions of Pleasure: Commerce and Culture in Ming China* (Berkeley: University of California Press, 1998), xix.

47. Pinto, *The Travels of Mendes Pinto*, 233.

48. Juan Gonzalez de Mendoza, *Historie of the Kingdome of China* (London: Hakluyt Society, 1853), 48.

49. Donald Lach comments incisively that Mendoza's discussion of the "secular, state-controlled and state-supported education" must have come as a shock to learned Europeans. Ming China offered low-cost and open education to all classes of people, something yet unheard of in Europe. Lach, *Asia in the Making of Europe*, Vol. 1, 781.

50. Mendoza, *Historie of the Kingdome of China*, 67.

51. Linschoten's account of China, based in part on Mendoza's, also stresses the law against begging (I, 135). Linschoten himself had not traveled in China, though he had spent five years in Goa and had briefly visited Southeast Asia. See John Linschoten, *The Voyage of John Huyghen Van Linschoten to the East Indies*, ed. Arthur Coke Burnell, Vol. 1 (London: Hakluyt Society, 1880).

52. Mendoza, *Historie of the Kingdome of China*, 113.

53. Donald Lach found a general shift in the European attitudes to China which corroborates the changes we observe in the discussions of the welfare system: "The earliest accounts stress the material wealth, technological skills and complex organization of Chinese society. Those who try after mid-century, like Cruz, Mendoza, or Maffei, to present a synthesis tend to emphasize the rational order prevailing in China's governmental, educational and social structure." Lach, 1, 821.

54. Pierre D'Avity, *The Estates, Empires, & Principallities of the World Represented by the Description of Countries, Maners of Inhabitants, Riches of Prouinces, Forces, Gouernment, Religion; and the Princes That Haue Gouerned in Euery Estate*, trans. Edward Grimstone (London, 1615), 737. Galeote Pereira's early

account of his captivity in China similarly gives credit for the excellent governance of the country to multiple levels of officials appointed to ensure justice.

55. D'Avity, *Estates, Empires, and Principalities*, 738.

56. Sebes lists that there were twenty-five Jesuits, twenty-two Franciscans, one Dominican, and one Augustinian who had visited mainland China from 1552 to 1583, but no one had stayed there for more than a few months. See Joseph Sebes, S. J., "The Precursors of Ricci," in *East Meets West: The Jesuits in China, 1582–1773*, eds. Charles E. Ronan, S. J. and Bonnie B. C. Oh (Chicago: Loyola University Press, 1988), 27-30.

57. Matteo Ricci, *China in the Sixteenth Century: The Journals of Matthew Ricci: 1583–1610*, trans. Louis J. Gallagher (New York: Random House, 1942), 57.

58. Ibid., 52. Gaspar da Cruz, writing about fifty years earlier, had similarly pointed to the bribery and corruption which sometimes prevented the carrying out of justice. Magistrates apparently paid and substituted an innocent man for a guilty person condemned to be whipped if the bribe was significant enough or if the magistrate was friendly with the guilty person. However, Cruz also points to the checks placed upon the magistrates—when there is evidence of the magistrates having accepted bribes, they are punished severely and stripped of their rank. See Cruz, in Boxer, 166–67.

59. Ricci, *China in Sixteenth Century*, 88.

60. Ibid., 57.

61. Ibid., 23.

62. Ibid., 86.

63. Botero, Giovanni. *Relations of the Most Famous Kingdomes and Common-wealths Thorowout the World Discoursing of Their Situations, Religions, Languages, Manners, Customes, Strengths, Greatnesse and Policies* (London, 1630). Available through *Early English Books Online*. Botero begins his portrait of China wholly condemning the various aspects of the country: "Their manner of life is most obscene and shamelesse, their idolatrie vile and vicious, their incantations ridiculous, the prostitution of Virgins to be deflowred of Idols abominable, their exorcismes damnable and the varietie of senselesse profanations most contemptible," 592.

64. Lach, Vol.1, Bk. 2, 709. Lach attests to the huge popularity of Botero's work in many languages, including the two English translations of 1606 and 1630, in Vol. 2, Bk. 2, 243.

65. Ibid., 593.

66. Richard Cocks, letter to Thomas Wilson, Secretary to Lord Salisbury, December 10, 1614, *Calendar of Japan Papers* 1614, reprinted in *Letters Written by the English Residents in Japan 1611–1623*, ed. N. Murakami and K. Murakawa (Tokyo: Sankūsha, 1900), 150.

67. Richard Trexler, "The Foundlings of Florence, 1395–1455." *History of Childhood Quarterly* 2 (1975), 260–61.

68. Valentina Tikoff, "'Not All the Orphans Really Are': The Diversity of Seville's Juvenile Charity Wards during the Long Eighteenth Century," *Raising an Empire: Children in Early Modern Iberia and Colonial Latin America*, ed. Ondina E. González and Bianca Premo (Albuquerque: University of New Mexico Press, 2007), 47.

69. Philip Gavitt, *Charity and Children in Renaissance Florence: The Ospedale Degli Innocenti, 1410-1536* (Ann Arbor: University of Michigan Press, 1990), 21.

70. Brian Pullan, *Orphans and Foundlings in Early Modern Europe*. The Stenton Lecture (Berkshire, UK: University of Reading, 1989), 5.

71. Gavitt, *Charity and Children*, 207.

72. Pier Paolo Viazzo, Maria Bortolotto, and Andrea Zanotto, "Five Centuries of Foundling History in Florence: Changing Patterns of Abandonment, Care and Mortality." In *Abandoned Children*, eds. Catherine Panter-Brick and Malcolm T. Smith (Cambridge: Cambridge University Press, 2000), 79.

73. Anne M. C. McCants, *Civic Charity in a Golden Age: Orphan Care in Early Modern Amsterdam* (Urbana: University of Illinois Press, 1997), 23.

74. Tikoff, "'Not All the Orphans,'" 44.

75. Nicholas Terpstra, *Abandoned Children of the Italian Renaissance: Orphan Care in Florence and Bologna* (Baltimore: Johns Hopkins University Press, 2005), 36.

76. Pullan, *Orphans and Foundlings*, 10.

77. Trexler, "Foundlings," 270.

78. T'ien Ju-Kang, *Male Anxiety and Female Chastity: A Comparative Study of Chinese Ethical Values in Ming-Ch'ing Times* (New York: E. J. Brill, 1988), 30.

79. Ann Waltner, "Infanticide and Dowry in Ming and Early Qing China," *Chinese Views of Childhood*, ed. Anne Behnke Kinney (Honolulu: University of Hawai'i Press, 1995), 202.

80. Terpstra, *Abandoned Children*, 35.

81. Timothy J. Coates, *Convicts and Orphans: Forced and State-Sponsored Colonizers in the Portuguese Empire, 1550-1755* (Stanford, CA: Stanford University Press, 2001), 16.

82. Gavitt, *Charity and Children*, 187.

83. See "The Jesuits in the Far East" in Samuel Purchas, *Purchas his Pilgrimes*, Vol. 12, 273.

84. D. E. Mungello, *Drowning Girls in China: Female Infanticide Since 1650* (Lanham: Rowman & Littlefield, 2008), 7. As Domingo Navarrete, a Dominican friar who lived in China from 1657 to 1665, discusses, he himself had tried to rescue several infants, but most of the requests for baptism were refused by Chinese parents; however, this was an important and perhaps easier way for the Christian church to swell its numbers in the resistant religious climate in China. See Domingo Navarrete, *The Travels and Controversies of Friar Domingo Navarrete, 1618–1686*, ed. J. S. Cummins (Cambridge, UK: Hakluyt Society, 1962).

85. Trexler, "Foundlings," 264.

86. Joanna Handlin Smith, *The Art of Doing Good: Charity in Late Ming China* (Berkeley: University of California Press, 2009), 74. Friar Navarrete cites cases of finding crying babies on the streets of China as well as right outside the parental home in the early Qing era.

87. Smith, *Art of Doing Good*, 118.

88. T'ien Ju-Kang, *Male Anxiety*, 30.

89. The Chinese only recognized the social existence of a child three days after its birth in a ritual called "lifting up" in which a male member of the family carried the baby out of the birthing chamber to present it to the father. There was also a bath on the third day that confirmed the social status of the new born. See Mungello, *Drowning Girls in China*, 5; Kinney, *Representations of Childhood*, 108–10.

90. Ping-Chen Hsiung, *A Tender Voyage: Children and Childhood in Late Imperial China* (Stanford, CA: Stanford University Press, 2005), 45.

91. Ibid., 33–47.

92. Smith, *Art of Doing Good*, 4.

93. Ibid., 8.

94. Kandice J. Hauf, "The Community Covenant in Sixteenth Century Ji'an Prefecture, Jiangxi," *Late Imperial China* 17, 2 (1996): 1–50.

95. Patricia Buckley Ebrey, *Women and the Family in Chinese History* (London: Routledge, 2003), 72–73.

96. Mungello, *Drowning Girls*, 46. Mungello sees the imperial or legislative involvement in the welfare of unwanted children disappearing during the Ming era, though early European visitors continued to claim that institutions of child welfare existed in China in vast numbers.

97. Terpstra, *Abandoned Children*, 66.

98. Ibid., 20.

99. Pinto, *The Travels of Mendez Pinto*, 1. Pinto begins his narrative talking about the "poverty and misery" he faced in his native land as a child, but no external evidence has survived that gives us an insight into his family's economic situation.

100. Timothy S. Miller, "The Early History of Orphanages: From Constantinople to Venice," in *Home Away from Home: The Forgotten History of Orphanages* (New York: Encounter Books, 2009), 37.

101. Brook, *The Confusions of Pleasure*, 163.

102. Ray Huang, *1587, A Year of No Significance: The Ming Dynasty in Decline* (New Haven, CI: Yale University Press, 1981), 119.

103. Burton, *Anatomy of Melancholy*, 353.

Qingjun Li, Belmont University

Of Golden Lilies and Gentlewomen: Constructions of Chinese Women in Early Modern European Travel Narratives

THE EARLY MODERN PERIOD IN ENGLAND WAS IN MANY ways characterized by great dynamism. Discoveries were being made of far away places such as China, where some of their customs and practices were regarded as strange and others were seemingly very familiar. Considerable attention has been given to the ways in which sixteenth- and seventeenth-century English literature represents and reflects the debate over gender identity with respect to the writers' use of biblical materials and reason. However, very little attention has been given to the subject of this paper: in what ways early modern English writers thought of their views on gender roles as universal truth in light of the new contacts with other cultures, specifically with China. From the thirteenth to the mid-eighteenth centuries, the source genre most widely cited by European writers providing information about women and gender in China was the travel narrative.

Just what understanding of China was available to the writers in England during the early modern period remains an area of vague assumptions and misconceptions. One misconception widely accepted until recently is the belief that with respect to literary output on other cultures by European writers between 1500 and 1750, the amount concerned with the Americas exceeded that on Asia. However, in *Asia in the Making of Europe,* Donald Lach and Edwin Van Kley have shown this assumption is false. They have identified over 1,500 works on Asia published in Europe between 1500 and 1750. Such a body of work actually dwarfs the amount of material published about the Americas during the same period.[1]

Another miscalculation made by many scholars studying this period is to read the presuppositions of nineteenth-century English colonialism back onto the sixteenth and seventeenth centuries, taking for granted that the English thought of themselves as nationally, morally, and racially superior to all Asian peoples. The assumption, then, made by many scholars applying postcolonial criticism to the works of early modern English writers is that they would not have looked to China for validation of their ideas about feminine conduct and roles. Instead, they would have thought civilizations such as China would have needed to learn from the British. That is to say, that what we find in the English colonial mentality is that English social patterns are superior to those found elsewhere, and that foreign peoples must be civilized by having these practices shown to them and infused into their cultural activities by the superior colonial power. This is certainly the pattern we see with respect to the Americas and the Pacific islands. However, employing this particular theoretical critique has some limitations with regard to how China was viewed by writers of the fifteenth and sixteenth centuries. In her work, *Colonialism/Postcolonialism,* Ania Loomba expresses the belief that European colonialism was by far the most extensive of the different kinds of colonial contact in the human history. She points out that by the end of the nineteenth-century 85 percent of the land surface of the world was covered by colonies or ex-colonies. Yet, she is very careful to exclude early modern Japan and China as major Eastern civilizations which were not under foreign colonial domination in the early modern period, even if China was indeed later semi-colonized, in the ways postcolonialists typically focus upon.[2] Her principal goal is to address two of the most pressing problems in postcolonial criticism: how to understand the concept of hybridity and how to recover the viewpoint of colonized subjects from a postcolonial perspective. Neither of these issues is directly relevant to the present project of understanding how writers over two hundred years before the rise of colonialism made use of travel narratives about a culture that was never a colony of Britain or any European power.[3]

Moreover, Lesley Cormack has shown that the formation of Britain's consciousness of itself as a global colonial power did not emerge until after the early modern period. This shift in consciousness occurred as the British encountered cultures that they considered uncivilized. For example, in his "Objects Ridiculous and August: Early Modern European Perceptions of Asia," M. N. Pearson argues that, in general, European travelers found India to be less well governed than China and the social patterns in China to be more reflective of what they considered universally right and true. He observes that a sense of European superiority does not replace this attitude until the late eighteenth century. [4]

Early modern English travel writers did not think of themselves or their culture as superior to that of China. The colonial mentality of the late eighteenth and early nineteenth centuries had not yet taken hold. David Porter argues that the writers and thinkers in pre-nineteenth-century England understood China to be possessed of a long history of accomplishment and advanced social structures and moral precepts that represented to them the sort of values that could be appropriated for English usage.[5] In "Making Something of It: Questions of Value in the Early English Travel Collection," Mary Fuller argues that China was not only the other side of the world, but also the other side of the coin as far as culture is considered. She says that the travel narrative writer, Richard Hakluyt (1589, 1600), often offered descriptions depreciating the Africans and indigenous Americans in travel collections, but that his comments on Chinese culture suggest that the English very much wanted to be taken seriously by that ancient and civilized country since England was emerging from a sense of its own conflict and even backwardness and was facing new challenges to traditional cultural roles and practices.[6] A closer look at early modern travel writing about China will bring these generalizations into tighter focus especially with respect to gender issues.

It is commonly believed that Marco Polo's *Le Divisament Dou Monde* (*Discovery of the World*, 1298) is the first travel account in a European language to discuss China, its people and culture, and that the understanding of China passed along to the Europeans in the early modern period came largely from this text. However, although Polo's account was better known and more influential, the distinction of being the "first" travel narrative about China actually belongs to the Franciscan friar William of Rubrick. William was dispatched to the Mongol capital in 1253 by King Louis IX of France in an attempt to secure aid against Islamic expansion. Although William did not make it to China, he did keep a journal encompassing the information he acquired from those who were Chinese or who had visited there.[7] Nevertheless, it is true, that in spite of debates over the accuracy and reliability of Polo's work on China,[8] it is still generally acknowledged that he provided Europe with the most comprehensive and authoritative account of China produced before the early modern period.[9]

Polo described the conduct and deportment of Chinese women to his European audience in this way:

> You ought to learn too that the girls of the province of Catai are beyond others pure and keep the virtue of modesty.... And if it happens that they go to some proper place, as perhaps the idol temples or to visit the houses of kinsfolk and relations, they would go in the company of their mothers, not staring improperly at people but wearing on the head certain pretty bonnets of theirs which prevent an upward look, so that in walking they always direct the eyes on the road before the feet. Before their elders they are modest, they never speak foolish words, nor indeed any in their presence, except when they have been asked. In their rooms they keep at their tasks and rarely show themselves to fathers and brothers and the elders of the house. And they pay no attention to suitors.[10]

Polo's depiction of Chinese women's dress, modesty, reserve, domesticity, and humility seems to conform well to what we know of the instructions given to girls and women in China during the period of the Yuan dynasty (1279–1368) which Polo is describing. The diverse literature instructing Chinese women and girls during the Yuan constructed gender identity and conduct expectations in much the same way as was done in Europe of the early modern period. Polo seems to describe just the kind of women recommended by the literature in the Chinese Confucian educational system written for girls and women. In China, many conduct texts worked together, mutually illuminating, supporting, criticizing, and balancing each other. None-theless, gender education was much more formalized and structured than in England. The most widely used works by all Chinese families to educate their daughters on feminine gender roles and conduct in Polo's day were the Nuerjing 《女兒經》 (*Classic for Girls*) and the Nujie 《女誡》 (*Precepts for Women*).

While the Nuerjing was anonymously authored, the Nujie was writ-ten by someone tradition considers to be the greatest female writer in Chinese history, Ban Zhao 班昭 (45–116). The Nujie has seven short chapters, including instructions on maintaining humility and modesty based on the fact that women are by nature yin 陰, passive, supple, and receptive. Among the behaviors the Nujie recommends to women are the following.

> Let her have ears that hear not licentiousness, and eyes that see not depravity. When she goes outside her own home, let her not be conspicu-ous in dress and manners. When at home let her not neglect her dress. Women should not assemble in groups, nor gather together for gossip and silly laughter. They should not stand watching in gateways. If a woman follows these rules, she may be said to have whole-hearted devotion and correct manners.[11]

The connection between what Chinese conduct books teach about women and the reports given by Polo raises anew the fundamental question whether the use of travel writing to supplement the discourse of history is reliable. Polo does observe how Chinese woman behave with pertinent manners; however, he does not unfold the reason why Chinese women cling to such rigid rules to the letter. He seems not to have noticed that the Confucian teachings about women in Confucian conduct books such as the Nuerjing have as profound an influence on Chinese women as the later early modern conduct books in England did on western women.

In his piece on travel narratives about Holland written by English writers in the sixteenth century, Christopher Gabbard argues that travel writing should not be treated as necessarily providing a window on a particular time and culture, but rather, as opening a textual space in which disparate cultures and worldviews meet, clash, and grapple with one another.[12] If we apply Gabbard's line of interpretation to Polo's writing, then we do not need to resolve the historicity of the account or even confirm that the sorts of practices he describes conform to those taught in Chinese conduct books. Rather it is his selection and valorization of just those features that validate traditional European views of women's conduct and place which matters most.

The English author John Mandeville[13] wrote several elaborate and deliberately romantic fictions about China in his *Travels of Sir John Mandeville* that circulated widely in the 1350s and which also played a significant role in constructing the European view of Chinese women prior to the early modern period. This work was tremendously popular both in England and throughout Europe. The extant manuscripts number around 300 whereas there are only 119 Marco Polo manuscripts now available. Versions remain in English, French, Spanish, Dutch, Danish, Irish, Bohemian, and Walloon. While there is little doubt that Mandeville never visited China or even the East, he nevertheless portrayed Cathay (i.e., China) as a utopia, not only because of its richness of land, but also because of its virtuous women who exhibited those traits that Polo had already mentioned: modesty, humility, obedience, and filiality.[14] Mandeville's fictions joined Polo's writings in creating the English consciousness of China as an idyllically well-ordered society in which women behaved according to the traditional expectations set for them in England and Europe. Throughout the fifteenth and into the sixteenth century, this understanding incubated the belief that there were transcultural norms for men and women.

Early Modern Travel Genre Materials

In 1511 the Portuguese captured Malacca and penetrated into southern China, and this new world opened to Europeans as never before. The Portuguese writer Mendes Pinto, who did visit the East, but not China, nevertheless wove stories about China from those he had been hearing and reading into his 1568 text *Peregrination*.[15] His descriptions of China occupy 120 pages of the 520-page volume. This work is a skillful literary piece written in four different narrative voices. In Pinto's section on China, the "innocent observer" who travels the world over in search of a civilization superior to his own, comes at last to find just such a place in

China. The Chinese are portrayed as being far ahead of their Western contemporaries in government, morality, and familial order. Chinese women are depicted as full of true virtue because they are submissive, quiet and full of gentility, and never aggressive or argumentative. They do not challenge male power or authority, nor question their role in culture and society.[16]

As Polo and Mandeville had done before the early modern period, we see Pinto attribute to Chinese women just the kinds of traits which were regarded as right and proper for women as shown both in the English conduct books for women written in the sixteenth and seventeenth centuries and embodied in the Chinese conduct books being used in the Ming period (1368–1644) as well. During the Ming, the women's conduct text *Nuerjing* was supplemented by a collection of four works known as the *Nu Sishu* 《女四書》 (*Four Books for Women*), which were all written by women and for women. These four texts included the previously mentioned *Nujie*; the *Nu Lunyu* 《女 論 語 》 (*Analects for Women*) by Song Ruoxin 宋若莘 and Song Ruozhao 宋若昭; the *Neixun* 《內訓》 (*Instructions for the Inner Court*) by Xu Shi, Empress Ren Xiao; and the *Nufan Jielu* 《女範捷录》 (*Short Records of Models for Women*) written in 1624 by Liu Shi, the mother of Confucian scholar Wang Xiang. Pinto, like those before him, was holding up an ideal of womanhood which was quite the opposite of the emerging feminine consciousness in Europe which was calling for greater freedom of women and asserting feminine rights. He was valorizing the Chinese model as evidence of a universal truth about gender roles.

Juan Gonzalez de Mendoza, an Augustinian monk, was author of another quintessential example of a European travel narrative unveiling China to the West. He produced one of the earliest and most influential chronicles of China in the sixteenth century. Although he did not visit China, he had as one of his main sources a fellow monk who did serve there. Gonzalez was ordered by Pope Gregory XIII to compose a history of all the things that were known about China.[17] His *L'historia del gran regno della China* (*The History of the Great and Mighty China*, 1588 Eng. trans.) is among the earliest European travel works to be devoted exclusively to that culture.[18] This work was translated from Spanish into English and almost all European languages before the end of the century. It was reprinted forty-six times in seven different European languages and was readily available in sixteenth-century England. Unlike the other writers on China before him, Gonzalez devoted an entire chapter specifically to an account of China's women and their behavior. He wrote, "And it is greatly to bee maruailed at, that the women of this kingdome are marueilous chast and discreet."[19]

Gonzalez praised the chastity and domesticity of Chinese women. He also described Chinese women as dedicated to the service of their husbands and families. Speaking of the burial of the male landlord about which he heard, Gonzalez reported that "[w]hen they should be buried, they command to kill all their seruants, or their wiues, those that best he loued in his life, saying they do it, that they should go with them to serue them in the other world, wheras they beléeue they shall liue eternally and die no more."[20] Gonzalez did not approve of the practice of husbands having their wives killed when they die in order that they can continue to serve them in the afterlife, but he presented this as an illustration of the seriousness with which Chinese women took their wifely duties. Gonzalez's approval of Chinese gender patterns creates a picture that Chinese women revere their husbands who are regarded as the backbone of family and the entirety of a woman's life. His portrayal of Chinese women's conduct joined with those of Pinto, Mandeville, and Polo to provide a growing picture of a transcultural gender pattern for femininity which fitted well with the literature arising in England written to suppress an emerging movement resisting the traditional model for women's conduct.

Actually, English writers both generated and reflected the struggle to understand the place of women in the new age being born in the sixteenth to seventeenth centuries. Received views of women and their roles were turned into ideals and vigorously defended by dozens of male writers. Attempts to move outside of the accepted gender models met with what can only be called misogynistic reactions. Reports and descriptions of exotic lands, including Asia, and especially the mysterious China, came into the English consciousness. The belief that European views of women could be regarded as transcultural gender truths began to find material support by authors who made use of travel narratives concerned with everyday life and the place of women in distant China.[21] Accordingly, the demands for greater gender equality by English women were conceived of as deviations from a universal pattern of women's conduct found in other cultures such as China and reported by the travel writers. To see just how this worked, some familiarity with what was being written about women in early modern England is required.

Women and Gender in the Early Modern English Conduct Books

Speaking of writings about the conduct and place of women in six-teenth- and seventeenth-century England, Joan Klein makes an insight-ful observation, "Because of the restrictions imposed on their speech and writing by law and custom, we know very little about the ways they [women] understood themselves and their relationships to their husbands, children, other relatives, and neighbors. . . . What we do pos-sess from this period, however, is a substantial number of books written by men and often to women."[22] These writings, known generally as "conduct books," set out the main outlines of the pattern for women and their domesticity as understood in the early modern period. With the advent of the printing press by William Caxton in 1476, there was a definite increase both in the number of treatises about female conduct written in English and in their widespread dissemination.[23] Suzanne Hull points out that "Between 1475 and 1640 approximately 170 dif-ferent books in some 500 editions were specifically addressed to females or dealt with subjects of direct concern to women. . . . If each of the 500 editions had a run of 1,000 copies—normal at that time—then 500,000 books for women came onto the market in that 165-year period."[24] Hull's statement emphasizes that the study of the "women's questions" were of great concern in England. Indeed, to underscore the importance of reflection on women's conduct in England, Hull has done a system-atic study of books by men addressed to women in her *Chaste, Silent and Obedient, English Books for Women 1475–1640*, and she has arranged the content of these works by topics such as "Rules for Wives" and "Rais-ing Daughters" in her *Women According to Men: The World of Tudor-Stuart Women*. These topics provide an explicit panorama of the expectations of women in early modern England and help organize a vast amount of writings on women's conduct in the period to serve as background for a study concerned with how China travel narratives were used in tandem with this corpus of material.[25]

One conduct text written by men for women is *An Homily of the State of Matrimony* which was included in *The Second Book of Homilies* (1563) required by King James I to be read in all of England's churches. King James's royal mandate makes it impossible to neglect this work in any study of the literature about gender roles in the early modern period because church attendance was obligatory in England until the late seventeenth century. Thus the entire English population would have been familiar with the *Homily*'s teachings about women.[26] As a result, this work took its place alongside the Bible, *Fox's Book of Martyrs*, and *The Book of Common Prayer* as the four best known books in England. It was in use during the time that the fictitious *Travels of Sir John Mandeville* was in wide circulation in England. The *Homily* was compiled by several male authors, and its seeming tolerance of women actually has behind it a clear estimate of feminine inferiority: ". . . the woman ought to have a certain honor attributed to her, that is to say, she must be spared and borne with, the rather from that she is the weaker vessel, of a frail heart, inconstant, and with a word soon stirred to wrath."[27] The *Homily* insists that a daughter obey her father and a wife be in submission to her husband.[28] While the authors forbid beating a wife as "the greatest shame" of a husband; nonetheless, they tell women that if they by fortune are matched to a man who beats them, "take it not too heavily, but suppose thou that thereby is laid up no small reward hereafter and in this lifetime no small commendation to thee if thou canst be quiet."[29] Of course, the *Homily*, as a Christian text, made no direct appeal to the *Travels of Sir John Mandeville*, nor to China, but the pattern it offered as divinely ordained closely resembled what was being reported of Chinese women in the travel narratives.

Of the important English texts concerned with the domestic duties and behavior of women in the early modern period, the one which did not make overt appeal to Christianity or the teachings of the church, was Richard Brathwaite's *The English Gentlewoman* (1631) addressed to Lady Arabella Wentworth.[30] The work was written one year after Brathwaite published *The English Gentleman*, and it was intended to be a companion to it.[31] Brathwaite does not begin his work with a description of Eve's fall, as do so many male authors of the religious-based conduct books of this period. Rather, he opens with a chapter on modest and pleasing fashion. For Brathwaite, it is the appeal of civility, not obedience to religious duty, which is the principal commendation of women. While Brathwaite surely believes his gentlewoman will be virtuous, he hopes that morality will be softened by gentility and polished by courtesy: "But lest by being too serious, she might become tedious, she will not stick to walk abroad with you into more pleasing groves or pastures of delight, where she will converse with you of love, and intermix her discourse with such time beguiling tales, as variety shall no less sharpen your attention, that the modesty of her method beget admiration."[32]

Brathwaite considers the feminine ideal to be a woman of calm restraint and confidence: "So as there is nothing in the whole posture of her behavior but with a native graceful propriety does infinitely become her . . . albeit every moving posture which comes from her may be a line of direction unto others to follow her."[33] This gentlewoman's chastity is "an inclosed garden" which should not be questioned "lest the report of her spotless beauty become soiled."[34] Yet, she must never lapse from her submission, "always being proportionate and discreet in her remonstration with father, husband, or lord."[35] When he speaks of honor, he does not define it as moral righteousness, but as gentility. For Brathwaite, the gentlewoman does honor to her parents, her husband, and her family. He admonishes the gentlewoman: "Retain those divine impressions of goodness in you that may truly ennoble you; display your gentility by such a coat as may best distinguish your family. So shall you live and die with honor and survive their fame, whose only glory it was to enjoy fortune's favor."[36] Brathwaite's text valorizes the sort of woman that Pinto's *Peregrination* and Gonzalez's *L'historia del gran regno della China* hold up as an example to Europe from Chinese culture, and both of these travel narratives were well known in Brathwaite's England.

While conduct books such as the *Homily* and Brathwaite's *English Gentlewoman* provide substantial evidence for early modern writing about women, in the middle of the sixteenth century, a genre of pamphlets was also in circulation in popular English culture written by both men and women, debating the traditional beliefs about feminine nature, role, and behavior. Male authors began this debate with two major works written in rhyme royal. The first of these was *The School-house of Women* (probably 1541), whose authorship is unknown. This text made a crude attack on women requiring them to keep silent and not dispute men: "Although women's reason is 'not worth a turd' since they are dominated by the senses, yet they constantly hinder men from speaking and insist on having the last word."[37] The author criticizes the "babble fast" gossiping of women who scold their fathers and husbands and considers every woman to be sexually lecherous and not able to be satisfied even by fifteen men. Husbands are encouraged to be firm with their wives and restrict all of their movements, and never to trust the tears of a woman because these are only crafty tricks.[38] *The Schoolhouse* does not present a model for a woman's behavior such as we find in *The Homily* or in Brathwaite's *English Gentlewoman*. It is an invective directed against women. Edward Gosynhill responded to *The Schoolhouse* with *The Praise of All Women, Called Mulierum Paean* (probably 1542), and a steady stream of popular pamphlets going back and forth on the nature and proper behavior of women followed. In 1595, Stephen Gosson wrote *Quips for Upstart, Newfangled Gentlewomen*, which attacked women's apparel and cosmetics as evidence of their moral depravity and lack of chaste modesty. Even so, women were not without their defenders even among male authors such as Lodowick Lloyd's *The Choice of Jewels* (1607) and William Heale's argument against wife beating, *An Apology for Women* (1609).

The other major work written for a popular audience that fanned the fires of debate about women's place in England was by Joseph Swetnam under the pseudonym Thomas Tell-Troth. It was entitled *The Arraignment of Lewd, Idle, Froward, and Unconstant Women* (1615). This pamphlet ran through ten editions by 1637, and it provoked responses from female authors for the first time in the controversy. Swetnam's writing was particularly harsh. He says simply, "Young men do not realize that women bring nothing but trouble."[39] Revealing a deep intolerance for any challenge to male authority, he writes that "[i]t is said that an old Dog and a hungry flea bite sore, but in my mind a froward woman biteth more sorer; and if thou go about to master a woman in hope to bring her to humility, there is no way to make her good with stripes except thou beat her to death."[40] According to Swetnam, women are subtle and dangerous, their beauties are mere bait, and their words are charms to bring men to ruin. "The pride of a woman is like the dropsy."[41] Swetnam finds no comfort in a woman who values her appearance. He remarks, "For commonly women are the most part of the forenoon painting themselves, and frizzling their hairs, and prying in their glass like Apes to prank up themselves in their gaudies."[42] He offers little hope that there are any virtuous women at all, and his exemplary women are very revealingly similar to those Chinese women that Gonzalez praises. One took her husband's place in prison, another built such a fabulous sepulcher for her husband that it became one of the wonders of the world, and one loving wife committed suicide with her husband as he died with a disease.[43]

Swetnam's contemptuous remarks on women received attacks, and actually three critical responses to Swetnam's work were written, all by women. This simple fact is perhaps most striking because between the start of English printing in 1476 and the year 1650 only roughly 125 women are known to have authored printed material of any kind. This is about 1 percent of the total number of works published.[44] The essays responding to Swetnam were by Rachel Speght (A Muzzle for Melastomus, 1617), by authors under the pseudonyms of Constantia Munda (The Worming of a Mad Dog, 1617), and by Esther Sowernam (Esther Hath Hanged Haman, 1617). Sowernam addresses Swetnam directly: "What have you gotten by publishing your Pamphlet? You have (perhaps) pleased the humors of some giddy, idle, conceited persons, but you have dyed yourself in the colors of shame, lying, slandering, blasphemy, ignorance, and the like."[45] She employed these severe words to attack the male-dominated world boldly. Her gesture clearly demonstrated her tendency to pursue a feminist viewpoint.

In 1620, at about the same time he ruled that the Homily should be read in all English churches, King James, perhaps impatient with the running debate over gender in the popular pamphlets, ordered his clergy "to inveigh vehemently in their sermons against the insolence of our women and their wearing of broad-brimmed hats, pointed doublets, their hair cut short or shorn, and some of them stilettos or poniards, and such other trinkets of like moment."[46] Shortly afterward, a viciously misogynistic tract appeared by an anonymous author under the title, Hic Mulier (The Man-Woman). The author attacks feminine assertiveness as an attempt to wear the breeches of the man, and posits a rational, physiological, and religious basis for restricting the movement of women in the public sphere and for their subordination in the domestic one. Hic Mulier says, "Those virtues that in women merit praise / Are sober shows without, chaste thoughts within, / True Faith and due obedience to their mate, / And of their children honest care to take."[47] In addition, the writer stresses how out of step from the universal pattern for feminine conduct English women are in asserting themselves and demanding greater rights and liberties in the following lines.

> [S]ee the modest Dutch, the stately Italian, the rich Spaniard, and the courtly French with the rest according to their climates, and you will blush that there cannot be found one piece of a Character to compare or liken with the absurdity of their Masculine Invention. . . . [indeed the one who] had liberty with his Shears to cut from every Nation of the World one piece of patch to make up his garment, yet amongst them all could not find this Miscellany or mixture of deformities.[48]

Although the writer does not mention China specifically, he claims that the absurdity of English women's assertiveness is contrary to the universal transcultural truths regarding women's behavior one can see simply by looking at other cultures. We can surmise that readers might have connected this universalist argument with the evidence the travel narratives provided since by the time of the writing of Hic Mulier a well-known picture of Chinese women was available through Polo, the Mandeville fictions, Pinto, and Gonzalez.

The sixteenth-century pamphlets such as Schoolhouse and Arraignment, along with responses by Speght, Munda, and Sowernam, represent an active struggle within English culture by members of all classes to create an understanding of how women should behave in society. However, Laura Gowing states, "The most neatly elaborated of cultural models for the household was . . . unwieldy for most people's use. The idealized orderly household, where hierarchical rules regulated every personal relationship, fitted few families' experiences. The detailed prescriptions for women's behavior that were listed in conduct books were just as hard to enforce."[49]

Assessing the Role of Travel Writings on Chinese Women to the Early Modern English Debate on Female Rights and Roles

The early modern English strictures which bound women to domesticity, modesty, chastity, silence, obedience, and restricted movement were, while being strongly reinforced, also being destabilized in the literature of sixteenth- and seventeenth-century England; however, there was fierce resistance to this tendency and desire to change. The conduct books and pamphlets are as much representative of this struggle as they are of its causes. Defenders of gender patterns and duties associated with biblical truth looked to works such as *The Homily*. Those who appealed to idealized English behavior for models found one at hand in Brathwaite's *The English Gentlewoman*. Attempts to move outside of the strictures of rigid gender models met with misogynistic pamphlets directed to a popular audience such as Swetnam's *The Arraignment* and the anonymous, *Hic Mulier*. The view expressed especially in *Hic Mulier* that the demand for greater gender equality on the part of English women went against the universal pattern of women's conduct found in all cultures, as indicated by its presence in far eastern China, forms the background for a study of just what sort of views of women in other cultures were available to English readers through the writings of European authors. Specifically, *Hic Mulier*'s examples were drawn from Europe, England's close neighbor. Finding similarity between the patterns for women's conduct in these cultures might be expected because the Dutch, Italian, Spanish, and French cultures had grown in the same religious and moral soil as had England. The logic of this argument continued. If the exotic culture of China in the Far East was found to have similar beliefs about women's conduct and role as those advocated in the conduct books, the hypothesis for transcultural gender patterns with universal application would simply be reinforced and strengthened.

    Peter Heylyn's work *Cosmographie* (1652) is a compilation of many travel sources. It is an attempt to describe in meticulous detail every aspect of the then-known cultures of the world, including their geography, climate, customs, achievements, politics, and belief systems.[50] His observations were based on firsthand descriptions of events offered by trade emissaries, and he used his descriptions to support his belief that there were universal truths about the moral order of gender roles.[51] He specifically lavished praise on the Chinese for their industry and government. In the second edition (1657) of his *Cosmographie*, published at a time when England was entangled in controversy about social order, Heylyn presented China as an example of how a complex society could function without succumbing to the internal cracks in social order that destroyed other empires.[52] Of China, he said that it is:

> [a] politick and judicious Nation; but very jealous of their women, and great tyrants over them, not suffering them to go outside the house, or sit down at the Table if any stranger be invited, unless he be some very neer kinsman. A tyranny or restraint, which the poor women give no cause for, being said to be very honest, and much reserved; not so much as shewing themselves at a window for fear of offence: and if they use painting, as most of them do, it is rather to preserve themselves in the good affections of their husbands, than for any other lewd respects.[53]

What is interesting here is that while Heylyn feels the restrictions on Chinese women may be extreme his reasoning is not what we might expect. He does not say that the Chinese limitations on women's conduct are tyrannical because they are unjust as we might find a defender of the growing women's movement in England arguing. Instead, he thinks them unreasonable because Chinese women give no cause for them. Chinese women are modest, dress only for their husbands, and they are reserved and honest. The restrictions on them are unnecessary in Heylyn's view because of the virtue of the women themselves. So, actually, Heylyn's point supports the traditional view of women's role and place and does so indirectly by an appeal to the Chinese model.

Like Heylyn, Johannes Nieuhoff wrote in 1673 interestingly and widely of the gender and family customs in China. He accompanied a European trade mission of the East-India Company from Canton to the court in Peking, thereby giving him the opportunity to observe Chinese women firsthand. He was quite impressed with the gentility he observed in the conduct of Chinese women. He expressed that "[a]ll the

Women are short, and low of Stature, and their chiefest Beauty (as they imagine) consists in the smallness of their Feet; and therefore when they are young, they bind and swath their Feet, they keep them from growing to their natural bigness, and by that means they become generally very small: But this is not all the care; for they are taught very young, That it is a principal part of modesty to keep within doors, and not to be seen frequently abroad in the Streets."[54]

Nieuhoff does not make any objection to the practice of foot-binding.[55] In fact, he takes it as part of the "care" Chinese women take to conform to their expected role in society. He stresses that the women of China are not only taught to bind their feet into what was known as "golden lilies" when they are young, but also to be modest and restrict themselves to their homes. As the Chinese conduct book, the *Nuerjing*, confirms, all girls should turn their feet into golden lilies in this manner: "Leave your bed when day is breaking, early thus begin the days. / Comb your tresses smooth and shiny, keep yourself both clean and neat, / Bind your lilies tight and tidy, never go upon the street."[56] Nieuhoff, like the *Nuerjing*, makes no apparent distinction between the behaviors of foot-binding, dressing in a clean and tidy manner, and never going out of the house. He seems to think that they are all ultimately good examples of proper feminine behavior.[57]

Patricia Ebrey notes that early modern European travel narratives, such as Nieuhoff's, approve of the Chinese practices of female seclusion; the discreet cut of women's clothing; the modesty, chastity, and meekness of Chinese women; and the gentleness of their behavior. She thinks that these narratives can be read as indirect criticisms of European ways or efforts on the part of women in Europe and England to change their place in society. She holds that it was not until the nineteenth century that an English writer (John Davis) challenged the practice of foot-binding and even then, principally because it was an imposed deformity against nature, and not because it was oppressive.[58] Early modern European travel genre writings provided descriptions of the duties and domestic roles of the women of China, valorizing them when they resembled practices being defended by the male authors of conduct books for women and the misogynistic pamphlets used in the popular culture of England of the early modern period.

An interesting development in the use of travel writings about China was marked by John Webb's 1669 work, *Essay Endeavoring a Probability that the Language of the Empire of China Is the Primitive Language*. Webb drew heavily on Nieuhoff's travel narrative to make his argument associating China with "the first knowledge of all things," including the proper nature and place of men and women. Webb actually wrote primarily to demonstrate that Chinese was the original or primitive language from which all other human languages emerged. Yet, he extended Nieuhoff's argument considerably, by claiming that from China "came the first knowledge of all things, and that the East parts of the world were the first civilized, having Noah himself for an Instructor, whereby the farther East to this day, the more Civil, the farther West, the more Savage."[59] For Webb, the civility exhibited in Chinese culture, including the conduct of China's women, is the expression of internalized moral principles that preserve the divine truth taught by Noah, from whom the Chinese descended just as the Hebrews did. Webb makes his point very clear: "But in all probability, *China* was after the Flood first planted either by *Noah* himself, or some of the sons of *Sem*. . . . For, such Principles of Theology, as amongst the *Chinois*, we shall shortly hear of, could not proceed from the wicked and idolatrous race of accursed *Cham*, but from those only that were, *de civitate Dei*, of the City of God."[60] Webb goes on to connect China with Israel in order to pull the knot that ties China's social and moral practices to the thread of God's truth:

> And how long soever the *Chinois* lived undiscovered to other Nations, it seems, that of old, they were not to the *Israelites* unknown, as may be collected from those words of the Prophet *Isaiah*, . . . Behold, these shall come from far: and lo, these from the North and from the West, and these from the land of *Sina. Isai. 49. v.* 12. But when you shall find so many reciprocally mutual customes between them, whether Theology, or Morality, or what else be respected, . . . you will, without all peradventure, assure your selves, that the *Chinois* immediately proceeded from one and the same stem *Noah*, as the *Hebrews* originally did.[61]

In his 2001 work *Ideographia*, David Porter argues that the interest in linguistic and cultural universalism exhibited in the work of early modern thinkers who drew on the travel narratives such as Webb had done demonstrated how China was used as a cipher for many types of European problems. For example, he argues that the chinoiserie fad was a way of giving China authority over aesthetics in much the same way that Webb does with respect to language and morality, including patterns of gender.[62] John Critchley shows that giving China an authoritative voice in European debates was not new, arguing that Polo's observations are actually designed to critique the calls for changing gender role expectations advocated in Venetian culture of the period.[63] Likewise, Robert Markley holds that writers such as Nieuhoff and Heylyn considered China's gender-inflected practices to be transcultural truths that overrode the linguistic and religious differences between the West and China.[64] Chung-shu Ch'ien gives a survey of the emergence of a European cult of Confucius and the authority of China over social and moral ideals.[65] In the mid-seventeenth century, the philosopher G. W. F. Leibniz gave voice to the growing authority of China in European writing and intellectual circles by saying,

> I fear lest we soon be inferior to the Chinese in everything that is deserving of praising . . . it is to be desired that we, on our side, should learn from them those things which hitherto have, rather, been lacking in our affair, especially the use of practical philosophy and an improved understanding of how to live—And so, I believe that if a wise man were chosen to pass judgment, not upon the shapes of goddesses, but upon the excellence of people, he would award the golden apple to the Chinese.[66]

It is in this stream of appropriating China as supporting evidence for positions taken in European debates that travel narratives about women in China were used as evidence for the transcultural truth of the patterns insisted on by the writers of the conduct books and popular pamphlets about women in the early modern period. Holding such a belief only strengthened the resistance in England to giving women greater rights and standing. As the number of travel narratives about China increased throughout the period, the authors' direct experience with Chinese women and their conduct in society also became more common. While there are substantial questions about the reliability of Polo's and Pinto's accounts of China, and about the extent to which Mandeville's writing about China is mere fiction, it is equally clear that Gonzalez,

Heylyn, and Nieuhoff all had some versions of eyewitness experience behind their accounts. It is difficult to say that the travel writers were motivated to describe China's women as they did by a desire to support the models of women's behavior and role found in the English conduct books. Nevertheless, Critchley and Markley seem to be right that these works were often used in that manner. Porter does not need to look any further than Webb's work for evidence that English writers were using the travel narratives as a basis for transferring authority to China, or at least to connect China's moral and social patterns with those of Europe's biblical heritage. The early modern travel narrative writers never constructed Chinese women as a "third-world woman" as we see in later colonial and imperialistic treatments of nonwestern cultures because the Chinese woman was used as a model for confirming behavioral guides not as someone to be liberated.[67]

While the European travel writers reported feminine behavior that was mirrored in the great Chinese conduct texts for women, what they neglected was any report of China's own gender debate occurring in the Ming and early Qing (1644–1912) dynastic periods. Bruce Robbins points out that a post-colonial theorist might hold that claims for the universality of beliefs and practices, such as how women are to behave and what is their proper role in society, is the principal myth of colonialism/imperialism because it systematically ignores specific cultural sensibilities and practices.[68] While there was an intense debate in sixteenth- and seventeenth-century England about women and gender, China was having its own internal struggles over the place of women during the same period. This struggle is manifested clearly and elaborately in two of the most popular dramas in the Ming dynasty: *The Peony Pavilion* 《牡丹亭》 (*Mudan ting*) and *The West Chamber* 《西厢記》 (*Xixiang ji*). The female protagonist Cui Yingying in *The West Chamber* attempts to search for her love by going beyond the established practice through writing poems and exchanging them with her lover. Great familial disharmony is hence caused due to her failing to stick to her womanly duties. Likewise, Du Liniang, the heroine in *The Peony Pavilion*, is portrayed as experiencing melancholy and dissatisfaction with her feminine role and duties. Pining for her freely chosen lover, instead of following the order of parents and the arrangement of the matchmaker advocated by the social tradition, results in her sad and tragic death. While these literary works make an endeavor to establish a voice for women breaking their supposed stereotypical civil roles, in the end, the heroines do not forsake the Confucian content of the instruction of women, the familial duties, and rights of women, which were so deeply rooted in the social ideology in that era.

The sixteenth- and seventeenth-century culture, both British and Chinese, used literature as the vehicle to express cultural struggles about proper feminine behavior. Through travel writings about China by those like Pinto, Gonzalez, Heylyn, and Nieuhoff, Europeans expressed their admiration of what they understood to be the submissive gentility and femininity of women in China. They embraced the values established for females in Chinese culture, regarding them as universal patterns for all humans, thereby finding a nonreligious basis for justifying the instructions in early modern conduct books, especially those in England. Webb went beyond this, using the travel narratives to defend China as the place of the original first truths about gender relations put into place by God and passed along to humanity by Noah after the flood. However, there is still a deeper truth and illumination which can be reached by a study of the intersection between the sixteenth- and seventeenth-century conduct books for women and European travel writings about China. The underlying truth is that women in each culture, no matter whether expressed in "golden lily" tiny feet in the East or the gentlewoman of the West, were defined by men and controlled by male ideology, and they were struggling to be free of this domination.

Notes

1. Robert Markley, *The Far East and the English Imagination, 1600–1730* (Cambridge: Cambridge University Press, 2006), 4.

2. Ania Loomba, *Colonialism/Postcolonialism.* 2nd ed. (London: Routledge, 2005), 3.

3. Of course, there were European and English influences on China as early as the seventeenth century, even though China was not a colony of any of the Western powers. Dawn Odell has written on the ways in which illustrations in travel books reflect the influence of China in the period before Chinoiserie, but also how trade affects a transformation in China's own self-representation in exports bound for Europe and England.

4. M. N. Pearson, "Objects Ridiculous and August: Early Modern European Perceptions of Asia," *Journal of Modern History* 68 (1996): 391.

5. Markley, *The Far East,* 1.

6. Mary Fuller, "Making Something of It: Questions of Value in the Early English Travel Collection," *Journal of Early Modern History* 10 (2006): 36.

7. Jonathan Spence, *The Chan's Great Continent: China in Western Minds* (New York: W.W. Norton, 1998), 1.

8. The arguments for and against Polo's actually being a resident in China from 1271–1295 are in Frances Wood, *Did Marco Polo Go to China?*

9. Donald Lach and Edwin Van Kley, *Asia in the Making of Europe*, 3 vols. (Chicago: Chicago University Press, 1993), 36.

10. A. C. Moule and Paul Pelliot, trans. *Marco Polo, the Description of the World*, 2 vols. (London: George Routledge and Sons, 1938), 304.

11. Zhao Ban班 昭, Nujie 《女誡》 (*Precepts for Women*). *Images of Women in Chinese Thought and Culture*. ed. Robin Wang (Indianapolis, IN: Hackett Publishing, 2003), 186.

12. In the particular cases of the two seventeenth-century texts by Fynes Moryson and Owen Felltham he studies, Gabbard holds that they reveal much about the differential between English and Dutch mentalities, cultural practices, and political systems. One writer portrays Holland's women as independent, and the other takes the figure of the "overbearing Dutch wife" as a common token of literary currency to call for greater control of women in England by emphasizing that Dutch republicanism had dangerous implications both for England's social and political hierarchy and for male ascendancy in the household (96).

13. The work generally regarded as the best summary of scholarly opinion on the identity of the author of this work and the extent to which it depended on other sources is Josephine Waters Bennett, *The Rediscovery of Sir John Mandeville* (New York: ML, 1954).

14. Lach, *Asia in the Making of Europe*, 79.

15. Spence, *The Chan's Great Continent*, 28.

16. Fernao Mendes Pinto, *The Travels of Fernao Mendes Pinto*. trans. and ed. Rebecca Catz (Chicago: University of Chicago Press, 1989), xv, xxv, xxxix-xl, xlii, 234–35.

17. Lach, *Asia in the Making of Europe*, 743.

18. Gonzalez's book was not the first European work devoted entirely to China. The first work was by the Portuguese Dominican father, Gaspar da Cruz, *Tractado em que se cotam muito por esteso as cousas da China* (1569), and the second was Bernardinao de Escalante's *Discurso de la navegacion que los Portuguese hazen a los Reinos y Provincias del Oriente, y de la notice q se tiene de las grandezas del Reino de la China* (1577). Cruz came to Canton, China, and spent a short time there, but Escalante had never visited China.

19. Juan Gonzalez de Mendoza, *The Historie of the Great and Mightie Kingdome of China, and the Situation thereof Togither with the Great Riches, Huge Citties, Politike Gouernement, and Rare Inuentions in the Same*, trans. Robert Parke (London: I. Wolfe, 1588), 373.

20. Ibid., 372.

21. For a discussion of the transformation of Asian and other travel narratives into a literary genre, please see Francis Jost, *Introduction to Comparative Literature* (New York: Pegasus, 1974), 109–16.

22. Joan Larsen Klein, ed., *Daughters, Wives, and Widows: Writings by Men about Women and Marriage in England, 1500–1640* (Urbana: University of Illinois Press, 1992), ix.

23. Katherine Usher Henderson and Barbara McManus, eds. *Half Humankind: Contexts and Texts of the Controversy about Women in England, 1540–1640* (Urbana: University of Illinois Press, 1985), 11.

24. Suzanne Hull, *Women According to Men: The World of Tudor-Stuart Women* (Walnut Creek, CA: AltaMira Press, 1996), 24.

25. Robert Shoemaker's work, *Gender in English Society, 1650–1850*, brings to light the value of giving attention to informal sources and other forms of printed materials than essays and books. He examines periodicals, popular pamphlets, ballads, plays, and novels. He also offers a careful survey of the popularity of the early modern conduct books, indicating which books had substantial publishing histories and wide distribution.

26. Klein, ed., *Daughters, Wives, and Widows*, 12.

27. Ibid., 16. The *Homily* makes quite explicit its claim to feminine weakness.

28. Ibid., 19.

29. Ibid., 21.

30. Klein observes that the *Dictionary of National Biography* reports that upon Lady Wentworth's death in 1631 the whole city had a face of mourning because she was loved and magnified by persons who had never even met her.

31. Ibid., 233.

32. Ibid., 234. Brathwaite believed feminine gentility could be shown through skillful conversation.

33. Ibid., 236.

34. Ibid., 247.

35. Ibid., 250.

36. Ibid., 256.

37. Ibid., 138. *The Schoolhouse* author has such a low view of women that he thinks they are dominated only by passion and cannot control or discipline themselves by use of reason.

38. Ibid., 146.

39. Joseph Swetnam, "The Arraignment of Lewd, Idle, Froward, and Unconstant Women" in *Half Humankind*, 195.

40. Ibid., 199.

41. Ibid., 196.

42. Ibid., 205.

43. Ibid., 211. Actually, these examples used by Swetnam could have easily found a place in tales of exemplary Chinese women as well.

44. Hull, *Women According to Men*, 25.

45. Esther Sowernam, "Esther Hath Hanged Haman" in *Half Humankind*, 242–43.

46. Henderson and McManus, 17.

47. "Hic Mulier" in *Half Humankind*, 276.

48. Ibid., 276.

49. Laura Gowing, *Domestic Dangers: Women, Words, and Sex in Early Modern London* (Oxford: Clarendon Press, 1996), 185.

50. Heylyn's work was placed on the 1711 edition of the *Index Librorum Prohibitorum*, the list of books banned by the Roman Catholic Church as not fit for the pious to read. The Church authorities believed that Heylyn took too favorable an attitude toward the barbarian cultures and his position on the universality of many values and practices threatened the distinctive revelation of the Christian faith.

51. Markley, *The Far East*, 58.

52. Heylyn's observation is obviously one-sided given that China had gone through a radical change of regime not too much earlier. The uprising of Li Zhicheng, the Battle of Shanhai Pass, the fall of Ming dynasty, and the rise of Qing dynasty had actually created enormous internal disturbance and chaos for then China.

53. Peter Heylyn, *Cosmographie in Four Bookes: Containing the Chorographie and Historie of the Whole Vvorld, and All the Principall Kingdomes, Provinces, Seas and Isles Thereof* (London: Henry Seile, 1652), 207.

54. Johannes Nieuhoff, *An Embassy from the East-India Company of the United Provinces, to the Grand Tartar Cham Emperor of China*, trans. John Ogilby (London: White-Friers, 1673), 181.

55. Nieuhoff is not the first writer to discuss foot-binding. Even Cruz, in the mid-sixteenth century, had thought of it as a useful device to keep women in doors.

56. Nuerjing 《女兒經》 (*Classic for Girls*), *Images of Women in Chinese Thought and Culture*, ed. Robin Wang (Indianapolis, IN: Hackett Publishing, 2003), 439.

57. Elizabeth Mazzola and Corinne Abate argue that the home and family in early modern England were mostly microcosmic versions of the state and church which were areas of surveillance over women's lives. The domestic world of the home became an arm of the patriarchal state and church even when it was presided over by women.

58. Patricia Ebrey, "Gender and Sinology: Shifting Western Interpretations of Foot-binding 1300–1890," *Late Imperial China* 20 (Dec. 1999): 3, 13.

59. John Webb, *An Historical Essay Endeavoring a Probability that the Language of the Empire of China is the Primitive Language* (London: Nath Brook, 1669), 21.

60. Ibid., 31. Webb's position connecting China to the Biblical record tied the earliest Chinese to God's natural and revealed truth in an even more direct way than Heylyn had done.

61. Ibid., 62–63.

62. In "China in 17th and 18th century Italy: Travel Literature, Scholarly/Reformist Writings, Theater" Adrienne Ward has done a study of the ways in which China functioned as an authority in cultural and artistic arenas in Italy. However, China was not regarded as an authority in all areas. Chi-ming Yang holds that in Europe's early modern turn to China for moral authority, European thinkers praise the superior wisdom of Confucius on the one hand, and condemn China's religious idolatry on the other.

63. John Critchley, *Marco Polo's Book* (Aldershot: Variorum, 1992), 107.

64. Markley, *The Far East*, 105.

65. Ch'ien, 352–54.

66. Quoted in Eui-Yeong Kim, *Thoreau's Orientalism: A Study of Confucian and Taoist Elements in Thoreau's Reading and Writing*, PhD diss. (University. of Illinois at Urbana-Champaign, 1990 AAT 9124441), 65.

67. Chandra Mohanty analyzes the production of the "third-world woman" as a singular monolithic subject, especially in the ways in which this construction has been used in some Western feminist texts. She is critical of the presupposition that all persons of the same gender, across classes and cultures, are to be treated as a homogeneous group that is identifiable prior to the process of actual analysis. She argues that images of third-world women are often built upon the colonial assumption that Western women are secular, liberated, and have control over their own lives. From this overdeveloped vantage point, writers define third-world women as oppressed and dependent.

68. Bruce Robbins, "Race, Gender, Class, Posteolonialism: Toward a New Humanistic Paradigm?" In *A Companion to Postcolonial Studies*, ed. by Henry Schwarz and Sangeeta Ray, (London: Blackwell, 2000), 556–68.

Part 2

Daniel Dooghan, University of Tampa

*E*arlier Moderns: The Novel Form as National Development in China and Europe

LITTLE WAS EARLY ABOUT CHINA'S MODERNITY DURING the so-called early modern period. The late Ming and early Qing dynasties saw imperial China at a zenith of civilizational achievement, according to visiting Europeans. Economically, technologically, and politically, China equaled or outpaced the West during this period. Western demand for silks and porcelain enriched China, and the European rage for chinoiserie motifs confirmed its cultural capital abroad. Culturally, the Europeans admired the intellectual and literary achievements of the Chinese. D. E. Mungello points out that this cultural difference was rooted in questions of epistemological foundations: "Additional evidence for the lack of European cultural superiority in the seventeenth century is shown by the intellectual challenge that China's history posed to European identity. Whereas theology was known as the queen of the sciences in Europe, in China this role was occupied by history."[1] Yet China's conception of history during this period in part represents the culmination of a millennium's creative adaptation and reformulation of the historical record. Contemporary with Europe's early encounters with China was the fulfillment of its own creative vision of history.

The medium in which this recasting of history plays out in both China and Europe is the long prose narrative. The novel in Europe and the long form *xiaoshuo*,[2] commonly glossed as novel, in China emerge within a couple of centuries of each other: China's *Sanguo Yanyi* in the late fifteenth century[3] and Spain's *Don Quixote* in 1605. In terms of literary history, the two novel forms are the products of vastly different antecedent trajectories. Long-form narrative in Europe has its roots in the epic and the romance, whereas the *xiaoshuo* narratives appear incrementally over centuries, drawing on historiography, oral performance, and drama.[4] Andrew Plaks downplays the historical differences of the two narrative traditions and argues instead for looking beyond formalisms to the broader cultural milieus that engendered each form: "In China such factors as rapid urbanization, the switch to a money economy based on new-world silver, increased trading possibilities opened up by maritime exploration, and the meteoric rise of great printing houses, indicate a clear link with the world of vernacular fiction, all the more so since these factors were largely concentrated in the cities of the Yangtze delta and the Southeastern coast where fiction publishing had its impetus in that period."[5] Much of the same could be said of the colonial European powers in which the early Western novel emerged. I would go beyond Plaks, though, and argue that these cultural shifts are visible formally within both the European and Chinese novels. Moreover, the rupture from and communication with the literary and historiographical traditions that precede both forms of the novel serve as sources of content for both novel forms: a playful awareness of the relationship with textual traditions is shared even though the particulars of each tradition are not. The two forms exhibit certain formal similarities that point to a self-awareness of contemporary cultural change.

The comparative inquiry into the novel thus leads to a preliminary definition of the early modern—if only on the literary front—as the nascent awareness of an emergent cultural tradition that is distinct from its antecedents while simultaneously drawing on them. Recent work on conceptualizing the early modern beyond Western Europe informs this definition. Regarding the early modern as perceived by the English, David Porter notes that they "presumably did not know that they were early modern. But they clearly did know that they were cosmopolitan: citizens of a global stage they shared with civilizations that were not only commensurable with, but by many measures, considerably more prosperous and powerful than their own."[6] This cosmopolitan consciousness is linked to the explorations and exploitations of the fifteenth and sixteenth centuries. "Against this background," Jason Scott-Warren argues, "the literary and linguistic expansionism of early modern England has also been recast. Far from being a natural self-expression of a country on the way to greatness, the 'renaissance' or 'golden age' of the later sixteenth century is now understood as a self-conscious project. While the English were asserting their rights of colonization in the New World, and subjugating the 'wild Irish' with their 'barbarous' language and customs, writers were constructing the modern literary canon that could bolster the country's claim to superiority."[7] Recognition of the other—or others—combined with often competitive cultural exchange are hallmarks of the early modern period in Europe.

This is no different in China of the same period. During the first half of the fifteenth century, the eunuch Zheng He led several naval expeditions that reached the Arabian peninsula. Although these did not result in colonial projects like the voyages of his European counterparts, the reports of subsequent cultural isolationism are overstated. The Jesuits were active in China beginning in the sixteenth century, and China had direct, intentional contact with South Asia at least as early as the seventh century.[8] Furthermore, China's literature also began to reflect cultural changes common to both Western Europe and East Asia. Ning Ma grounds the development of both the early English and Chinese novels in "an ideological crisis caused by the rapid commercialization of society," which "relocates literary landmarks previously confined to 'national' or 'civilizational' traditions to the transcultural context of early modern economic development across the Eurasian landmass."[9] Thus it is against this background of a consciousness of intercultural exchange and awareness that the novel's cross-cultural similarities emerge.

Modern, national cultures began to appear among the European states with the early works of vernacular literature. Dante, Rabelais, and Luther, among others, established the potential for cultural production tied not to Latin and the Catholic Church but to the various peoples of Europe. Europe, however, was not alone in its development of vernacular literature. Roughly contemporary with the beginning of the modern period in Europe was the printing of the four major

Ming dynasty vernacular novels.[10] One of the major foundations of modernity, the printing industry, appears much earlier in China than in the West. Woodblock printing began at the latest during the eighth century in China,[11] with movable type appearing in the eleventh century.[12] Furthermore, Gutenberg's fifteenth century press likely owes a debt to earlier Chinese technology. Tsien Tsuen-Hsuin's study of the topic notes that speculation over an Asian origin of European printing emerged soon after the birth of Western printing, and remains inconclusive but strongly suggestive.[13]

In addition to its development of printing technology, China also establishes a vernacular storytelling tradition as early as the Tang dynasty. Rather than fabricating tales out of whole cloth, professional storytellers embellished existing narratives. Jaroslav Průšek, following a contemporary classification, identifies four groups of storytellers based on their source materials: "tellers of shorter secular tales, *xiaoshuo*; narrators of histories, usually long workings-up of various chronicles; expounders of Buddhist scriptures, probably also long texts; and narrators of religious stories of Buddhist character."[14] The religious categories here point to an evangelistic quality in the storyteller's craft: that of disseminating canonical works, both secular and religious, to a broad audience. Indeed, as Průšek notes, "the terms used for storytelling, such as *shuoshu*, 'to interpret books,' *yanyi*, 'to explain the sense,' and others, indicate that one of the primary functions of this activity was to expound works of recognized literature to the masses."[15] Although each storyteller likely presented the materials differently, printed versions of the stories appeared as early as the Song dynasty. Fantastic stories of Xuanzang,[16] the Tang era Buddhist monk who retrieved and translated Buddhist texts from South Asia and historical basis for the Ming novel *Xiyou Ji*, or *Journey to the West*, appeared in these texts within a few centuries of his actual journey. Průšek remarks that this work "still dates perhaps from the time of the Northern Song and is as yet only a brief and fairly primitive storyteller's manual, containing seventeen episodes. Already in this version, a miraculous monkey appears as the monk's guide, but he does not yet bear the name Sun Wukong."[17] Though other scholars place this text slightly later in the Southern Song, its existence shows that the fundamental elements of the Ming novel *Journey to the West* were circulating by the thirteenth century, and widely too: this text was housed in a Japanese monastery.[18] Moreover, based on references found in a seventeenth century Korean primer of Chinese, Glen Dudbridge asserts that by the fourteenth century, the narrative of *Journey* was well established: "As far as we may use the *Pak t'onsa ŏnhae*'s sketch of a lost text as evidence of a trend, it appears that the *Xiyou Ji* story, now well known in published form, was progressively assuming an accepted and less variable form."[19] Though occurring much earlier than in Europe, the dissemination of common narratives to a wide audience in China suggests a similarly fertile ground for the emergence of national consciousness.

Invoking the nation to describe imperial China is perhaps ill advised. The term ignores indigenous conceptions of the state form and appears anachronistic in light of the explicit nationalism of the late Qing and Republican eras. The term is common, if unexamined, in much of the scholarly literature, though, and is analytically productive under certain conditions.

Benedict Anderson offers a useful definition of the nation as an "imagined political community," though the conditions of its utility must be specified.[20] Although Anderson privileges a European model in his definition of the nation, a demonstration of its applicability to China can perhaps serve to recuperate the "nation" until the development of a genuinely global technical vocabulary occurs. Anderson views the emergence of the nation as concurrent with the rise of print capitalism: "the convergence of capitalism and print technology on the fatal diversity of human language created the possibility of a new form of imagined community, which in its basic morphology set the stage for the modern nation."[21] Appealing as this is as a theoretical framework, it rests entirely on European models. Tellingly, he dismisses China's publishing industry entirely with a footnote: "It is worth remembering in this context that although printing was invented first in China, possibly 500 years before its appearance in Europe, it had no major, let alone revolutionary impact—precisely because of the absence of capitalism there."[22] In this unsubstantiated dismissal, Anderson conflates the means by which national consciousness manifests with the consciousness itself. Not only were Chinese fictional narratives widely distributed, in both oral and printed forms, but also, according to Průšek, in a socioeconomic climate that "bears some resemblance rather to Europe in the era of early capitalism."[23]

Anderson argues that the novel "is clearly a device for the presentation of simultaneity in 'homogeneous, empty time,' or a complex gloss upon the word 'meanwhile,'"[24] and cites several texts to confirm that this phenomenon does in fact occur. The disparity of the texts he chooses suggests that he sees the representation of simultaneity present in them as indicative of something more fundamental. Yet this phenomenon is taken for granted. Anderson does not see a causal link from national consciousness to simultaneity, but the reverse; the novel form is opaque. The development of the European novel and its representation of simultaneity during the sixteenth and seventeenth centuries is simply a given. This opacity combined with the foreclosure of any discussion of a Chinese national identity allows Anderson to elide the question of whether or not the Chinese novel or its predecessor forms exhibit the same features as its European counterpart and thus banish China to the non-national and premodern. Rather than follow Anderson's conclusions, we might instead follow his method and look at the Chinese novel for evidence of a national consciousness.

The modern appears not as a reaction to an external threat but as a reframing of one's own cultural history. Through a comparative analysis of Miguel de Cervantes' *Don Quixote* and *Journey to the West*, attributed to Wu Cheng'en, we can see that this reframing occurs in China just as it does in Europe, and earlier. The formal elements of the European novel that undergird its modernity, according to its critics, are also present and operative in both the Chinese novel and the narrative tradition that enables it. If we are to consider the development of the novel as a signifier of cultural modernity and nationhood in Europe, then we must take it as such in China.

The capacity of the Chinese novel to indicate a modern, national culture was observed by no less a promoter of a European national culture than Goethe. Seeing the success of vernacular literature as central to a national project, Goethe argued for what he saw as the salutary effects of translated literature on the development of local culture: "The plain prose translation surprises us with foreign splendors in the midst of our national domestic sensibility; in our everyday lives, and without our realizing what is happening to us—by lending our lives a nobler air—it genuinely uplifts us."[25] These sentiments were common among the German intelligentsia of the early nineteenth century.[26] What is extraordinary is that he recognizes a Chinese novel as the equivalent of contemporary European literature, comparing it to his "*Hermann und Dorothea* as well as to the English novels of Richardson."[27] The favorable reaction—assuming that he approves of his own work—suggests that he saw the Chinese novel as an instructive source for the German writer seeking to create modern, nationally conscious literature, in line with his thoughts on translation cited above. His comments also demonstrate the respect the Europeans had for China's literary achievements: when asked if this novel was somehow exceptional, he replied with apparently unintentional hyperbole, "Not at all [. . .] the Chinese have them by the thousand and already had them when our ancestors were still living in the forests."[28] What is more, the discussion of the unnamed Chinese novel is famous for its inauguration of the term "world literature." Goethe senses not only superficial similarities among the works, but also sees in them signs of an epochal rupture: "I like to look around in foreign nations and advise everyone to do the same on his part. National literature means little these days; the epoch of world literature is at hand, and everybody must endeavor to hasten its coming."[29] That the works he cites as evidence of this new epoch are novels is no accident, for this rupture is inherent to the novel in both its Chinese and European forms. Plaks sees this rupture in the Chinese novel in even greater relief when compared to its sources: "the relation of the novel to various antecedents is of far less consequence than is the radical structural transformation and revalorization of meaning effected on these materials when they are recast in the new generic mold."[30] The structure of the novel offers a new way to represent the world.

    The European novel's modernity is a function of both its form and its content, and is subsumed under the name of realism. This is not realism in the sense of Dickens or Balzac but a shift in emphasis from the ideal, relatively ahistorical fiction of earlier periods to the experience of daily life that appears in the novel. Ian Watt argues that "the novel is surely distinguished from other genres and from previous forms of fiction by the amount of attention it habitually accords both to the individualisation of its characters and to the detailed presentation of their environment."[31] The novel is populated by people who dwell in specific places rather than generic types without home or history outside of their narratives. In addition to the emergence of the potentially historical individual as an actor in the novel, the form also concerns itself with the rhythms of daily life. A possible world emerges in the pages of a novel that is persistent. One might imagine its characters going about their business until the narrative compels them back to directed action, in line with Anderson's notion of simultaneity. In the premodern epic, by contrast, Homer's Odysseus fights and feasts, but it would be difficult to envision him actually working after his return to Ithaka; he exists only within the space of the narrative.[32] Don Quixote, on the other hand, suffers through so many bodily indignities that were it not for his death at the end of Part II, he would likely go on bumbling about even if Cervantes never wrote another word. In fact, when Cervantes did not write

any more after the publication of Part I, so compelling was Quixote's life and world that a spurious sequel appeared. A similar phenomenon occurred in China: *Journey to the West* and other classic novels also spawned false sequels. By defining the novel's modernity in terms of a rupture from the ideal or at least the generic, we can set the standard of cultural and literary modernity at an adequation of cultural production with potentially lived experience.

By this standard, one might be tempted to discard *Journey to the West* as neither modern nor novel, given its invocations of the supernatural. Despite the presence of ghosts and demons in some Chinese novels, this does not necessarily exclude them from a broader category of realism. The supernatural, as it appears in the Chinese novel, is not exclusive of the human world. The verisimilitude that Watt praises in the early English novel has been a part of Chinese fiction since the Tang dynasty *chuanqi* stories. In these tales, grounding the accounts in a specific time and place naturalizes the supernatural rather than granting it a transcendent nature. In keeping with Watt's realism, *chuanqi* stories are often framed by affirmations by their narrators that the events described did in fact occur.[33] Even the demons of *Journey*, ostensibly supernatural figures, are realized in such detail that, "most of the work's important demons are fictional *characters* not mere flat types."[34] Rob Campany suggests that the demons's realistic appearance is the necessary pendant to their illusory nature, supporting a reading of Buddhist allegory in the work.[35] However, many of the *chuanqi* stories also feature supernatural creatures in detailed, even domestic representations, so the realism of the demons in *Journey* need not be solely the product of a theological maneuver.

The supernatural appears not as an indicator of an ideal vision of the world as in Augustine, but as an extension of the human order in that it appears as a parallel of the human world. Furthermore, the supernatural world, as it exists in Chinese fiction, does not offer a Platonic model for life on earth. In fact, it often mirrors the vagaries of mortal existence. The first seven chapters of *Journey to the West* concern events of the supernatural world, but were it not explicitly identified as such, it would not appear to be different from the description of the mortal world that follows. Sun Wukong's rise as the Monkey King appears in the mundane detail of a political record rather than a fantastic tale: "From that moment, the stone monkey ascended the throne of kingship. He did away with the word 'stone' in his name and assumed the title, Handsome Monkey King [. . .] The Handsome Monkey King thus led a flock of gibbons and baboons, some of whom were appointed by him as his officers and ministers."[36] Certainly there is a heavenly (and subterranean) order in the novel, but it is neither perfect nor immutable. Sun Wukong's antics in the heavenly palaces disrupt the heavenly order much in the same way that a rebellion might upset imperial control on Earth.

This order does suggest that a type of universalism could be at work in the text, in that all relations potentially exist in a hierarchical, harmonious system in the mortal world and beyond. This, however, is not the primary focus of the text. The text makes explicit that this order is not universal when the Tang Monk passes out of the imperial domain. Immediately upon reaching the frontier, any sense of order is lost: "It soon became exceedingly difficult for them to find their way. As they had to poke around in the grass to look for a path, they began to worry that they might be heading in the wrong direction. In that very anxious moment, they suddenly tripped; all three of them as well as the horse tumbled into a deep pit. Tripitaka was terrified; his companions all shook with fear. They were still trembling when they heard voices shouting, 'Seize them! Seize them!' A violent wind swept by, and a mob of fifty or sixty ogres appeared, who seized Tripitaka with his companions and hauled them out of the pit."[37] Following this encounter, Sanzang meets Liu Boqin, a helpful hunter, who further emphasizes the locality of order in contrast to the potentially chaotic wilderness. Liu first identifies himself as a compatriot of Sanzang, saying, "If you have come from the Tang empire, you are actually a native here, for this is still Tang territory and I am a Tang subject. You and I both live off the land belonging to the king, so that we are in truth citizens of the same nation."[38] Slightly later though, Liu admonishes Sanzang for his ignorance of the boundaries of that polity: "You do not realize, Elder [. . .] that this mountain is called the Mountain of Two Frontiers; the eastern half belongs to our great Tang domain, but the western half is the territory of the Tartars. The tigers and wolves over there are not my subjects, nor should I cross the border. You must proceed by yourself."[39] Sanzang's passage through borders within the world of the text marks the hierarchical order of the novel's opening chapters as particular rather than universal.

Those borders indicate awareness in the text of distinct aesthetic and political realms. In his structural analysis of the novel, Roderich Ptak stresses the importance of this boundary as one of "the magic thresholds in the quest adventure which, in a metaphorical sense, delimitate the mundane sphere from the nether world."[40] Although many supernatural encounters follow the traversal of this boundary, what precedes it is hardly mundane. In the context of the quest narrative, which is the target of Ptak's analysis, the passage marks the start of the quest proper. Earlier forms of the narrative did not have the extensive prefatory sections of the novel,[41] in which the quest is not the sole object of narrative interest. The structure of the novel and its explicit mention of the limits of the Tang state point to the manifestation of a political division rather than just a structural feature of the quest narrative. Given the development of the *Journey* narrative, linking the structural division to a political one serves to emphasize the limitations of that political order.

The particularity of that order to the Tang Empire—China—reveals a nascent national consciousness. This does not necessarily belong to the Tang Chinese, but at least to the Ming era author who ascribes that order to the Tang, and possibly to his predecessors as well. Anderson argues that nations are inherently limited, "because even the largest of them, encompassing perhaps a billion living human beings, has finite, if elastic, boundaries, beyond which lie other nations. No nation imagines itself coterminous with mankind."[42] By noting the boundary of an ideological system, or imagined community, and just as important, acknowledging the existence of other ideological systems, the text adduces one component of a Chinese national identity. This differs from earlier understandings of the other in China. The Han dynasty historian Sima Qian constructs an influential vision of China in his *Shiji*, the archetypical Chinese history, by assembling a collection of short narratives about events in Chinese history, but not about China itself as a state actor among comparable entities. Sima Qian's China is not a nation any more than is Homer's vision of Hellenic culture. Beyond the borders of Sima Qian's China lie the nomadic Xiongnu; beyond Homer's proleptic Greece, the barbarians. The opposition in both texts is between an assumed universal civilization and groups that are marked as uncivilized rather than as competing or collaborating cultures. In *Journey to the West*, by contrast, we encounter other literate civilizations throughout the text. Most notable among them is the South Asian culture that produced the religious texts sought by the travelers.

The cultural origin of those texts is a paradox in *Journey*, because their contents, Buddhism, appear completely domesticated even though the animating force of the narrative relies on Buddhism's foreignness: the travelers must get the scriptures from India. The opening chapters of the novel see the Buddha seamlessly integrated into a Chinese pantheon. Moreover, Buddhist references appear alongside Daoist allusions without comment. In a memorable example, the Buddha traps the Monkey King through illusion before imprisoning him in "Five-Phases Mountain."[43] The illusory nature of the material world is a common Buddhist theme, and the five phases recall Daoist alchemy. Syncretism is common in Chinese literature and philosophy, but *Journey* complicates any syncretism by stressing the foreign origin of Buddhism.

The presence of the Monkey King in the text underscores the presence of the foreign. Sun Wukong's remarkable but ultimately untraceable resemblance to Hanuman the monkey deity in the Sanskrit epic *Ramayana* is one of the great unresolved problems of comparative literature. However, not all find the similarities compelling; Jing Wang notes, "Those who uphold the theory of Monkey's indigenous origin draw upon the evidence of a local monkey-cult in the Fujian area that is known to have existed in the late Tang period."[44] Nevertheless, Jing does not see the two schools as irreconcilable, seeing in *Journey* a productive synthesis of the two traditions because it is "a narrative that transforms the earlier sensual and 'half-civilized' ape into a vehicle capable of engendering its own opposite image—the spiritual and the cultivated—while recontaining all of its original attributes of the sensual and the sexual."[45] Sun Wukong is a Chinese invention, but a dialectical one. In him we see the sublation of the encounter between East and South Asia, in which the Chinese text decisively recasts its South Asian source material. The presence of Sanzang's monkey companion in the earliest extant forms of the *Journey* narrative suggests that this recognition of the other was underway long before the appearance of the novel.

The syncretism evident in *Journey* marks it as epochally separated from the events it nominally describes. Near the end of the novel, after the travelers have finally obtained the scriptures from the Buddha, they realize that the texts they are carrying are devoid of any writing, and so return to the Buddha to complain. The Buddha admonishes them: "But these blank texts are actually true, wordless scriptures, and they are just as good as those with words. However, those creatures in your Land of the East are so foolish and unenlightened that I have no choice but to impart to you now the texts with words."[46] Qiancheng Li argues that this is not actually a slight against Chinese culture, but a reflection of theological debates, beginning with the Chinese language *Platform Sutra*, over whether Buddhist enlightenment happens suddenly or gradually,[47] concluding, "It has taken the pilgrims fourteen years to reach their destination, and they have to bring something material back to China. In the final analysis, it would seem, gradual liberation is the structuring principle of the book."[48] Fundamentally, *Journey* could not be written without those debates having already happened. Yet Buddhism's foreignness was, as Průšek mentioned, an animating principle behind the development of expository, evangelical storytelling tradition that produced the *Journey* narrative. In it Buddhism appears as an already indissociable part of a Chinese cultural identity, for much of the text would be impenetrable without an understanding of Buddhist mythology and philosophy. Plaks sees in the novel's syncretism not a support for Buddhism over Daoism or vice versa as many commentators have claimed, but an expression of the Neo-Confucian synthesis prevalent during the sixteenth century, emphasizing the distinction of the novel from the texts that informed it.[49] Even though the text recognizes Buddhism's foreign origin, it assumes the narrative telos before the start: Buddhism has come into its own in China, and is treated more or less equivalently, varying by the sympathies of each critic, with Daoism and Confucianism. *Journey* recognizes the South Asian other in order to assert its own cultural identity.

The recognition of the limitations of the nation is present in the early European novel as well. *Don Quixote* in particular reflects an understanding of Spain as a discrete entity among others. Given that the Reconquista occurred only a little over a century prior to its publication, and Cervantes himself was captured by North African pirates, it would be difficult for the novel to present its world as universally applicable. The text's recognition of the Islamic other happens somewhat ironically, but the recognition occurs nonetheless. What is more, the text's Spanish narrator must rely on a Muslim interlocutor to produce the complete story of Don Quixote: "With this in mind I urged him to read me the title, and he proceeded to do so, turning the Arabic into Castilian upon the spot: History of Don Quixote de la Mancha, Written by Cid Hamete Benengeli, Arabic Historian."[50] In this the novel acknowledges Spain's still recent emergence as a nation and addresses the history of that emergence by positing the Muslim not as a voiceless other, but as a member of a literate civilization different from that of Spain.

Nationhood and verisimilitude aside, what appears as most modern about the novel in both its European and Chinese contexts is its ability to synthesize various historical literary genres into a single coherent narrative. Although this is not common to all novels, it appears in many early works in the genre: Cervantes most notably and self-consciously, but also, for example, in the formal experiments of Sterne's *Tristram Shandy*. The popularity of epistolary novels is also suggestive of this formal synthesis. With the possible exception of *Don Quixote*, though, the extent of this generic synthesis in the European novel does not approach that of the Chinese novel. Nevertheless, the extended narrative of both novelistic traditions affords an opportunity to archive and celebrate prior literary styles. The strongest evidence for the novel as both a modern and national form is in its capacity as an archive.

The Chinese novel is not the first genre within Chinese literature to exhibit synthetic tendencies. The dynastic history, for example, collects various narratives into a single work. However, the history differs from the novel in that it provides no overarching narrative to unite its constituent subnarratives. The dynastic history offers chronologies, but they serve a more referential rather than narratological function. However, the Chinese novel is indebted to the historiographical tradition. The first of the Ming novels, *Sanguo Yanyi*, derives its source material from a third century historical record. The core of *Journey* appears in Xuanzang's account of his actual expedition. Although *Journey* departs from the historical in many ways, in so doing it does not reject its historical sources in contradistinction to the other major novels, as Anthony Yu suggests.[51] Instead, according to Martin Huang, the Chinese novel beginning with *Sanguo* "creates a special narrative form incorporating all the forms of traditional historiography in order to demonstrate the narrative limits of these forms; it shows, in a novelistic gesture, where traditional historiography fails, paradoxically, by exhausting all of its possibilities."[52] *Journey* simply represents the culmination of this movement away from orthodox historiography in which "the dominant comic spirit or 'joy of relativity' that is so unique to the novel contributed greatly to the general 'carnivalization' of the 'sacredness' of traditional historiography and thus to the ultimate triumph of the novel as an independent literary genre."[53] The novel becomes an archive of historiographical and fictional elements to be reshaped at will.

The archival qualities of the Chinese novel are often spurious. Tropes and genres are deployed within the novels, but the text that sustains the generic borrowings is itself not necessarily part of any extant archive of Chinese literature outside the novel. This blending of genres does not originate with the Chinese novel, but is also visible in its antecedent genres. Hsiao-Peng Lu sees the origin of this generic mixing in the demands of oral storytelling: "That in each round (*hui*) of storytelling, a story is adjusted for the particular occasion, adapted to the specific composition of the audience, and extended or cut as dictated by the ability and interest of the storyteller abolishes the possibility of finding an original version of the story."[54] The *bianwen*, or records, of these stories mix "Tang heptasyllabic poetry, earlier pentasyllabic poetry, the alternating tetra-heptasyllabic *bianwen* parallel prose, classical prose, half-baked vernacular speech, and rhapsody (*fu*)."[55] This early form of fiction celebrates anachronism, and though borrowing from the historiographical tradition, "it explodes the slim, fixed framework of historical representation and unleashes, in addition to the pleasure of oral discourse, and orgiastic free play of textual productivity (in the sense of *jouissance de texte*). The singularity and unity of the Chinese worldview of the former historical discourses is now thoroughly dialogized in the *bianwen* story so as to accommodate multiple worldviews, languages, cultures, and temporal sequences."[56] At its earliest moments, the narrative tradition that would culminate in the novel had the admixture of genres at its core.

Journey's frequent invocation of a poem by *shi yue* resembles a reference to the Confucian classic *Shijing*. This referential invocation paradoxically aligns itself with literary history by offering a poem as evidence of the narrative's veracity, while repudiating that tradition by inserting a poem of contemporary composition. Frequently, the verse content of the novel imitates that of the Tang and Song dynasties, with many penta- and heptasyllabic *shi* compositions.[57] Ci poetry also frequently appears throughout the work. The opening of chapter 10 consists of an extended series of *ci* and other poems recording the conversations of a woodcutter and fisherman that are not present in earliest forms of the text,[58] suggesting a late and conscious insertion of anachronism. Intermediate forms, too, are substantially less developed, even if the material is present in brief.[59] These forms of lyrical exchange "are part of a curious allusion occurring with great frequency in songs from Xanadu [a Yuan dynasty capital],"[60] pointing to further temporally marked material in the novel. Průšek sees the insertion of historically accurate but contemporarily anachronistic poems as a feature of the early narrative tradition too, though in that case the poems are not necessarily playful adductions of the veracity of a given event, but examples of historical flavor lending support to the story's overall historical verisimilitude.[61]

Yet verse styles are not the sole generic imitations in the novel. The account in chapter 9 of Chen Guangrui's rescue of a magic fish and its consequences, for instance, resembles a Tang or Song *chuanqi* tale. The material in this chapter does not appear in earlier forms of the *Journey* narrative, or even in all the recensions of the novel, indicating that this process of adaptation was ongoing even late in the narrative's development. Alsace Yen points out, "This cluster of motifs enjoyed a great vogue in popular tradition, underwent rigorous recasting, and resulted in several literary genres from the Tang classical Chinese tale, to Yuan play, down to Chapter 9 of the *Xiyou Chi*, Ming drama and short story."[62] This continuous rewriting, especially in the latest stages of the novel's development, gestures toward a conscious recognition of the literary tradition as open for playful reorganization, as seen in its subordination to the structure of the novel. Such generic syntheses present in the novel demonstrate not only a mastery of the Chinese literary tradition, but also recognition of it as tradition. For the novel to create such an archive of pseudo authentic works marks it as a new stage of that tradition.

Much later, Cervantes engages in the same practice in *Don Quixote* and even admits as much. In the novel's preface, the author's persona complains,

> I have no citations for the margins, no notes fore the end. To tell the truth, I do not even know who the authors are to whom I am indebted, and so am unable to follow the example of all the others by listing them alphabetically at the beginning, starting with Aristotle and closing with Xenophon, or, perhaps, with Zoilus or Zeuxis, notwithstanding the fact that the former was a snarling critic, the latter a painter. This work will also be found lacking in prefatory sonnets by dukes, marquises, counts, bishops, ladies, and poets of great renown; although if I were to ask two or three colleagues of mine, they would supply the deficiency by furnishing me with productions that could not be equaled by the authors of most repute in all Spain.[63]

In his plaint the author demonstrates his knowledge of both tradition and convention by gesturing toward an assumed need for intertextual references both ancient and modern. His invocation of the obscure Greeks "Zoilus or Zeuxis" suggests his desire to be known not only as a student of tradition but also as its master. This mastery is further evinced by his interlocutor's suggestion to write the conventional prefatory material himself.[64] The author does just this, taking as his spurious sources characters from chivalric romances.[65] Cervantes makes frequent reference to other literary genres and does so to showcase his skill in the contemporary high literary genres—a possible parallel to *Journey to the West*. However, the interweaving of the various genres—sonnet, epic, pastoral, epistolary, etc.—into a continuous narrative allows the novel as a form, again, to distinguish itself from its predecessors.

This characteristic is especially pronounced in *Don Quixote*, since many of the work's plots concern literary criticism, whether of actual works or of those related within the diegetic space of the novel. Of the former, a prominent example occurs in chapter 6, in which two minor characters, the barber and the curate, debate the merits of the eponymous hero's library before consigning it to the flames, sparing of course Cervantes's *Galatea* in a fine bit of self-promotion.[66] Of the latter type, the curate passes judgment on the "Story of the One Who Was Too Curious for His Own Good," related in chapters 33–35. He declares, "I liked this tale well enough [. . .] but I cannot persuade myself that it is true. If it is pure invention, then the author is to blame; for I cannot imagine a husband so foolish as to make such a costly experiment as Anselmo did. If it were the case of a gallant and his mistress, that might do, but as between a husband and wife it is lacking in plausibility. As to the method of telling the story, I have no fault to find with that."[67] As the author of both the story and its criticism, Cervantes dismisses the tale as outmoded while championing its presentation, which is his own. These literary critical interventions within the novel allow it to subsume the older genres under its overarching narrative structure.

The source material for these works did not spontaneously emerge with their publication. Both *Journey to the West* and *Don Quixote* have many antecedents in their respective traditions. Although the novels reshape this material, its presence renders the narrative thrust ambiguous. *Don Quixote* has no discernable narrative telos; Quixote's death ends the narrative, but it does not fulfill the project he set before himself at the novel's outset. Sanzang and his companions do eventually find the Buddha and retrieve the scriptures, but this occurs only after hundreds of pages of discrete episodes. The narrative ambiguity in these works, however, does not deny their internal consistency, but is instead a precondition of their synthetic capability.

The formative years of Chinese fictional narrative produced a mechanism that could synthesize disparate literary constructs into a coherent narrative without imposing a narrative telos. The partially oral origin of the narrative in *Journey to the West* is largely responsible for its meandering structure. On a basic level, the hundreds of years between the work's sixteenth century publication and the actual Tang monk's journey to India allowed for the accretion of additional narrative content and generic adaptations. By the time of the novel's publication in the sixteenth century, however, all of that information appears as subordinate to its overarching structure, as the text's allegorical intricacy suggests. Henry Zhao identifies *Journey to the West* as belonging to the "rewriting" period of vernacular Chinese fiction, during which texts "are changed so much that they can hardly be considered to be of the same text."[68] We have, however, consistent modern editions of the text, which indicates that the process of rewriting was ultimately able either to encompass or discard the variants. This is consistent with Zhao's argument that the variable authorship engendered the emergence of a powerful narrative frame: "As there was no authoritative source of the narrative message, the narrator assumed a responsibility comparable to that in oral performance; thus in this simulated oral narrative frame, the authorship could be left out of consideration, as in oral performance, in which authorship is almost irrelevant."[69] Zhao's distinction between narrator and author allows for the construction of a powerful narrative frame while maintaining the independence of the episodic components of that narrative.

The absence of a clearly identifiable author did not undermine the perceived unity of the text, but prompted instead the explication of that unity by contemporary critics. In conjunction with efforts to raise the status of fiction as a whole, traditional commentators ascribed authors to texts. With regard to *Journey to the West*, David Rolston notes that "not even a pseudonymous author had been widely associated with this text before the Wang Xiangxu and Huang Zhouxing commentary made the claim that Qiu Changchun was its author."[70] Although other novels were attributed to particular authors, Rolston shows that, in cases of infelicitous content, commentators "would absolve the 'original' author of responsibility and attributed the blame to some later editor or author."[71] The attempt to clarify or invent an author for the novel suggests a growing acknowledgment of the novel as a legitimate genre unto itself. In addition to its powerful narrative frame, the development of its author function imparted a hermeneutic unity to the text.

Though literary criticism has largely moved beyond the idea of an authoritative interpretation, the positing of an author by critics points to the recognition of the work as a complete, consistent text. To argue for the thematic unity of *Journey to the West* seems like a fool's errand given its complex amalgam of genres and themes; nevertheless, critics did just that, seeking out and endorsing Daoist and Buddhist numerologies and allegories in the text. About two centuries after its publication, Daoist priest Liu Yiming produced a commentary that examined the text from several philosophical positions, with a subtle emphasis on a Daoist interpretation. He states, "In *The Journey to the West* is to be found an exhaustive treatment of the principles of the mundane world and of the Tao, of the seasons of Heaven and the affairs of men [. . .] Only he who knows this can read *The Journey to the West*."[72] Liu ascribes this unity to an authoritative creative effort: "In *The Journey to the West* each episode has its own meaning, each chapter has its own meaning, and each word has its own meaning. The Adept [Qiu Changchun] never spoke without purpose or used a superfluous word. The reader must pay attention to every line and every phrase, not even a single word should be permitted to slip by."[73] This positing of the purported author's creative genius is not unlike the Romantic idea of the author as *alter deus*. With the establishment of author functions and authoritative interpretations, *Journey to the West* emerges not only as an archive of literary history, but also as a recognized, consistent, and contemporary text in its own right.

Don Quixote also exhibits authorial ambiguity within an established narrative frame. The proliferation of authorial voices and personae within the text makes it difficult to ascertain who is actually speaking at any given point. Cervantes, however, is a master storyteller. He links the various episodes through the overarching frame of the parody of chivalric romance. Yet this frame hardly drives the narrative. It frequently fades into the background as other authors emerge in the text to recount their own stories. Robert Bayliss argues that "the yield of the novel's narrative complexity and hyperactivity is an absence, a lack of authorial adjudication in Cervantes's text, or a refusal on the author's part to prescribe how his work is to be read."[74] This is not to say that the novel's many readers have not established authoritative interpretations of the text. Like that of *Journey to the West*, *Don Quixote*'s internal ambiguity has left the task of unifying the manifold to its critics.[75]

Through this combination of narrative consistency and authorial ambiguity, both works allow their literary traditions to speak equivocally. *Don Quixote*'s primary narrative may be a parody, but what about the myriad subnarratives in different genres? *Journey to the West*, as a novel, may be written in a marginalized genre, but it contains many compositions in high literary genres. This generic synthesis is not so much a profanation of privileged forms of literary production as it is the creation of a new genre through the admixture of historical forms marked by the mingling of authorial voices.

The novel's ability, in both its Chinese and European forms, to deploy literary history within its narrative has the effect of flattening that history. Unlike the anthologist or the historian, whose works either lack consistent narrative or who subordinate it to the demands of chronology, the novelist can create a literary space with a narrative that can be self-sufficient without explicit reference to external events. By placing literary history in the service of this narrative, the novel can efface the contours of that history within its pages and thus rob the historical of its categorical difference when deployed within the novel. History is no longer history in the novel, but rather relief for its own narrative map. That Cervantes and the author(s) of *Journey to the West* use pseudo-historical works as supposedly historical gestures alongside actual literary references underscores this point. The mastery of historical forms appears as a strategy to make the world of the novel verisimilar, even though it is anything but. The novel, in its deployment of literary history, reduces that history to an ahistorical construct by employing it to support what is not real. We can read *Journey to the West* and point out, for example, a *ci* poem, but that poem cannot exist just as a *ci* poem in the context of the novel since it is always circumscribed by the novel's narrative.

With the flattening of history, time becomes homogeneous. In the space of the novel, with its command over literary history, all events are expressible in terms of the narrative. This is not the temporal space of the classics, Chinese or European, which is marked by epochal ruptures, but it instead allows for the possibility of simultaneity. The juxtapositions of literary genres in these novels may be anachronistic, but they signify the preconditions for a national identity. Benedict Anderson argues, "Why this transformation should be so important for the birth of the imagined community of the nation can best be seen if we consider the basic structure of two forms of imagining which first flowered in Europe in the eighteenth century: the novel and the newspaper. For these forms provided the technical means for 're-presenting' the *kind* of imagined community that is the nation."[76] Bracketing out his problematic account of print history, Anderson suggests that the novel's ability to display to us a world in which separate narrative events go on simultaneously is essential for the formation of a national community. Both *Don Quixote* and *Journey to the West* fulfill this requirement. Yet, this does not explicitly account for how history itself becomes part of the novelistic narrative. When Anderson notes "That all these acts are performed at the same clocked, calendrical time, but by actors who may be largely unaware of one another, shows the novelty of this imagined world conjured up by the author in his readers' minds," it is not just the imagined world that is represented to the readers, but their world as well.[77]

Furthermore, the structure of the novel that allows for the simultaneous presentation of historical genres speaks to its contemporaneity. Theodor Adorno stresses the role of form as an expression of a historical moment: "Aesthetic expression is the objectification of the non-objective, and in fact in such a fashion that through its objectification it becomes a second-order nonobjectivity: It becomes what speaks out of the artifact not as an imitation of the subject."[78] That the novel, with its archival capacity, emerges as a genre in both China and Europe indicates, following Adorno, that its authors, readers, and critics recognized their era as markedly different from its predecessors. The "second-order nonobjectivity" here refers to the artwork's ability to speak about its historical moment independently of its content. In the case of these texts, the novelty of their form suggests the cultural awareness of a break from tradition.

The long development of Chinese fictional narrative that sees its consummation in the Ming novel indicates a consolidation of Chinese national identity distinct from the historiographically defined cultural polity of the premodern era. That the European novel is also a product of temporally and spatially local concerns speaks to the national identification that enables its production. Neither Defoe nor Dante could have written *Don Quixote* any more than Sima Qian or Sanzang himself could have written *Journey to the West*. Still, literary precedents and cultural others find expression in both forms of the novel, the recognition of which is the condition of their possibility. However, *Don Quixote* inaugurates a formal tradition that is already mature in *Journey*. The early appearance in China of so many of the formal elements of the novel in other generic forms suggests that the novel itself signals the close of early modernity in China, rather than its opening.

Notes

1. D. E. Mungello, *The Great Encounter of China and the West, 1500–1800*, 3rd ed. (Lanham, MD: Rowman and Littlefield, 2009), 93.

2. Romanizations have been standardized to Hanyu Pinyin, excepting titles of cited works.

3. This dating is contested, with some arguing for a fourteenth century composition. I follow Andrew Plaks here, who summarizes the debate. See Andrew H. Plaks, *The Four Masterworks of the Ming Novel: Ssu Ta Ch'i-Shu* (Princeton, NJ: Princeton University Press, 1987), 361-76.

4. C.T. Hsia, *The Classic Chinese Novel: A Critical Introduction* (New York: Columbia University Press, 1968), 6–12.

5. Andrew H. Plaks "Full-Length *Hsiao-Shuo* and the Western Novel: A Generic Reappraisal," *New Asia Academic Bulletin* 1 (1978): 166.

6. David Porter, "Sinicizing Early Modernity: The Imperatives of Historical Cosmopolitanism," *Eighteenth-Century Studies* 43, no. 3 (2010): 304.

7. Jason Scott-Warren, *Early Modern English Literature* (Cambridge: Polity, 2005), 162.

8. Cf. Xuanzang, *Da Tang Xiyu Ji* (Shanghai: Shanghai Renmin Chubanshe, 1977). This is the written record by the Tang Monk Xuanzang of his journey to South Asia to retrieve the Buddhist scriptures that in part forms the basis of the novel *Journey to the West*.

9. Ning Ma, "When Robinson Crusoe Meets Ximen Qing: Material Egoism in the First Chinese and English Novels," *Comparative Literature Studies* 46, no. 3 (2009): 463.

10. *Sanguo Yanyi, Shuihu Zhuan, Xiyou Ji,* and *Jin Ping Mei.*

11. Tsien Tsuen-Hsuin, *Paper and Printing*, ed. Joseph Needham, vol. 5.1, Science and Civilisation in China (Cambridge: Cambridge University Press, 1985), 146–49.

12. Ibid., 201.

13. Ibid., 313–19.

14. Jaroslav Průšek, "Urban Centers: The Cradle of Popular Fiction," in *Studies in Chinese Literary Genres*, ed. Cyril Birch (Berkeley: University of California Press, 1974), 265–6. Lu Xun notes in his *Brief History of Chinese Fiction* that these categories come from the Song dynasty text *Ducheng Jisheng*. Lu Xun, *Lu Xun Quanji*, 18 vols. (Beijing: Renmin Wenxue Chubanshe, 2005), 9:117.

15. Průšek, "Urban Centers," 263.

16. Alternatively Sanzang, Tripitaka, or Tang monk.

17. Průšek, "Urban Centers," 266.

18. Anthony C. Yu, *Journey to the West*, 4 vols. (Chicago: University of Chicago Press, 1977–83), 1:7.

19. Glen Dudbridge, *The Hsi-Yu Chi: A Study of Antecedents to the Sixteenth-Century Chinese Novel* (Cambridge: Cambridge University Press, 1970), 74.

20. Benedict Anderson, *Imagined Communities: Reflections on the Origin and Spread of Nationalism*, Revised ed. (London: Verso, 1991), 5–6.

21. Ibid., 46.

22. Ibid., 44.

23. Průšek, "Urban Centers," 259.

24. Anderson, *Imagined Communities*, 25.

25. Johann Wolfgang von Goethe, "Translations," in *The Translation Studies Reader*, ed. Lawrence Venuti (New York: Routledge, 2004), 65.

26. Cf. Wilhelm von Humboldt, "From the Introduction to His Translation of *Agamemnon*," in *Theories of Translation: An Anthology of Essays from Dryden to Derrida*, eds. Rainer Schulte and John Biguenet (Chicago: University of Chicago Press, 1992). and Friedrich Schleiermacher, "On the Different Methods of Translating," in *The Translation Studies Reader*, ed. Lawrence Venuti (New York: Routledge, 2004).

27. J. P. Eckermann, *Conversations with Goethe*, trans. Gisela C. O'Brien (New York: Frederick Ungar Publishing Co., 1964), 92.

28. Ibid., 94.

29. Ibid.

30. Plaks, *Masterworks*, 186.

31. Ian Watt, *The Rise of the Novel: Studies in Defoe, Richardson and Fielding* (Berkeley: University of California Press, 1957), 17–18.

32. Erich Auerbach, *Mimesis: The Representation of Reality in Western Literature*, trans. Willard R. Trask (Princeton, NJ: Princeton University Press, 1968), 7.

33. See, for example, Shen Jiji, "Ren the Fox Fairy," in *Selected Chinese Short Stories of the Tang and Song Dynasties* (Beijing: Foreign Languages Press, 2001), 22.

34. Rob Campany, "Demons, Gods, and Pilgrims: The Demonology of the Hsi-Yu Chi," *Chinese Literature: Essays, Articles, Reviews* 7, no. 1/2 (1985): 108.

35. Ibid., 115.

36. Yu, *Journey*, 1:72.

37. Ibid., 1:284–85.

38. Ibid., 1:289.

39. Ibid., 1:296.

40. Roderich Ptak, "Hsi-Yang Chi: An Interpretation and Some Comparisons with Hsi-Yu Chi," *Chinese Literature: Essays, Articles, Reviews* 7, no. 1/2 (1985): 129.

41. Dudbridge, *Antecedents*, 189. Dudbridge's précis of the earliest extant text demonstrates that the quest is already underway at the start, though the first section of the text is lost.

42. Anderson, *Imagined Communities*, 7.

43. Yu, *Journey*, 1:174.

44. Jing Wang, *The Story of Stone* (Durham, NC: Duke University Press, 1992), 229. Many have weighed in on this debate, which Dudbridge carefully explains in Dudbridge, *Antecedents*, 114–38. and more recently in Glen Dudbridge, *Books, Tales and Vernacular Culture* (Leiden: Brill, 2005), 254–74.

45. Wang, *The Story of Stone*, 231.

46. Yu, *Journey*, 4:393.

47. Qiancheng Li, *Fictions of Enlightenment* (Honolulu: University of Hawai'i Press, 2004), 74–75.

48. Ibid., 80.

49. Plaks, *Masterworks*, 243–76.

50. Miguel de Cervantes, *Don Quixote De La Mancha*, trans. Samuel Putnam (New York: Modern Library, 1998), 82.

51. Anthony C. Yu, "History, Fiction and the Reading of Chinese Narrative," *Chinese Literature: Essays, Articles, Reviews* 10, no. 1/2 (1988): 14.

52. Martin Weizong Huang, "Dehistoricization and Intertextualization: The Anxiety of Precedents in the Evolution of the Traditional Chinese Novel," *Chinese Literature: Essays, Articles, Reviews* 12 (1990): 55.

53. Ibid., 68.

54. Hsiao-Peng Lu, "The Fictional Discourse of Pien-Wen: The Relation of Chinese Fiction to Historiography," *Chinese Literature: Essays, Articles, Reviews* 9, no. 1/2 (1987): 56–57.

55. Ibid., 61.

56. Ibid., 64.

57. These *shi* poems consist of two quatrains of five or seven characters with complicated rhyme schemes. *Ci* poems and *qu* poems have roots in musical performance. Here I follow Zong-qi Cai's argument that the popularity of Chinese poetic genres loosely follows the dynastic cycle, and offers a convenient basis for the periodization of the Chinese verse tradition. Cf. *How to Read Chinese Poetry*, ed. Zong-qi Cai (New York: Columbia University Press, 2008), 4–5.

58. Hsia, *The Classic Chinese Novel: A Critical Introduction*, 119–20.

59. Dudbridge, *Antecedents*, 59.

60. J. I. Crump, *Song-Poems from Xanadu* (Ann Arbor: University of Michigan Center for Chinese Studies, 1993), 107.

61. Průšek, "Urban Centers," 271.

62. Alsace Yen, "A Technique of Chinese Fiction: Adaptation in the "Hsi-Yu Chi" with Focus on Chapter Nine," *Chinese Literature: Essays, Articles, Reviews* 1, no. 2 (1979): 208.

63. Cervantes, *Don Quixote*, 12–3.

64. Ibid., 13–4.

65. Ibid., 18–24.

66. Ibid., 57–64.

67. Ibid., 377.

68. Henry Y. H. Zhao, *The Uneasy Narrator: Chinese Fiction from the Traditional to the Modern* (Oxford: Oxford University Press, 1995), 11.

69. Ibid., 45.

70. David L. Rolston, *Traditional Chinese Fiction and Fiction Commentary: Reading and Writing between the Lines* (Stanford, CA: Stanford University Press, 1997), 120.

71. Ibid., 114.

72. Liu I-ming[Yiming], "How to Read *the Original Intent of the Journey to the West*," in *How to Read the Chinese Novel*, ed. David L. Rolston (Princeton, NJ: Princeton University Press, 1990), 301.

73. Ibid.

74. Robert Bayliss, "What *Don Quixote* Means (Today)," *Comparative Literature Studies* 43, no. 4 (2006): 390.

75. Ibid., 384–87.

76. Anderson, *Imagined Communities*, 25.

77. Ibid., 26.

78. Theodor Adorno, *Aesthetic Theory*, trans. Robert Hullot-Kentor (Minneapolis: University of Minnesota Press, 1997), 111.

Ning Ma, Tufts University

"𝒜 Strong Resemblance": Samuel Richardson, Chinese Talent-Beauty Novels, and a Secret Origin of "World Literature"

IN HIS WIDELY READ CONVERSATIONS OF GOETHE, JOHANN Peter Eckermann reports the following dialogue with the poet on January 31, 1827: "Dined with Goethe. 'Within the last few days, since I saw you,' said he, 'I have read many things; especially a Chinese novel, which occupies me still and seems to me very remarkable.' 'Chinese novel!' said I; 'that must look strange enough.' 'Not so much as you might think,' said Goethe; 'the Chinese think, act, and feel almost exactly like us; and we soon find that we are perfectly like them, except that all they do is more clear, pure, and decorous, than with us.'"[1]

On the basis of this observation Goethe reached a daring conclusion: "National literature is now rather an unmeaning term; the epoch of world literature is at hand, and everyone must strive to hasten its approach."[2] Nearly two centuries later, the term "world literature" Goethe first coined here has become a familiar part of today's reality of global mobility and exchange. As a harbinger of the multicultural world we now inhabit, Goethe's percipient formulation of the emergent "epoch of world literature" has received copious critical attention, and is often considered as an origin of the modern discipline of comparative literature.

What then is the particular "Chinese novel" that motivated Goethe's famous commentary? Eckermann's report does not give the precise title, but based on the few details Goethe recalled from the book, it is clear that Goethe had in mind an anonymous novel titled *Hao qiu zhuan* 《好逑傳》 (*The Pleasing History*), which was probably written during the 1650s and happens to be the first full-length Chinese fictional work introduced to Western readers.[3] Apart from *Hao qiu zhuan*, we know that around this time Goethe was also reading an 1826 French translation of *Yu Jiao Li* 《玉嬌梨》 (*Jade-Charming-Pear*), another seventeenth-century Chinese novel of unidentified authorship.[4] It is possible that in his conversation Goethe might have been thinking about this book as well.

Given the high opinion Goethe held of these Chinese novels, we might expect them to enjoy comparable esteem in their native culture. While *Hao qiu zhuan* and *Yu Jiao Li* were indeed widely popular in China from the seventeenth through the nineteenth centuries, their appeal came to an abrupt end with the drastic political and cultural shifts of the early twentieth century. Now rarely read even by students of Chinese literature, they vaguely register in today's scholarly discourse as examples of the so-called talent-beauty novel, a type of love narrative modern critics often find unpalatably formulaic, unrealistic, and didactic. This critical disregard explains why *Hao qiu zhuan* and *Yu Jiao Li* have so far received little attention in discussions of Goethe's notion of "world literature." One might conclude that the enthusiasm these texts garnered from Goethe and many of his contemporaries is chiefly attributable to the sheer dearth of translations of Chinese literary texts available to them.

I believe, however, that Goethe's interest in such "minor" works as *Hao qiu zhuan* and *Yu Jiao Li* stems from much more than an accidental misreading of Chinese culture. The key to uncovering the deeper significance of this curious cross-cultural response lies in a brief yet striking comment Goethe made to Eckermann—that there is a "strong resemblance" between the Chinese novels he read and the works of Samuel Richardson, the eighteenth-century English writer whose distinctively "sentimental" style enjoyed phenomenal success across Europe from the mid-eighteenth to the early nineteenth centuries. Given the tremendous literary influence Richardson then had, any similarity between the talent-beauty novels of China and his writings would work effectively to dissolve the otherwise considerable distance between these foreign texts and European readers of the time.

Furthermore, the sentimental novel in general and Richardson's works in particular are regarded by many modern critics as constituting "a watershed in the evolution of modern consciousness."[5] It is my contention that to an extent the kind of cultural transformation embodied by the sentimental novel can be likewise detected in the rise of the talent-beauty novel, a still much-neglected subject within the field of Chinese studies.[6] The most crucial point of convergence is that both the sentimental novel and the talent-beauty novel exemplify a structural shift from a "public" to a "private" definition of virtue in their respective culture. By the term "public definition of virtue" I refer to a moral system premised on the assumption that the highest form of truth resides in the proper maintenance of political order and religious faith, an assumption that implicitly posits a fundamental correspondence between social and moral hierarchy, hence working to justify status distinction. A "private definition of virtue," on the other hand, asserts that personal and subjective experiences, instead of external roles and duties, constitute the ultimate signifier of an individual's moral character.

105

The following sections first expound in more detail my argument regarding the shift from "public" to "private" conceptions of virtue and then move on to illustrate my thesis through readings of Richardson's *Pamela* and *Clarissa* and three representative works of the talent-beauty novel—*Yu Jiao li, Hao qiu zhuan*,[7] and *Jin Yun Qiao zhuan* 《金云翘傳》(*The Tale of the Golden Hairpin*). The essay ends with a hypothesis that the correspondence it uncovers between the Chinese and English texts are more than coincidental: roughly simultaneous, they might well be what Joseph Fletcher once percipiently termed "horizontal continuities"—that is, basically speaking, parallel and transcultural phenomena not necessarily related in themselves, but can be attributed to "the same ultimate source."[8] To establish the possibility of such a horizontal link is to imagine a different way of writing literary history. An exploration into this new comparative perspective is precisely what this essay, however modest in scale, attempts at by delving into an overlooked background of Goethe's otherwise well-studied notion of "world literature," a concept whose birth—as I hope to illustrate—registers not just the meeting of previously separated literary worlds, but also the contour of a world-historical moment shared by what seems to be the most distant places.

A New Structure of Virtue

In European cultural history, the public definition of virtue is inherent in aristocratic ideology and social structure. As Michael McKeon has pointed out, at the core of aristocratic ideology is the notion of "honor," which refers both to external circumstances such as ancestry, wealth, and political power, and to "an essential and inward property of its possessor, that which the conditional or extrinsic signifiers of honor exist to signify": "In this respect, honor is equivalent to an internal element of 'virtue.' This notion of honor as a unity of outward circumstances and internal essence is the most fundamental justification for the hierarchical stratification of society by status, and it is so fundamental as to be largely tacit. What it asserts is that the social order is not circumstantial and arbitrary, but corresponds to and expresses an analogous moral order."[9]

In contrast to the aristocratic ideology, the Confucian principles that governed traditional China are mostly meritocratic: they emphasize moral cultivation rather than birth and lineage as the passport to virtue. However, it is important to note that, despite this crucial difference, Confucianism and the aristocratic ideology do share one common pattern in similarly insisting on the coherence of the social and moral orders. In other words, they both affirm what I have previously termed the "public definition of virtue." In the Chinese tradition, this ideological structure is best illustrated by a core passage in the Neo-Confucian canon The Great Learning (Da Xue 《大學》, which theorizes the process of moral cultivation "in terms of a set of concentric circles of ever-broadening significance,"[10] proceeding from the rectification of the mind (zheng xin 正心), the cultivation of the self (xiu shen 修身), the management of the household (qi jia 齊家), to the right-government of the state (zhi guo 治國), and eventually of the universe (ping tianxia 平天下). As exemplified by this passage, the correction of the mind-heart, or xin, naturally leads to the cultivation of shen, the identity and repute of a person shaped through social interaction. Since the cultivation of *shen* is asserted to have an expanding chain of influence in the extrinsic milieu of the individual, from the family to the entire Chinese land, this supposed unity of body and mind further serves to link the order of the self with the order of the world. Culminating in administrative service, virtue is portrayed in this passage as essentially a political duty. Thus the human subjects who exemplify virtue are necessarily those granted political powers.

This equation of moral and political merit in the Confucian worldview, as expressed in *The Great Learning*, was institutionalized through the civil examination system (*ke ju* 科舉), which recruited state officials on the basis of their performance in tests on the Confucian classics. The founding premise of the civil examination system arose from the belief that the learning of the classics perforce produces moral character, and that moral character directly translates into administrative leadership. Given this premise, men who succeeded in these exams and assumed public office—known as scholar-officials—embodied a moral authority that justified their political prestige. In this respect, although Confucian ideology differs from aristocratic ideology in fundamental ways, it similarly postulates that the public organization of power represents an essential moral order, and that the socially privileged class personifies the highest standard of human worth.

107

The public definition of virtue, however, seems to have been severely eroded by rapid socioeconomic shifts in both China and Europe from the sixteenth century onward. Elsewhere I have discussed in detail that, as reflected by the first "realistic" Chinese and English novels—the sixteenth-century anonymous Chinese text *Jin Ping Mei* (*The Plum in the Golden Vase*) and Daniel Defoe's (c. 1659–1731) *Robinson Crusoe*, widespread commercial developments in Chinese and European societies around the time rigorously undermined their traditional value systems as wealth emerged as an increasingly visible determinant in the organization of social and political power. Whereas *Jin Ping Mei* treats the severance between virtue and power as occasioning an irreversible moral decline, *Robinson Crusoe* confines moral judgment to the purview of the individual, hence reinventing the pursuit of wealth as "private virtue" instead of "public vice." Though pronouncing contrary judgments, both texts record a tremendous sense of rupture that signals the profound cultural destabilization of the time.[11]

The sentimental novel and the talent-beauty novel responded to this sense of rupture with an analogous strategy: they both carve out a subjective space of feeling to accommodate a moral order divorced from social reality. This interiorized conception of virtue on the one hand acknowledges the disintegration between virtue and power, and on the other hand proffers a new conceptual possibility—that the separation of virtue from the actual operation of the world marks not the end but the beginning of morality. In this way, these texts reinvent the moral order as a subjective and internal realm that bears no relation to the public organization of power and service, thus marking a cross-cultural rise of the "private definition of virtue" during the early modern time.

Reinventing Chastity

In both the Chinese and European cases, a notable corollary of the internalization of moral agency is the feminization of subjectivity. One of the radically new aspects of both the talent-beauty novel and Richardson's works, as has been observed by earlier scholars, is their idealization of women.[12] Nancy Armstrong has discussed this phenomenon in eighteenth-century English fiction in terms of the "rise of feminine authority," which she attributes to women's traditional exclusion from sociopolitical activities. Women's consequent disfranchised status meant a separation, and thus freedom, from the hierarchy of social power, by virtue of which they paradoxically obtained a privileged status as the embodiments of an ideal moral order.[13] Given that traditional Chinese society was likewise patriarchic, Armstrong's thesis offers an equally cogent explanation for the exalted status of women in the talent-beauty novel. In both cultures morality became affiliated, and even identified, with domesticity, subjectivity, and femininity in contradistinction to the materialism that was becoming increasingly determinant of social and political relations.

As a result of the feminization of moral agency, virtue in the English and Chinese texts examined in this chapter came to be defined primarily as the specifically female virtue of chastity. Indeed, the focus on chastity in these novels is so predominant that they typically strike modern readers as moralistic and sexually repressive. Careful attention to the texts involved, however, leads one to argue that they in fact radically reinvent the code of chastity and in doing so constitute a turning point in European and Chinese literary representations of human nature and subjectivity. To understand the new significance of chastity in the sentimental novel and the talent-beauty novel, we need first to briefly review what came before.

In European cultural history, the code of female chastity had its origin in the patrilineal kinship structure of aristocratic pedigree. As April Alliston has noted, the notion of chastity emerged to assure a "reproductive fidelity" between father and son. Furthermore, in addition to preserving the supposed genetic "purity" of family bloodline, women's subordination and allegiance to men in domestic and sexual life symbolically echo analogous bonds in the male, political world— most important, the vassal's military fealty to the feudal monarch.[14] Alliston's observations are pertinent to establishing a comparative framework for our discussion of the Chinese case. As I shall elaborate later, the structure of chastity in European aristocracy has an analogy in the Confucian principle of the "Five Cardinal Relations" (*wu lun* 五倫), according to which a woman's pledge of loyalty to her husband carries the dual functions of physically sustaining the patrilineal lineage and symbolically reinforcing the organization of power in the social realm, which in imperial China chiefly depended on the minister's political devotion to the sovereign.

These parallel structures of chastity in traditional European and Chinese cultures will be referred to herein as the "patriarchic" model of chastity, which represents the penetration of the public definition of virtue into the domestic sphere. The private domain regulated by this model functions less for its own sake than to legitimatize the political system. This ideological pattern, as we shall see in the following analyses, is notably subverted in both Richardson's novels and talent-beauty novels like *Yu Jiao Li* and *Hao qiu zhuan*, in which the discourse of chastity is reinvented to generate a privatized, feminized, and eventually interiorized center of moral identity *vis-à-vis* the spiritual vacuum that shrouds social and political life. At its most extreme, as we see in *Clarissa* and *Jin Yun Qiao zhuan*, the narrative's intense focus on moral interiority propels it to destroy the heroine's physical chastity to affirm her spiritual chastity, hence representing virtue as a purely subjective quality that needs no correspondent in material reality.

From Pamela *to* Clarissa

Pamela, Richardson's first major work, provided eighteenth-century English readers with an unprecedented portrait of the superior virtue of a maidservant, the novel's eponymous heroine who unflinchingly resists the sexual advances of her master. Deployed in this context, the discourse of chastity, instead of corroborating social hierarchy as in the patriarchic model, becomes the core of a symbolic self by reference to which the heroine is empowered to transcend her political subordination. This radically new function of chastity can be clearly seen in the following passage, originally part of Pamela's refutation written on a contrast of terms her master offers to buy her as a mistress: "And to lose the best Jewel, my Virtue, would be poorly recompensed by those you propose to give me. What should I think, when I looked upon my Finger, or saw, in the Glass, those Diamonds on my Neck, and in my Ears, but that they were the Price my Honesty; and that I wore those Jewels outwardly, because I had none inwardly?"[15]

In this passage, by comparing her chastity to her "best jewel," Pamela purposefully twists her master's original terms that promise her actual jewels once she agrees to be his mistress. This juxtaposition of the literal and figurative meanings of the term "jewel" sets the moral idealism of the heroine against the commodity value her master offers. In this way, the imagery of an interior self whose value is independent of external authorities emerges through the heroine's resistance to the greater political and economic power of her master.

Paradoxically, the deep appeal the interiorized realm of virtue depicted in *Pamela* held for its readers is demonstrated by the controversy surrounding the book. This controversy concerned Pamela's eventual reconciliation with and marriage to her master, who has ultimately reformed, a happy ending presaged by the novel's subtitle "virtue rewarded." Calling themselves "anti-Pamelists," critics of the novel argued that, given that her "reward" is the prestige and profit associated with marrying a gentleman, the virtue the heroine displays is after all merely a duplicitous scheme to secure an economically and socially advantageous marriage.[16] The anti-Pamela controversy indicates the profound degree to which the moral and social orders became separated and antagonized in the cultural consciousness of the period. As the anti-Pamelists assumed, virtue, if authentic at all, cannot coexist with worldly rewards. Given this assumption, the two realities *Pamela* deliberately separates and places in opposition—the ideal reality and the social reality—cannot be reconciled without contradicting and undermining the novel's moral message.

The ideological dilemma of Richardson's first novel, as exposed by the "anti-Pamela" controversy, was carefully resolved in his second major work, *Clarissa*, published seven years after the first edition of *Pamela*. Like Pamela, the heroine of *Clarissa* faces the persistent harassment of a rakish hero, Lovelace. This analogous narrative conflict, however, ends on a much darker note: the heroine, rather than converting Lovelace with her virtue, is unknowingly drugged and raped by the hero. After she realizes she has been raped, Clarissa begins, in Lovelace's words, a "courtship of death,"[17] which eventually takes her life. Clarissa's death seals the moral truth that exists only as a claim in *Pamela*—that a woman's loss of chastity is equal to a "fate worse than death." In this manner, the deprivation of the heroine's bodily chastity in *Clarissa* is turned into the very means to attesting her virtue, her spiritual chastity. No longer chaste according to physical or social definitions following the rape, Clarissa transforms virtue entirely into a creation of her interior will and sentiment.

The radical break between virtue and the material world enacted in *Clarissa* may account for its nearly universal approval among eighteenth-century readers. In *Clarissa*, the ideological contradiction of *Pamela* is resolved through the dissolution of all linkages between the ideal and the real, the inward and the outward, the heart and the body. Consequently, in this later novel, chastity, the last embodiment of virtue, becomes a state of mind rather than a physical condition. This drastic reformulation of the idea of chastity implies that in the European culture of this time the perceived center of moral truth—having already retreated to the private, feminine realm—was further interiorized into pure psychology and personal conviction, no longer bearing any definite relation to extrinsic signifiers, be they political power, economic rewards, or the chaste female body.

Yu Jiao Li and the Redefinition of the "Five Cardinal Relations"

In parallel with the European case examined above, the idea of chastity and marriage portrayed in the seventeenth-century talent-beauty novel is essentially different from the "patriarchic model" codified by the "Five Cardinal Relations," which resemble European aristocratic ideology in imposing on conjugal life a domestic hierarchy that corresponds to the political system of authority and subordination. A classic formulation of the code of the Five Cardinal Relations can be found in a passage in *Mencius*, which teaches the correct ordering of five fundamental human relations: between father and son, sovereign and minister, husband and wife, elder and younger brothers, and friends.[18] In this passage the key to the proper relation between husband and wife falls on their "separate functions" (*bie* 別), which literally means "difference." This emphasis on separation stems from the assumption that the attachment between a man and a woman is necessarily sexual and hence a self-serving and materialistic desire that holds the potential to corrupt the moral order if not properly controlled. Subsequently, the only appropriate way for the two sexes to interact with each other is through parentally arranged marriages aiming at preserving the patriarchic family line. In short, in traditional Confucian culture, male-female relations either fall into the category of disciplined, orthodox marriage, or that of illicit sexual passion—there is no middle ground.

Furthermore, the gendered difference prescribed by the code of the Five Cardinal Relations essentially denotes the husband's higher authority in relation to his wife. This definition of conjugal life symbolically reinforces the regulatory bonds of other cardinal relations, especially a son's filial piety toward his father, and a minister's loyalty toward his sovereign. All requiring the uttermost devotion of one party to the other, these familial, marital, and political ties were regarded as the core of the Five Cardinal Relations, and were often singled out as the "Three Bonds" (*san gang* 三綱). By juxtaposing the subordinate roles of a wife, a son, and a minister, the principle of the Three Bonds encodes the family as a microcosmic embodiment of the state. Thus in Confucian ideology the private and public spheres of life are perceived not as separate cultural domains, but as constituting a totality governed by the same moral pattern.

Based on this overview, the seventeenth-century talent-beauty novel's subversion of the established view of love and marriage becomes immediately clear if we turn our attention to the following excerpt from *Yu Jiao Li*, in which the novel's hero Su Youbai 蘇有白, a Chinese "man of feeling,"[19] reflects on his situation in life:

> There are "Five Cardinal Relationships" in human life. I am an unfortunate orphan who lost his father and mother at a young age. Neither do I have brothers. Two of the "cardinal relationships" are inherently absent in my life. The meetings between sovereign and minister, and between friends, depend on chance and occasion. If I cannot marry an exceptionally accomplished and beautiful woman, then I, Su Youbai, live in vain a life immersed in books and poetry—for what good can the name of a talented scholar do for me, if I cannot find someone to share the passion and yearning that fill my chest? [Without an ideal wife,] I will not be appeased even if I die.
>
> 人生有五倫，我不幸父母早亡，又無兄弟，五倫中先失了兩倫。君臣朋友間遇合有時，若不娶一個絕色佳人為婦，則是我蘇友白為人在世一，空讀了許多詩書，就做一個才子也是枉然，叫我一腔情思向何處去發？便死也不甘心. (5:36)[20]

While citing the principle of the Five Cardinal Relations, the hero's monologue interprets the meaning of the canonical code in a radically unorthodox manner. Casually dismissing the sovereign-minister bond as a matter that depends on "chance and occasion," hence circumstantial rather than essential in life, Su Youbai reveals a noncommittal attitude to the official duty traditionally perceived as the ultimate destiny of a Confucian scholar. In this way, the hero frees himself from the political loyalty that traditionally controlled the symbolic patterns of other cardinal relations. Once distanced from the social organization of power, marriage becomes an independent realm of private life. In *Yu Jiao Li* and many other talent-beauty novels, the autonomy of marriage is further stressed through the hero's orphaned status, which renders the question of parental authority irrelevant in his choice of spouse. The perception of marriage as a self-contained unit naturally yields a more personal understanding of the nature of conjugality: as Su Youbai's words demonstrate, for him the fundamental importance of marriage rests in companionship, a notion largely incompatible with the orthodox marital system that emphasizes the hierarchical and functional distinctions between husband and wife.

The idea of companionate marriage in Yu Jiao Li is accompanied with the novel's deliberate de-eroticization of love. In the narrative this process goes so far that the lovers' physicality virtually disappears in the process of their courtship. As the plot of the novel proceeds, Su Youbai falls in love with Bai Hongyu 白紅玉, the principle heroine of the story, not because of her beauty but because of her poetry. Ignited by the sheer communicative power of the heroine's words, Su Youbai's passion grows in a nonphysical manner. With the help of Bai Hongyu's maidservant, he begins to exchange poetic writings with the heroine without actually meeting her in person. Bai Hongyu reciprocally falls in love with the hero on the sole ground of her appreciation of his literary talent and lyrical sensitivity. After many twists and turns, the hero and the heroine are eventually united as husband and wife. Before the wedding that concludes the novel, the two lovers, despite their deep commitment to each other, have never met face to face. In the end, rather unsurprisingly, Bai Hongyu turns out to be a great beauty, yet her physical attractiveness, unknown to the hero throughout their courtship, has been entirely displaced by her internal qualities expressed through poetry.

The desexualization of love in Yu Jiao Li must be viewed against the explicit eroticism of earlier vernacular novels, such as the famous Jin Ping Mei.[21] On a larger level, Yu Jiao Li's creation of a chaste romance offers a solution to the larger ideological question alarmingly exposed in Jin Ping Mei: that is, to put it simply, the nature of individual freedom and its consequence. Jin Ping Mei primarily treats individual freedom in terms of material egoism, which leads to economic and sexual corruption. Yu Jiao Li, however, rationalizes and domesticates the free mobility of human desire by expunging its physical and material components, thus turning that freedom into the very force of moral containment and generating a new order in face of the collapse of traditional values. To become the new vehicle of meaning and personal identity, love must be categorically desexualized to signify a purely idealistic value, as well as an authentic selfhood unadulterated by material desires of all kinds.

The Virtuous Match

In *Yu Jiao Li*, the hero and heroine embody such a perfect lyrical subli-mation of desire that sexual complicity hardly appears an issue in their relationship. Though tacit, the narrative's insistence on the maintenance of the characters' chastity is unmistakable. For a much more pronounced example of the importance of chastity in seventeenth-century talent-beauty novels, we should turn to *Hao qiu zhuan*.[22] In fact, the preemi-nence of the matter of chastity in this Chinese text might well be the main reason that it reminded Goethe of Richardson's works: one detail Goethe remembered from this Chinese novel is an episode in which the hero and heroine "showed such great purity during a long acquaintance that, when they were on one occasion obliged to pass the night in the same chamber, they occupied the time with conversation and did not approach one another."[23] This episode occurs around the midpoint of the narrative of *Hao qiu zhuan* and sets up the main conflict to be resolved in the novel's second half, which in principle narrates the hero and heroine's unremitting efforts to prove to the world their chaste behavior during that compromising night. To this end, the two protagonists even avoid all physical contact after their wedding ceremony, until the hero-ine's virginity is vindicated in the imperial court.

By spending a night together in the heroine's chamber, the pro-tagonists of *Hao qiu zhuan* are put in a situation that in nearly all aspects incriminates them as a pair of unlawful lovers. Facing this accusation, the heroine Shui Bingxin 水冰心 compares the immoral appearance of her behavior to "floating clouds," and argues that what is truly funda-mental to the "purity" (*qing bai* 清白) of her person is the intention of her "heart" (*xin*), which constitutes the "foundational essence" (*ben* 本) of a human being.[24] This emphasis on moral interiority is a consistent theme of *Hao qiu zhuan*, and the narrator of the novel at one point even claims, in poetic form, that the true character of a person cannot be seen until it is tested by incriminating circumstances: "What is hidden beneath an overturned basin cannot be seen in broad daylight; Nowhere else but in the kitchen can one know the heart of a magic carp. Say not that 'boring a hole to steal a sight' is a shameful act; For otherwise how can we tell between the chaste and the unchaste?" (青天不睹覆盆下，廚中方知靈鯉心。　莫道鑽窺非美事，不然何以別貞淫.)[25]

"Boring a hole to steal a sight" (*zuan kui* 鑽窺) is a phrase derived from *Mencius*. In the original context, the term means that, once men and women give free reign to their desires, they would abandon the proper procedure of courtship. Rather than waiting for "the bidding of parents and the words of matchmakers," as convention requires, they would go so far as to bore a hole in the wall, steal a sight of the other sex, and eventually cross the wall to elope with one another.[26] This teaching from *Mencius* reveals that the strict control of cross-gender contact in Confucian morality is underlain with a fear of the collapse of boundaries and limits. The narrator of *Hao qiu zhuan*, however, argues that the disintegration of such boundaries is precisely a necessary condition to manifest a person's moral character, which is—as described by the metaphors in the first two lines of the poem cited—normally concealed from the public eye. By this argument, the hero and heroine's late-night meeting is not an inexcusable crime but, in the words of Magistrate Bao who takes charge of the case, "the critical moment that reveals the chaste or licentious nature of a person" 《貞淫大關頭》.[27]

With this new stress on subjective ethical sensibilities, however, it also becomes particularly exigent for the hero and the heroine to socially evince their inner rectitude. In the hero's words to the heroine, "Only you and I know that we are guiltless of all charges of dishonesty and indecency. Apart from ourselves, who else could vouch for our innocence?" 《夫人與卑人之無欺無愧，惟有自知，此外則誰為明證.》[28] This much needed proof is eventually provided by the heroine's virginity: as the protagonists agree, to completely clear their name, the heroine must preserve "a body that shall evince [their] innocence" (*ke bai zhi shen* 可白之身),[29] even after their marriage. The moment of vindication the protagonists anticipate soon arrives when the emperor is notified of their case and decides to find out the truth by letting the court ladies test the heroine's virginity. This test, issued by the highest authority imaginable, demonstrates that Shui Bingxin indeed still possesses her "original body" (*yuan ti* 原體).[30] Thus through the private signifier of female virginity the protagonists' moral autonomy, which

116

allows them to transgress the ritual prescription on gender segregation, finally receives its social validation.

If *Hao qiu zhuan* somewhat resembles *Pamela* in using female chastity as the physical signifier of an interiorized, more fundamental form of moral agency, another well-known seventeenth-century talent-beauty novel *Jin Yun Qiao zhuan* parallels *Clarissa* in sacrificing the heroine's physical chastity to generate a more absolute affirmation of her spiritual chastity. In this last example we are going to examine, the defilement of the heroine's body paradoxically sets the stage for her moral apotheosis. Such a narrative design polarizes the ideal and the real, the heart and the body, and signals the logical extreme of the division between subjective and objective experiences in the cultural imagination of the time.

The Saintly Prostitute in Jin Yun Qiao zhuan

Attributed to a certain Qingxin cairen [青心才人],[31] *Jin Yun Qiao zhuan* is based on the "Wang Cuiqiao story complex" that emerged during the sixteenth century.[32] According to these earlier accounts, Wang was a late Ming courtesan who became the favorite concubine of the powerful pirate lord Xu Hai 徐海 (d.1556). She played a crucial role in persuading Xu Hai into accepting the Ming government's amnesty, without knowing that this official pardon was in fact a trap. The pirate lord was detained and executed soon after his surrender. Believing herself complicit in Xu's death, Wang Cuiqiao eventually committed suicide by drowning herself.

Using this story as its basic source, the novel *Jin Yun Qiao zhuan* at the same time adds many new events to relate Wang Cuiqiao's complex personal history before she meets Xu Hai. In fact, in the book Xu does not appear until the final three chapters. Due to this narrative design, as Martin Huang has noted, "the private life of Wang Cuiqiao rather than her public role in quelling the formidable pirate force becomes the narrative focus."[33] The novel's new emphasis on the heroine's individual existence is connected with its aim to construct an idealized quality of the "heart" (*xin*) separated from all significations associated with the "body" or a person's external persona (*shen*). This agenda is pithily summarized by Tianhuacang zhuren's[34] 天花藏主人 in his preface to the novel: "A person who has an unsullied body [or, lives an unsullied life] yet degraded heart is unchaste despite being chaste; a person who has a degraded body yet blameless heart is chaste despite being unchaste" 身免矣，而心辱焉，貞而淫矣；身辱矣，而心免焉，淫而貞矣.

It is noteworthy that, by underscoring the antithetical relation between "body" and "heart," Tianhuacang zhuren breaks the assumed unity of an individual's inner and outer selves in the canonical teachings of *The Great Learning*. The narrative of *Jin yun qiao zhuan* represents this rupture through Wang Cuiqiao's drastic transformation from a chaste maiden, who very much resembles Bai Hongyu in *Yu Jiao Li* and Shui Bingxin in *Haoqiu zhuan*, to "a wife of one thousand men" (*qian ren fu* 千人婦).[35] As the story begins, the heroine is the oldest daughter in a scholarly family of declining fortune. In the manner of a conventional romance, she secretly falls in love with her neighbor Jin Zhong 金重 after she catches a glimpse of the young man during a family outing. Living in two adjacent households, the lovers, in a way that almost literally recalls the "hole-boring" elopers condemned in *Mencius*, stealthily meet each other through a secret passage they opened up between the two family gardens. Meeting in this furtive manner, they nevertheless choose to avoid all physical intimacy due to the heroine's resolve to preserve her chastity before marriage. Here *Jin Yun Qiao zhuan* resembles *Yu Jiao Li* and *Haoqiu zhuan* in asserting the lovers' ability to act morally beyond prescribed codes of conduct. In comparison to the other two novels, *Jin Yun Qiao zhuan* nevertheless involves another radical turn, as it later destroys the heroine's chaste body that formerly signified her moral agency, thus dissociating the virtue she embodies from all external correlatives.

As it happens, shortly after Wang Cuiqiao and Jin Zhong begin their secret trysts, a sudden misfortune befalls the Wang household as the heroine's father is falsely charged in a lawsuit. To save her father from the death penalty, the heroine decides to sell herself to raise the required bail of three hundred taels of silver. Seeing her chaste body as the essential substance of her person, the heroine equates the selling of that body to death, and thus describes her action in terms of the ancient phrase *sha shen cheng ren* 殺身成仁—"to die for a just cause," or, more literally, "to kill one's own body for the sake of virtue."[36] The symbolic death of Wang Cuiqiao's body comes the moment it is turned into an object for sale. During the trading process, the heroine begins to refer to her body as her "physical body" (*rou shen*肉身), as mere flesh. Treating her body as a commodity alienated from her true person, the heroine reveals a businesslike cool-headedness in dealing with her buyer, as she bargains for the best price, and makes sure that the payment is not amiss in the slightest.[37]

As it turns out, the living death Wang Cuiqiao must endure is still worse than what she first expects: she is in fact sold as a prostitute rather than a concubine. After a failed suicide and many harrowing trials, the heroine finally succumbs to her fate as a "public woman" and thus becomes irrevocably parted from her former self inscribed in the discourse of female chastity. Yet, on the other hand, the material degradation of the heroine's body conversely functions to bear out her inherent moral sentiment. An important device employed in the novel to this end is its inclusion of a large number of song lyrics Wang Cuiqiao composes to express her suffering and deep sense of alienation from her environment. Words and music enable the heroine to create a symbolic self opposite to the sordid role she is forced to play, a symbolic self whose lack of objective signifier renders its truth all the more absolute. Thus, in accordance to Tianhuacang zhuren's preface, the ordeals the heroine undergoes result in a sharp opposition between her "body" and "heart."

Toward the end of the novel, this body-heart distinction leads to yet another twist. After complex misadventures, the heroine, as in preexisting versions of her story, becomes Xu Hai's concubine and later drowns herself out of her feelings of guilt about Xu's execution. Only that in *Jin Yun Qiao zhuan* she is miraculously rescued from the river by an earlier acquaintance. Finally, she manages to return home and reunite with her parents as well as her former lover Jin Zhong, who, by Wang's request before she is sold away, is married to her younger sister Cuiyun 翠雲. As a way to compensate the sacrifices Wang has made for the family, her parents and sister arrange for her to marry Jin as another principle wife. Though still deeply in love with Jin, the heroine on their wedding night nevertheless refuses physical contact with her lover, who has now become her lawful husband.[38] As the heroine explains, her body "has degenerated and should have been dead a long time ago" 此身殘敗, 應死久矣. To use such a deteriorated, broken body to serve her husband, in the heroine's mind, is a shame she cannot bear. Hence the

heroine supplicates Jin to "pity her and keep her whole" 乞郎憐而保
全之. Like her former self, Wang is still obsessed with her "wholeness."
Yet at this point that "wholeness" is no longer about her physical chastity, but about a spiritual integrity understood in terms of its categorical
separation from the materiality of her body.

This interiorized view of virtue underlies the heroine's claim to
her "chastity after defilement" (*shou ru zhi zhen* 受辱之貞). To preserve
her imagined chastity, the heroine is compelled to keep her defiled body
away from the conjugal relation she regards as the defining center of her
moral being. At this point, as in the opening of the novel, the heroine's
virtue is expressed through the desexualization of her relation to Jin.
Yet the difference made through the course of the story is that the body
the earlier Wang Cuiqiao cherishes with all her being is no longer an
integral part of her sense of self at the end of the novel. She becomes
pure "heart," hence transcending the female role her body essentially
denotes: as Jin exclaims after the heroine's speech, "Now I see that
you are in fact not a woman, but belong to the order of great saints and
heroes" 原來夫人非女子也，竟是聖賢豪傑中人.[39] Jin's conclusion
effectively sums up the radical implication of the body-heart opposition
that emerges through the narrative of *Jin Yun Qiao zhuan*, an opposition
that makes it possible for a former prostitute to assume a saintly stature
after she has endured what is probably the most debasing kind of experience in the traditional Confucian value system.

Epilogue: Goethe's Misreading Revisited

The analyses of the previous sections are meant to illustrate—to use
Goethe's words—a "strong resemblance" between the sentimental
novel of eighteenth-century Europe and the talent-beauty novel of
seventeenth-century China. Specifically, I argue that they similarly
reflect a gradual division between spiritual and material realties and
concomitantly a growing emphasis on the private, internalized, and feminized self. This cross-cultural convergence may partly explain Goethe
and many of his contemporaries' enthusiastic response to those Chinese
talent-beauty novels now dismissed as "secondary" and "unreadable."
Living in a time of radical cultural transformation, eighteenth-century
European intellectuals such as Goethe tended to regard the ideal moral

sentiment they found in the Chinese novels as the reflection of a timeless Chinese "spirit." As already discussed, however, the talent-beauty novel emerged in the near wake of *Jin Ping Mei*'s apocalyptic vision of the fall of Confucian civilization in a world where material desires reign supreme. The genre's "purity" thus in fact parallels the sentimentalism of Richardson's novels in being produced by a pressing sense of moral crisis and consequently involves an intricate process through which established cultural boundaries were questioned and redrawn.

Emerging from a similar context, the parallels between the sentimental novel and the talent-beauty novel are not only textual but also structural, since they exhibit a comparable correlation between the literary and the extra literary domains. Even more arresting is the approximate *simultaneity* of their appearance at the two ends of Eurasia, a fact that leads one to suspect that they are after all linked by certain common historical factors. Such a suggestion seems to defy all sense of reason if we follow the conventional wisdom that the histories of China and Europe remained essentially separate until the late nineteenth century. However, as cogently demonstrated by the works of Joseph Fletcher, Andre Gunder Frank, Kenneth Pomeranz, and other world historians, in real historical terms various world civilizations developed *interdependently* long before the diffusion of European colonialism.[41] Their studies debunk the myth of European exceptionalism by showing that, on the one hand, Europe was by no means the most economically or institutionally advanced area in the world up to as late as around 1800, and on the other, the so-called rise of the West was a highly contingent progress dependent upon a combination of global conjunctures. As Frank in particular emphasizes, a crucial cause for the growth of early modern European economy and commerce rests in the European exportation of newly discovered American silver to China for considerable arbitrage.[41] Meanwhile, this massive influx of probably at least a quarter of the world's total production of silver into China,[42] where it was used as currency, likewise stimulated "spectacular" economic expansion in Chinese society from the mid-sixteenth century onward.[43] In the succinct phrase of Frank, during those centuries when silver flowed across the globe to China, "money went around the world and made the world go around."[44] In fact, the increasing interrelatedness of the two ends of

Eurasia due to the silver trade was already noted by a famous contemporary witness—that is, Adam Smith, who thus writes in *The Wealth of Nations*: "Since the first discovery of America, the market for the produce of its silver mines has been growing gradually more and more extensive . . . [and] the greater part of Europe has been improved. . . . The silver of the new continent seems . . . to be one of the principle commodities by which the commerce between the two extremities of the old one is carried on, and by means of it, in great measure, that those distant parts of the world are connected with one another."[45] Could this silver connection between what seems to be the most widely separated societies, one wonders, be the very *same* historical force that brought about the rapid socioeconomic shifts of early modern China and Europe and catalyzed the literary parallels discussed in this essay?

If this hypothesis stands, the comparability between the sentimental novel and the Chinese talent-beauty novel is no longer just a curious coincidence; rather, it may be characterized as an example of what Fletcher once termed "horizontal continuities"—unrelated parallels attributable to a common cause. For anyone who is convinced that literature is an ingrained part of history, Fletcher's idea of "horizontal continuities" opens up an exciting possibility for comparative literary research beyond the well-trodden paths of "influence" study either within the "West," the "East," or any cultural system itself, or from the West to the rest of the world after the rise of Europe's global hegemony. However valid and valuable these earlier frameworks are, they replicate the conceptual process by which history has nearly always been arranged and written—that is, to emphasize only vertical and often hierarchical relations either through time or from a civilizational core to its peripheries. This kind of vertical imagination by necessity limits critical inquires to a local perspective that implicitly encourages Eurocentric or other ethnocentric assumptions. To provide a corrective to this deep-seated historiographic one-sidedness, Frank has repeatedly urged that the task of the present generation of historians is to rewrite history, and that the key method to do so is to make efforts to "relate different things and places at the same time in the historical process." As Frank asserts, "the very attempt to examine and relate the simultaneity of different events in the whole historical process or in the transformation of the whole system—even if for want of empirical information or theoretical adequacy it may be full of holes in its factual coverage of space and time—is a significant step in the right direction."[46] It would be hard to disagree with Frank's plea, unless one can imagine a map with only vertical but no horizontal coordinates.

It is beyond the scope of this essay to further probe the methodological implications of a horizontal comparison. Yet, beginning with Goethe's much-quoted statement about the coming of the age of "world literature," our inquiry has reached a conclusion that echoes its point of departure in intriguing ways. There is little doubt that the optimistic universalism expressed by Goethe's reading of the Chinese talent-beauty novel has now become a thing of the past. Wary of the analytical sin of mutilating non-Western cultures by the Procrustean bed of dominating Western models, critics today have developed an entrenched predilection for difference rather than similarity. Unquestionably, cultural differences are real and should be valued. However, it would be mistaken, even treacherous, to imagine them as natural, essential, and unsurpassable. After the discourse of difference has long engendered the disciplinary divide that compartmentalizes and institutionalizes various "area studies," it seems time to remind us once again, however tentatively, the possibilities of envisioning commonalities across national, cultural, and civilizational lines. In the illuminating words of Frank, it is necessary to "help construct an intellectual basis for accepting *diversity in unity* and celebrating *unity in diversity*."[47] Maybe one would even agree with Goethe that there is after all a common humanity, except that it is not the timeless essence he assumed, but historical and constantly changing. To chart the trajectory and interrelations of these changes would be a direction for the term "world literature" to realize its full significance, for, instead of being just a collection of "great books" of various national origins, the notion suggests an integrative whole—a *macro* literary history. For the goal of mapping such a larger structure—or what Fletcher describes as "a tentative schema of the continuities, or, at the least, parallelism in history,"[48] it seems that, almost two centuries after Goethe's hopeful pronouncement that "the epoch of world literature is at hand," the need to "hasten its approach" is still as urgent, if not more.

123

Notes

1. Johann Peter Eckermann, *Conversations of Goethe*, trans. John Oxenford (New York: Da Capo Press, 1998), 164.

2. Ibid., 165–66.

3. As early as 1761 an English translation of the book in four volumes, under the title *Hau kiou choaan; or, The Pleasing History*, came out in London; within the next two years, French, German, and Dutch versions of the novel based on the English rendition were published in Paris, Leipzig, and Amsterdam. See Zhongshu Qian, "Thomas Percy and His Chinese Studies," in *Vision of China in the English Literature of the 17th and 18th centuries*, ed. Adrian Hsia (Hong Kong: The Chinese University Press, 1998), 301–25, and Ros Ballster *Fabulous Orients: Fictions of the East in England 1662–1785* (New York: Oxford University Press, 2005), 236–41.

4. Jean-Pierre Abel Rémusat, *Iu-kiao-li, ou, Les deux cousines* (Paris, Moutardier, 1826). For reference to Goethe's reading of *Hao qiu zhuan*, *Yu Jiao Li*, and other translated Chinese texts, see Patricia Sieber, *Theaters of Desire: Authors, Readers, and the Reproduction of Early Chinese Song-Drama, 1300–2000* (Palgrave Macmillan, 2003),14.

5. G. J. Barker-Benfield, *The Culture of Sensibility: Sex and Society in Eighteenth-Century Britain* (Chicago: University of Chicago Press, 1992), xxxiv.

6. For two notable recent studies that contain extensive discussion of the talent-beauty novel, though not from a comparative perspective, see Keith McMahon, *Misers, Shrews, and Polygamists: Sexuality and Male-Female Relationships in Eighteenth-Century Chinese Fiction* (Durham, NC: Duke University Press, 1995), MA and Martin Huang, *Desire and Fictional Narrative in Late Imperial China* (Cambridge, Mass.: Harvard University Press, 2001).

7. The Chinese title *Yu Jiao Li* (literally, Jade-Charming-Pear), following the convention established by the famous *Jin Ping Mei*, is a combination of the main characters' names. The name *Hao qiu zhuan* is based on a well-known phrase from the Confucian classic *Shiji* 《詩經》 (*The Classic of Poetry*). In view of this allusion and the content of the book, I propose that we more accurately translate it as *The Virtuous Match*.

8. Joseph Fletcher, "Integrative History: Parallels and Interconnections in the Early Modern Period, 1500–1800" [1973], in idem *Studies on Chinese Islamic Inner Asia*, ed. Beatrice Forbes Manz, pt. X. (Aldershot, England: Variorum Press, 1995), 2.

9. Michael McKeon, *Origins of the English Novel* (Baltimore: Johns Hopkins University Press, 1987), 131.

10. Andrew Plaks, *The Four Masterworks of the Ming Novel: Ssu ta ch'i-shu* (Princeton, NJ: Princeton University Press, 1987), 138.

11. Please see my article "When Robinson Crusoe Meets Ximen Qing: Material Egoism in the First Chinese and English Novels," *Comparative Literature Studies* 46.3 (2009): 443–66.

12. For an account of the idealization of woman in talent-beauty novels, see Keith McMahon, "The Chaste 'Beauty-Scholar' Romance and the Superiority of the Talented Woman," in *Misers, Shrews, and Polygamists*, 99–125.

13. Cf. Nancy Armstrong, *Desire and Domestic Fiction: A Political History of the Novel.* (New York: Oxford University Press, 1987), 108–109.

14. April Alliston, *Virtue's Faults: Correspondences in Eighteenth-Century English and French Women's Fiction* (Stanford, CA: Stanford University Press, 1996), 56.

15. Samuel Richardson, *Pamela: Or, Virtue Rewarded* (London: Oxford University Press, 2001), 190.

16. This controversy can be summarized by the following comment by Peter Shaw: "There are Swarms of Moral Romance. One, of late Date, divided the World into such opposite Judgements, that some extolled it to the Stars, whilst other treated with Contempt. Whence arose, particularly among the Ladies, two different Parties, Pamelists and Anti-Pamelists. . . . Some look upon this young Virgin as an Example for Ladies to follow. . . . Others, on the contrary, discover in it, the Behavior of an hypocritical, crafty Girl in her Courtship; who understands the Art of bringing a Man to her Lure." See Peter Shaw, *The Reflector: Representing Human Affairs, as They Are: And May Be Improved* (London: T. Longman, 1750), 14.

17. Samuel Richardson, *Clarissa, or the History of a Young Lady* [1747–1748] (Harmondsworth: Penguin Books, 1985), 189.

18. A canonical definition of the "Five Cardinal Relations" can be found in *Mencius*, Book III, part I, 4.8. See "Mencius," trans. Irene Bloom, in *Sources of Chinese Tradition*, vol. 1, ed. Wm. Theodore de Bary and Irene Bloom, 2nd ed. (New York: Columbia University Press, 2000), 133 for a translation of this passage.

19. In contrast to the sexual struggle dramatized in *Pamela, Clarissa,* and many other eighteenth-century English novels, the talent-beauty novels of seventeenth-century China are typically structured upon a perfect symmetry and reciprocity between lovers, who are virtually like-minded souls of equal moral and aesthetic sensibilities. In other words, the typical hero of the talent-beauty novel is from the outset the type of "Man of Feeling"—as fittingly described by the title of Henry McKenzie's popular 1771 novel—made prominent in European novels by such authors as McKenzie and Lawrence Stern in England, Jean-Jacques Rousseau in France, and J. W. Goethe in Germany. Villainous rakes do exist in talent-beauty novels, and very often they resemble Mr. B or Lovelace in possessing considerable social and economic advantages due to family connections. Yet, in the Chinese talent-beauty novel this type of character is generally relegated to a subsidiary role. He for the most part exists as an external threat to the union of the lovers, a threat that is usually overcome at the end of the story through the hero and heroine's joint effort. In this narrative structure, the conflict between worldly and ideal values is represented not as the lonely resistance of a single woman, but as the camaraderie of virtuous lovers who together confront the onslaught of a corrupt world.

20. Chapter and page references to the Chinese original of the book are based on the *Zhongguo gudian xiaoshuo mingzhu baibu* 《中國古典小說名著百部》 edition (Beijing: Huaxia chubanshe, 1995). Translations of the Chinese talent-beauty novels in this essay are mine.

21. This connection is clearly indicated by *Yu Jiao Li*'s preface penned by a certain "Master of the Hall of Pure Governance" (Suzhengtang zhuren素政堂主人), who condemns the "filthy words and dissolute books" 穢言浪藉 that debased the notion of romance. For a complete translation of this preface, see the appendix in Richard Hessney, "Beautiful, Talented and Brave: Seventeenth-Century Chinese Scholar-Beauty Romances." Ph.D. dissertation, Columbia University, 1979.

22. Page references to the Chinese original of the book are based on the *Zhongguo gudian xiaoshuo mingzhu baibu* 中國古典小說名著百部 edition (Beijing: Huaxia chubanshe, 1995).

23. *Conversations of Goethe*, 165. In the novel, the heroine Shui Bingxin 水冰心 is forced by her greedy uncle to marry the good-for-nothing son of a court dignitary. The resourceful heroine manages to circumvent her uncle's plan and presents grievance to the local magistrate. The hero Tie Zhongyu 鐵中玉 hears about this case and, as the true knight-errant he is, tries to persuade the magistrate to rule in the heroine's favor. Finding Tie an obstacle to their scheme, Shui Bingxin's uncle and her suitor secretly poison him, and their misdeed is soon discovered by the heroine. To save the hero who has fallen seriously ill, Shui Bingxin takes him to her home to convalesce, thus breaching the ritual prohibition of direct contact between unmarried men and women.

24. *Hao qiu zhuan*, 6:37.

25. Ibid., 7:39.

26. *Mencius*, Book III, part II, 3.6.

27. *Hao qiu zhuan*, 18:105.

28. Ibid.

29. Ibid., 17:98.

30. Ibid., 18:106.

31. Qingxin, the pseudonym of this anonymous author, puns on "the passionate heart." Page references to the Chinese original of the book are based on the *Zhongguo gudian xiaoshuo mingzhu baibu* 《中國古典小說名著百部》 edition (Beijing: Huaxia chubanshe, 1995).

32. For a discussion of these earlier accounts, see Huang, *Desire and Fictional Narrative*, 211–13.

33. Huang, 214.

34. "Tianhuacang zhuren" played an important role in the emergence of seventeenth-century talent-beauty novels. He was the editor, publisher, and prefacer of at least sixteen examples of the genre, including *Yu Jiao L*. According to Liu Ts'un-yan, Tianhuacang zhuren was likely active during the second half of the seventeenth century and "had extensive connection with the book trade in the lower Yangtze at that time" (Quoted in Hessney, "Beautiful, Talented and Brave," 18).

35. *Jiin Yun Qiao*, 11:168.

36. Ibid., 4:140.

37. Ibid., 4:142.

38. Ibid., c.20.

39. Ibid. 20:220.

40. See Joseph Fletcher, "Integrative History: Parallels and Interconnections in the Early Modern Period, 1500–1800" [1973]; Andre G. Frank, *ReOrient: Global Economy in the Asian Age* (Berkeley: University of California Press, 1998), and Kenneth Pomeranz, *The Great Divergence: Europe, China, and the Making of the Modern World Economy* (Princeton, NJ: Princeton University Press, 2000).

41. See Richard von Glahn, "Myth and Reality of China's Seventeenth-Century Monetary Crisis," *The Journal of Economic History* 56.2 (1996): 429–54, and Frank, *ReOrient*, 143–49 for detailed discussions of this phenomenon.

42. This figure is based on von Glahn's rather conservative estimate in "Myth and Reality." See Frank, *ReOrient*, 149.

43. Frank, *ReOrient*, 150.

44. This is the title of the third chapter of Frank's *ReOrient*.

45. Adam Smith, *The Wealth of Nations* [1776] (New York: Random House, 1937), 202, 204, 207. Quoted in Frank *ReOrient*, 131.

46. Frank, *World Accumulation, 1492–1789* (New York and London: Monthly Review Press and Macmillan Press, 1978), 21. Quoted in *ReOrient*, 227.

47. *ReOrient*, 359. Italics in the original.

48. "Integrative History," 4.

Part 3

"Magicians, Enchanters, and Professional Crooks": Early Modern Understandings of Daoism

MY RESPECTED COLLEAGUE, T. H. BARRETT, WRITES IN HIS 129 "Chinese Religion in English Guise," that the English-language world sustained a description of China in its early depictions that was "at very considerable variance with the facts."[1] The substantial responsibility for this distortion is usually laid on the backs of the Jesuit missionaries of the early modern period, which in Chinese terms we may consider as extending from Francis Xavier's arrival off the west coast of China in1552 during the period of the rule of the Ming dynasty's Jiajing 嘉靖 Emperor to the Qing Qianlong 乾隆 Emperor's death (1793). Barrett's claim is not a new one. The position that the Jesuits misrepresented China first surfaces early in the seventeenth century after the Jesuits' publication of a Latin version of the Nestorian Monument text found in Xi'an. The Jesuits were accused of distortions by Georg Horn, Gottlieb Spitzel and Domingo Navarrete.[2] Adam Smith in his *An Inquiry into the Nature and Causes of the Wealth of Nations* in 1776 appraises the travel writings of the Jesuits as the reports of "stupid and lying missionaries," and this evaluation has continued as a virtually unchallenged assumption down to the present.[3]

The importance of the early Jesuits' descriptions of Chinese Daoism specifically may perhaps be best explained by one simple observation: only persons who were especially concerned with the interaction between their own religious beliefs and those of the Daoist way paid any serious attention to that tradition. Merchants, traders, and even diplomats had little, if any, reason to take note of Daoism. Accordingly, for almost two centuries, the persons living in China whose spiritual moorings prompted them to pay close attention to Daoist belief and practice were the participants and leaders of the Jesuit mission.[4] When we understand this, we know better why George Dunne, writing of what the Jesuit fathers of the late Ming dynasty accomplished with respect to understanding the belief systems of China, calls them a "Generation of Giants." Indeed, by the end of the eighteenth century, the Western lens for viewing Daoism had already been ground by the Jesuits and it was inherited by virtually every European and English intellectual attracted to China and its belief systems down to the twentieth century. An argument can be made that the primary reason there was no critical examination of this lens by European intellectuals was because their interest was directed primarily toward Chinese Confucianism and what it might contribute to both an understanding of China and to various aspects of social values in the West.[5]

130

Indeed, among the great eighteenth century philosophers of the West only Voltaire (Francois-Marie Arouet, 1694–1778) paid attention to Daoism. He relied on the Jesuit construction of Daoism as a weapon against the Catholic Church which he hated. He picked up the Jesuit ridicule of Daoist practices and beliefs, analogically comparing it to what he took to be the corruption and perfidy of the church with which he was familiar.[6] As Daniel Cook and Henry Rosemont amply demonstrate, G. W. F. Leibniz's (1646–1716) writings on China are dominated by his explorations of Neo-Confucianism and he shows no interest at all in Daoism.[7] Immanuel Kant (1724–1804) referred to Daoism only as "the monster system" of Laozi and he believed that the old master taught that nothingness was the highest good and advocated as its life philosophy a perpetual nonaction.[8] G. W. F. Hegel (1770–1831) seemed prepared to take Daoist thought more seriously and it appears that his work on the tradition benefited from a direct knowledge of the *Daodejing*. He even drew tentative parallels between Daoism and pre-Socratic philosophy. But Hegel consigned Daoism to "philosophy's infancy," saying in his *Lectures on the History of Philosophy* that it was stuck in an elementary stage of Spirit.[9]

In this paper, I will reconstruct the Jesuit portrayal of Daoism during the early modern period, demarcated in the West as roughly 1450 to 1800. I will set these sources alongside what we now know about this great Chinese spiritual tradition from Matteo Ricci's arrival in the mid-Ming dynasty (c. 1582) to the publication of Jean Baptiste Du Halde's *General History of China* in the mid-Qing (1736).[10] Finally, I will invite the reader to consider whether having our current knowledge about Ming and Qing Daoism requires a reexamination of the long standing assessment of the Jesuit testimony about Daoism as distortions and even outright lies.

The Jesuit Portrayal of Chinese Daoism and Its Context

I construct the Jesuit portrayal of Daoism in the early modern period by using the earliest Western accounts of first contact with the tradition contained in the travel journal of Matteo Ricci (1552–1610, Li Madou 利玛窦) published in 1615 and describing his twenty-eight years in China from 1582 to 1610.[11] In addition to Ricci, I draw on Alvaro Semedo's (1585–1658, Zeng Dezhao 曾德照, earlier Xie Wulu 謝務祿) *Empire of China* (*Imperio de la China* 1642) based on his twenty-six years in China from 1610 to 1636 and his knowledge of a large number of missionary reports coming to his attention in virtue of his position as Procurator of the Jesuit mission for almost twenty years. I include as well Charles Le Gobien's *History of the Emperor of China's Edict Favoring the Christian Religion* (1698), a work based on his selection of missionary reports from China during his service as Procurator of the French mission to China. Additionally, I consider Jean-Baptiste Du Halde's *The General History of China* (1736), which he wrote based on correspondence available to him from seventeen Jesuit missionaries serving in China. Du Halde's work is a prime example of sinophilic, early eighteenth-century travel literature. Although he had not gone to China, Du Halde used the letters to write an overview of Chinese history, culture, and society. Benjamin Penny opines, "It is hard to escape the impression that Europeans in China at the beginning of the nineteenth century travelled with a copy."[12] The volume was widely read and arguably may be considered the most thorough description of China published by that time in Europe.[3] These materials are all necessary components in any reconstruction of the Jesuit travel corpus and I believe them to represent the essential source texts for the Jesuit version of Daoism delivered to Europe in the early modern period.[14]

According to the *History of the Ming* (*Ming shi* 明史), the first emperor, Zhu Yuanzhang朱元璋 (r.1368–1399, a.k.a., Taizu太祖) had a number of Daoist advisors and sought to use the masters of the Zhengyi (正一) lineage for his political ends (De Bruyn 2004, 594). He appointed the forty-second Celestial Master (*Tianshi* 天师) Zhang Zhengchang張正常 (1335–1377) as administrator of all matters related to Daoism, giving clear precedence to the Zhengyi lineage of the Celestial Masters rather than to that of the Complete Perfection or Quanzhen (全真) branch. Later, he created under the Board of Rites (*libu* 禮部) a ministry called the Bureau of Daoist Registration (*Daolu si* 道錄司) charged with the responsibility of the management of all levels of Daoist activity in the empire. The *History of the Ming* confirms that Daoist masters who frequented the court of the Ming emperors were known for their healing and divination abilities, as well as their skills in calendrics, the alchemy of immortality, and the performance of ritual power.

The third Ming emperor, Zhu Di朱棣 (r. 1403–1425, a.k.a., "the Yongle Emperor"), studied Daoist techniques, learning talisman-making and alchemy from two different *daoshi* masters. As the Song emperors had done generations before, Zhu Di also patronized the Daoist spirit being known as the Perfected Warrior (Zhenwu真武), who was the numinal being manifesting himself on Wudang mountain. In fact, the Ming dynasty became the period of Zhenwu's greatest popularity and influence. Upon Zhu Di's ascent to the throne, the great Daoist master Li Suxi李素希 (1329–1421), respected for his reclusive lifestyle on Wudang, sent the emperor pieces of fruit from a sacred tree on the mountain that was supposedly created by Zhenwu himself. Li's act seen as an auspicious sign for Zhu Di's upcoming reign, and Zhenwu was subsequently promoted throughout the empire as the numinal protector of the dynasty. Zhu Di forced his sons to make offerings to Zhenwu at the Northern gate of Nanjing whenever they visited the capital, and he believed the teachings of the *Revelation Record of the Emperor of Dark Heaven*

(*Xuantian shangdi qishi lu*) 《玄天上帝啟示錄》. According to that text, Zhenwu was actually the eighty-second transformation of Laozi.[15] Zhu Di built many temples to Zhenwu, and the complex constructed between 1412 and 1413 on Wudang was called by the same name later given to the imperial palace in Beijing: "The Purple Forbidden City" (*Zijin cheng*紫禁城).[16] It was also Zhu Di who gave the order to compile a new canon of Daoist scriptures and it was printed in 1445.[17] The Daoist lineage that was most influential in the Ming dynasty was that of Zhengyi, and many masters from the lineage center located on Dragon-Tiger mountain (Longhushan龍虎山) married women of the Ming imperial family, weaving Daoism into the descent line of the Ming rulers.

In the years leading up to Ricci's move to Beijing, the influence of Daoist masters in the families of the Ming court was continued in many ways. Zhu Gaozhi朱高熾 (r. 1425–26, a.k.a., Renzong 仁宗), Zhu Di's eldest son, who was infamous for canceling the expeditions of the great Chinese maritime master Zheng He鄭和, died after only one year of rule as a result of ingesting a Daoist elixir of immortality. Zhu Jianshen朱見深 (r. 1465–1488, a.k.a., Xianzong憲宗) gave great authority to Daoist masters (*daoshi* 道士) claiming extraordinary powers, and so when his son Zhu Youtang朱祐樘 (r. 1488–1506) came to power, he tried to rid his court of all Daoist influences. However, this vacuum was soon filled. Empress Zhang 章, wife of the Hongzhi 弘治 emperor (r. 1488–1505) was ordained as a Daoist priestess. Very soon thereafter, Zhu Houcong 朱厚熜 (r. 1521–1566, a.k.a., Shizong世宗) became known as "The Daoist Emperor." Zhu Houcong was an adept of several Daoist masters during his reign. Even the Confucian officials who worked in various bureaucratic offices in his court were required to study Daoist techniques and teachings in order to be promoted. Daoist masters became political advisors as a result of their use of "blue paper prayers" (*qingci* 青詞), the prayers used in imperial *jiao* 醮 rituals.

The significance of all this history of Ming royal family is apparent if we remember that "The Daoist Emperor" ruled less than three decades before Matteo Ricci's arrival in Beijing. The Ming dynastic rulers looked to Daoism, and specifically to Zhenwu of Wudang for their protection. By the time Ricci arrived in Beijing, the fingerprints of Daoism were not only to be found on the lives of the common people, but also on civil ceremonies and government as well. While some later Ming rulers, such as Zhu Yijun朱翊鈞(r. 1562–1620, a.k.a. the Wanli 萬曆emperor) were turning toward Confucianism and seeking greater control over Daoist beliefs and practices, they did not turn away from a reliance upon it as a guide to spiritual power, physical transformation, and immortality. One indication of Daoism's abiding influence is that the great masters of the Ming dynasty Zhe School (浙派) of literati art all painted many Daoist images.[18]

The rough outline of Ricci's mission to China is relatively familiar and so I will sketch it only briefly. Ricci began his work in Macau, having arrived there in 1582. In 1583, he received permission to settle in Zhaoqing, and then he later moved his mission to Shaoguan (both in Guangdong province). From 1595 to 1598, Ricci lived and worked in Nanjing, and in 1598 he made a bold but fruitless attempt to establish himself in Beijing. Rebuffed by the authorities and forced to return to Nanjing in February of 1599, he began his role as a teacher. However, he continued to feel that the Christian mission would not be secure in the provinces until it was established and authorized in the capital. Accordingly, on May 18, 1600, Ricci again set out for Beijing and, just when it seemed that once again he would not be given entry, he presented the emperor with the gift of a chiming clock. Shortly thereafter, on January 24, 1601, he received an invitation from the Wanli Emperor to present himself at the imperial court. Thus it was that Ricci became the first Jesuit missionary to reach Beijing (1601) and the first Westerner to be invited into the Forbidden City (*Zijincheng* 紫禁城, literally "Purple Forbidden City"), and one of the first Westerners to master classical Chinese.

Although Ricci was given free access to the Forbidden City, he never met the reclusive Wanli Emperor. However, he was granted patronage and a generous stipend that helped him remain in Beijing for the remaining ten years of his life. He associated himself with the scholar-bureaucratic class (*ru* 儒) and his years in Beijing were arguably the most productive and influential of his career. He died in Beijing in June 1610 at the age of fifty-eight. According to the code of the Ming dynasty, foreigners who died in China had to be buried in Macao. However, the Jesuits made a special plea to the imperial court, requesting a burial plot in Beijing in view of Ricci's contributions to China. Permission was granted by the emperor, and in October 1610, Ricci's remains were transferred to his tomb in Beijing.

If we set down in Ricci's travel journal in search of his descriptions of and judgments about Daoism our focus should be principally, but not exclusively, on two chapters in book 1: chapter 9, "Concerning Certain Rites, Superstitious and Otherwise," and chapter 10, "Religious Sects among the Chinese."[19] I say that our focus should be "principally" on these two chapters, because there are neglected records of events throughout Ricci's *Journal* that are quite revealing about late Ming dynasty Daoist belief and practice and his interpretations of them. For all their other merits the standard accounts of Ricci's *Journal*, such as David Mungello's *Curious Land* (1989), tend to overlook the importance of these embedded narratives to a full picture of Daoism in China as Ricci experienced and reported it.

In chapter 9, Ricci describes what he calls the superstitious reliance on calendrics and astrology pertaining to the observance of auspicious and inauspicious days and hours. He associates other forms of divination with the moment of birth (i.e., the star or astrological signs of one's birth) and with numerology. In his description of the practice of determining the days on which one should begin to build a house, start a journey, and make a marriage, Ricci is clearly referring to the work of masters who stand in the lineages of Daoist practice.[20] During the period of Ricci's work in the Ming dynasty, Daoists were using a combination of different methods of calendrics, including the *jianchu* 建除, *liuren* 六壬, and *dunjia* 遁甲 strategies.[21] But Ricci has disdain for all such practices observing,

> Fraud is so common and new methods of deceiving are of such daily occurrence that a simple and credulous people are easily led into error. These soothsayers frequently have confederates in a gathering who declare to a crowd that everything that was told them by the performer came to pass just as he had predicted it. . . . The result is that many deceived by this trickery, have their own fortunes told and accept what is predicted for them as the certain truth.[22] Although divination was never an exclusively Daoist practice, many Daoist texts represent its most careful

refinement and the training of Daoist masters always included one or more methods of discernment.[23]

Ricci also laments other practices we may associate with Daoism's role in Chinese culture in this way:

> In choosing a place to erect a public edifice or a private house, or in selecting a plot of ground in which to bury the dead, they study the location with reference to the head and the tail and the feel of the particular dragons which are supposed to dwell beneath that spot. Upon these local dragons they believe that the good and bad fortune, not only of the family but also of the town and province and of the entire kingdom, is wholly dependent. . . . This might happen when some public building or a monument is to be erected and the machines used for that purpose are to be placed so that public misfortune might be avoided and good fortune attend the undertaking. Just as their astrologers read the stars, so their geologists reckon the fate or the fortune of a place form the relative position of mountains or rivers or fields, and their reckoning is just as deceitful as the reading of the stargazers.[24]

136

There can be no mistake about which of the Daoist practices Ricci is here criticizing. He means to condemn *fengshui* 風水, the art built on beliefs about the energy (*qi* 氣) of space and location deeply embedded in Daoist history. In Daoist history "true" charts and diagrams of holy mountains were cherished by lineages and their masters, one example of which is *The Chart of the True Shape of the Five Sacred Mountains*.[25] Daoists such as Kou Qianzhi 寇謙之 (365–448) followed these techniques to implement a new administrative structure of power centers for his Daoist theocracy. Later Daoist writings codify such practices of early masters and provide specific instructions about how to determine sites for altars and instructions called "opening a mountain" (*kaishan* 開山) or "mountain methods" (*shanfa* 山法). Daoists made geomantic charts showing how and where the cosmic energies of a place were concentrated. In fact, this practice was so well established in Daoism by the time of Ricci that an entire section of the 1445 Ming dynasty *Daoist Canon of the Zhengtong Era (Zhengtong daozang)* 《正統道藏》 is devoted to "Charts."[26] Moreover, a collection of various *fengshui* methods of the Ming dynasty, which is dated about the year of Ricci's entrance into China, was quite reflective of the practices of the period closely associated with *fengshui*.[27] Of all this, Ricci says, "What could be more absurd than their imagining that the safety of a family, honors, and their entire existence must depend upon such trifles as a door being opened from one side or another, as rain falling into a courtyard from the right or from the left, a window opened here or there, or one roof being higher than another?"[28]

Ricci concludes chapter 9 with an account of "what are aptly styled two very foolish practices of the Chinese, common in every part of the land and especially so among the more influential classes."[29] Actually, both of these "foolish practices" are related to the Daoist art of alchemy. The first is the effort to produce silver from other metals and the second is the attempt to escape death and to become immortal by rendering one's living being indestructible. Ricci traces both endeavors to "certain celebrities who are now numbered among the blessed," by which he almost certainly means the Daoist immortals (*xian* 仙). Indeed, since he refers to "certain celebrities" he may be referring specifically to the famous Eight Immortals (*baxian* 八仙) of Chinese history. Ricci knows that Chinese believed such persons to have lived extended lives, until such time as they became weary of worldly existence and were taken up into heaven. Moreover, although Ricci does not mention any titles, he observes that there are a "tremendous number of books in circulation" that treat of what he calls, "these two occult sciences." He says these are daily and public practices in the pursuit of which the wealthy are reduced to poverty. He characterizes the obsession with alchemy as a form of insanity, and observes, "Here in the province of Pekin, in which we are living, there are few, if any of the magistrates, of the eunuchs, or of others of high station, who are not addicted to this foolish pursuit."[30]

In book 1, chapter 10, Ricci turns his attention to "China's Three Religious Sects": the literati or *rujiao* 儒教 (i.e., what we know as the Confucians); Buddhism; and that of Lauzu (i.e., Laozi 老子) or the Daoists. Ricci reproduces the widely believed account that Daoism originated with an actual historical person named Laozi who was a contemporary of Confucius. However, he says that Laozi left no writings, leaving open the question whether he does not know the tradition that the *Daodejing* was ascribed to Laozi, or that he does not accept it.

He makes no mention whatever of the *Zhuangzi*, or the writings of the massive Ming dynasty Daoist canon, the compilation of which was surely one of the major events of the century preceding Ricci's coming to China. It is Ricci, and not James Legge, who offers the first Western version of the distinction between the philosophy of Laozi and the religious cult of the Taufu, the masters of which he calls "low and dishonest." He traces the genesis of the Taufu to its "original high priest," Ciam (i.e., Zhang 張, as in Zhang Daoling 張道陵, 34–156), whom he describes as "a certain magician" who passed down the secrets of his art to his descendants.

Ricci makes clear that Daoist masters in his own day, especially the head of the Celestial Masters lineage, had direct access to the emperor and chief ministers of the government.[31] He also shows he is well acquainted with Daoist activities other than alchemy noting that Daoists use meditations (i.e., sitting positions, *zuowang* 坐忘), prayers, and medicines to make themselves immortal, sometimes reducing their followers to poverty through the quest.[32]

If we stopped here with an analysis of Ricci's *Journals* on Daoism, as is typically done, we would have a snapshot of the first contacts of a Westerner with Daoism. But embedded in the narration of various events in Ricci's life we find records that enliven the comments of book 1, chapters 9 and 10 and increase our understanding of Ricci's contribution to a picture of Daoism. One such account is the description of the acquisition of the first permanent mission house in Nanjing. According to this narrative, a city commissioner offered a palace (*gong* 宮) to Ricci. The story that the official told Ricci goes as follows:

> "A short time ago," he said, "I built a palace, at public expense, for my colleagues; the staff of my tribunal. As soon as it was finished and given over to them, ghosts and devils took possession of it, and no one could live there without being harmed . . . if you are not afraid of ghosts, it is yours to purchase and there will be no wrangling about the price, because you may determine that yourself, as you see fit."[33]

Ricci accepted this offer, paid for the palace, and conducted a Christian ritual, parading through the building carrying a crucifix and sprinkling holy water, with the result that "the evil spirits made no further appearance."[34] The *Journal* reports that Daoist masters had tried to live in the house previously and had resorted to every means available to expel the spirits. There were talismanic markings on the walls and pillars still visible when Ricci took possession of the building. The story ends by recounting a later conversation between Ricci and the commissioner, in which the official is reported to have said, "Now, I can understand why the demons took possession of it. It was because Father Matthew's God commanded them to let no one live there, other than Father Matthew himself."[35]

Clearly the purpose of Nicolas Trigault's inclusion of this account into the *Journals* in the third person "about Ricci" is to demonstrate the providence of God, the superiority of Ricci's divine master, and the bankruptcy of the Daoist practices. What we can draw out of this account for our purposes is a sort of confirmation of the kind of thing that Daoist masters were doing in the late Ming. Ricci records the work of Daoist masters in driving out demons and ghosts, calling this their "special duty" and noting that the rituals associated with this work were even performed in the secret chambers of the imperial palace.[36]

139

Spellbinding of ghosts was an ancient practice in Chinese religion and some Daoist texts, including the *Zhuangzi* (Watson 1968, 203–204), report Daoist masters engaged in it. Likewise, Ming dynasty literary sources such as Tang Xianzu's 汤显祖 (1550–1616) play *Peony Pavilion* (*Mudan ting*) 《牡丹亭》 has a Daoist character who uses talismans to bind demons and ghosts, indicating that this was a practice known widely among common Chinese audiences of the play. In the play, the *daogu* (道 姑, i.e., female Daoist master) of the Purple Light Temple (*Ziyang gong* 紫阳宫) is commissioned to write a talisman (*fu* 符) and to bind the ghost believed to be living in the garden of the home of Du Liniang, the heroine.[37]

Tang Xianzu was only two years older than Ricci. His career as an official consisted principally of low-level positions near areas in which Ricci also lived and worked in southeastern China. He successfully participated in the provincial examinations at the age of twenty-one and in the Imperial examinations at the age of thirty-four. He even held official positions in Nanjing and in Guangdong province. He wrote four "dream plays," each with a prominent character who is a Daoist master. A great deal of the action in these plays required for understanding quite a good background in the rituals and teachings of Daoism, showing that these details must have been very familiar to Ming dynasty audiences. The *Peony Pavilion* was first performed in 1598, almost exactly the same time as Shakespeare's completion of *Romeo and Juliet*. In Tang Xianzu's play, lovers who seem to be star-crossed are actually destined by a marriage affinity (*yin yuan* 姻緣) to be together. In this play, there are detailed descriptions of Daoist rituals performed by the female master known simply as Shi Daogu (石道姑). Shi Daogu figures significantly throughout the most important scenes of the play. She is able to use amulets to cure, has talismanic power to call on the spirits of the Big Dipper (*beidou* 北斗), has skills in exorcism, knows the rituals for summoning numinal spirits (*shen* 神) from the ghost world, is gifted in the alchemy of making mercury pills to preserve the body even in death, and knows how to perform the rituals and concoct the elixir that can bring one back to a revitalized life.[38] In addition to the powers of the *daogu*, Tang weaves into the tale the details of a trip to the ghost world by Du Liniang, and in so doing confirms what we know from other sources to be the Daoist teachings about the hells ritualized in the network of Eastern Peak Temples (Dongyue miao 东嶽廟) throughout China during the late Ming and early Qing.[39] The great spirit of this mountain (i.e., Dongyue dadi 东嶽大帝, a.k.a. Taishan 泰山) controlled all the bureaucracy of numinal beings who administered death and the earth prisons and who judged each individual's moral life.

Ricci's *Journal* not only confirms spellbinding practices by Daoist masters, but also it seems unreasonable to me to believe that Ricci was unaware of the massive crowds of pilgrims and participants in the various festivals and observances dominated by Daoist Zhengyi ritual masters. Nanchang, where Ricci lived from about 1595–1598, is not far from the Wudang mountains, the point of manifestation of the numinal power Zhenwu, who was believed to protect the Ming. The annual trek from Suzhou in Eastern China to Wudang drew tens of thousands of people who traveled over 2,000 miles over a six-week period and many who joined this group came from the Nanchang and Nanjing regions.[40] These pilgrimages were in some ways not unlike the sort of experience one may read about in Chaucer's *The Canterbury Tales*. Along with the devout participants, there were acrobats, actors, musicians, cooks, traders, charlatans, and vacationers.[41]

Pilgrims likewise came to Beijing where Ricci spent the last ten years of his life. In the first lunar month, the annual Ninefold Festival of Yan (*Yanjiu jie* 燕九節) in Beijing was attended by at least 40,000 persons, all of them following Daoist practices. On the twenty-eighth day of the third lunar month each year, the Daoist celebration of the birthday of the Great Emperor of the Eastern Peak (i.e., Dongyue dadi or Taishan) drew massive crowds to Beijing. Susan Naquin tells us that it was probably the biggest such celebration in the capital city.[42] The numinal spirit being honored on this day was Dongyue dadi or Taishan, the god of Mt. Tai, Daoism's Eastern Peak and the deity venerated at the Eastern Peak Temple in Beijing. The huge ritual drew thousands and included the washing of the statues of Taishan and other numinal beings in the temple ambulatory. Among the crowds were always many blind persons who were taught that the water used in washing the statues would take on talismanic powers and would heal them if applied to their eyes. Other worshippers came to make offerings to the gods of Taishan's ghost world bureaucracy, who controlled the punishments and destinies of all persons. At the celebration, Daoist masters "paced the dipper" to bring good luck to aspiring business men and women, and "overthrew the hells" to reassure family that their deceased loved ones would be spared misery in the ghost world.

In an extraordinary irony (or what Trigault considers "an act of divine providence") we are reminded in Ricci's *Journal* that the palace ground given for Ricci's burial place was taken from a royal eunuch who had lost the favor of the emperor and the temple on those grounds was originally a Daoist Eastern Peak Temple probably associated with the Goddess of the Morning Clouds (Bixia Yuanjun 碧霞元君), the daughter of Taishan or Dongyue dadi. She was honored because of her willingness to show mercy to those destined to be punished by her father's ghost world bureaucracy. The eunuch originally given the palace had placed an image in this temple of Di Zang, the Buddhist Bodhisattva whose specific charge it was to descend into Hell and save those being punished there. But Trigault's description of the temple's iconography reveals that it represented the Daoist ten hells and the punishments administered there. Trigault carefully recounts how all the icons, frescoes, and hangings were purged in order to transform the temple into a church open to the public next to Ricci's tomb.[43]

Alvaro de Semedo was a Portuguese Jesuit missionary in China. He arrived in Macau in 1610, the same year of Ricci's death in Beijing. In 1613, he moved his mission to Nanjing, but was imprisoned during the anti-Christian campaign of 1616 and was then sent back to Macau. In 1621, he changed his Chinese name and re-entered China, working in the Jiangsu and Jiangnan areas. In 1636, he was called back to Europe as a procurator for the mission, charged with the responsibility of recruiting new missionaries for China. As a part of his work as procurator, he published *The Empire of China* (*Imperio de la China*) in Spanish at Madrid in 1642. This work was published in Italian (1643), French (1645), and English (1655), making it one of the most successful versions of China by one who had lived there and wrote of his travels in that period.

Semedo devotes chapter 18 of *The Empire of China* to Chinese religions and chapter 19 to the "superstitions and sacrifices" of the Chinese. The Daoist masters and lineages that were most active in the late sixteenth and early seventeenth century Chinese life and culture witnessed by Semedo expressed their religious practices through local community traditions of ritual and belief. Daoist masters were numerous and they were based in villages, urban neighborhoods, and connected to various families and temples. While Daoism's great Zhengyi and Quanzhen lineages had their founders, centers on sacred mountains, scriptures, and rules for ordination, by far the greatest numbers of practitioners were hearth-dwelling masters (*huoju daoshi* 火具道士) of the Zhengyi lineage who performed rituals and activities for the common people and whose work cannot be readily separated from what is often called "popular religion."[44]

These masters emerged from within the long overlapping lineages of masters coming from the original Celestial Masters in Sichuan and even before. During the period of training and initiation they learned the rituals, names of numinal spirits who reside both in the cosmos and his own body, and the techniques for calling upon and controlling these spirits through formulas, talismans, and hand gestures.

Semedo says in chapter 18 that the Daoists (romanized as "Tanfi," "Tansi" by Semedo) acknowledge one Great God and other lesser ones, all corporeal. Like Ricci, Semedo mentions that Daoists acknowledge Heaven and Hell, but he makes clear that they think of Heaven ("glorie") as joined to a bodily form, not only in "the other life" but also in this. Semedo knows well the traditional beliefs about Daoist immortals and their powers, referring specifically to "spirit immortals" (*xin sien*, i.e., *shen xian* 神仙). He writes,

> Fighning, that by meanes of certaine exercifes and meditations, one may come to make himfelfe a child, and young, and others to become *xin sien*, that is, the fortunate ones of the earth, obtaining by this meanes what-foever they defire, and to be able to transferre themfelves from one place to another, although never fo diftant, fpeedily an eafily; and other fuch like fooeries."[45]

When speaking of rituals, Semedo emphasizes that Daoists are skillful in music and the making of sacrifices. He is referring to the elaborate combination of singing, chanting, recitation, and dance that characterizes Daoist rituals. These were performed to drum, gong, cymbal, strings, and woodwinds. Adepts usually began their training as members of the musical band. Daoist rituals lasted for days, with only brief rests between rites for sleeping and eating. By the time of the Ming, there was a tendency to integrate and synthesize the ritual traditions of the many Daoist lineages of masters. The *Corpus of Daoist Ritual (Daofa huiyuan)* 《道法會元》, was collected for this end and in use during Semedo's work in China. By this time, the ritual categories of *jiao* 醮 (communal sacrifices), *gongde* 功德 (requiem services), and *xiaofa* 小法 (exorcisms and other minor rites) were already established.

While Semedo reported on religious and "superstitious" rituals he witnessed in local city festivals and ceremonies, such rituals were also performed at court under the rule of almost all Ming emperors, including Zhuanglie 莊烈 (r. 1627–1644, a.k.a., Zhu Youjian 朱由檢), the last emperor of the dynasty. Zhuanglie was very interested in Daoism and while he did not ingest Daoist elixirs, he did use Daoist advisors and diviners to aid his selection of sexual partners and sought their

143

assurance that Zhenwu was still supporting the Ming in the face of its waning power.[46]

The three-to-five day celebrations known as *jiao* rituals involved weeks or months of preparation, careful organization, the mobilization of large numbers of people, and hiring outside specialists such as musicians and opera performers. Sponsoring families or associations had to coordinate their activities with surrounding villages. Operas based on traditional stories were performed in the day and evening. Festivals were lively and "hot and noisy" *renao* 熱鬧, a kind of "collective effervescence" formed by the presence of thousands of worshippers and onlookers crowded tightly together.[47] The Daoist masters recited scriptures and conducted rituals known only to the trained specialists. They called spirits into ritual vessels and transformed substances such as water and wine to perform healings and exorcisms. They performed ceremonies to control the weather and guarantee success in business. They had their own ritual formulas, implements, and calendric guidelines. Over half of the texts in the Ming Daoist canon had their origin with just such practices.

Although Semedo does not mention any ritual specifically, we have extensive documentation of the kinds of *jiao* ceremonies being performed in the Ming and Qing by Daoist masters. We may take as examples the previously mentioned birthday celebration for the Great Emperor of the Eastern Peak on the twenty-eighth day of the third lunar month and the annual Ninefold Festival of Yan. Additionally, in the fourth lunar month, a magnificent festival was held in honor of the Goddess of the Morning Clouds on Mt. Miaofeng (Miaofeng shan 妙峰山) located in the outskirts of Beijing. The occasion created a highly popular pilgrimage culminating in a huge ritual observance which could not have gone unnoticed by those associated with the Jesuit mission.[48]

Semedo objects to Daoists who "pretend to be sooth-sayers" and promise to bring wrath down and to drive away devils from places that are haunted. Of the efficacy of such practices, Semedo concludes that Daoists "are able to do nothing; and fometimes at fuch undertakings they are fouly routed by the devils: I gret droughts them promife raine, and oftn prolong fo much time in praying for it, that at length the time of raine commeth."[49] Of the work of Daoists in bringing rain, Semedo reports the following incident which happened in Beijing.

> In Pekim, in the yeare 1622, there feel out a pleafant Accident, although troublefome. There happened a great drought, prayers were made, penninces and fafts were kept: but all to no end. At length certain Tanfi offered themfelves to procure raine without faile, and appinted a fet day and houre, the offer was accepted with great applaufe, joy, and good hope of the event: then they in a great piazza, or marketplace made a theater compofed of little tables, which, as they have many there of a equall height and breath, they did fet one upon another, beginning at bottom with a great many, and faifing it up by degrees higher, ftill with a fewer tables, till at length, the machine came to end in one only, obferving an handform proportion and reafonable height. On this laft and higheft ftood the cheife of them, parying and fupplicating; and the reft went round about him, doing the fame, like Baals Priefts, (although they did not wound themfelves; for in that they had great regard, as thofe who fought not bloud, but water. The pople ftood all round about, expecting the event: and the Minifters obferving fo great an auditory, which was almoft infinite, redoubled their prayers, their whiftlings, and ceremonies. When the day and houre appinted was come, prefently the sky began to be overcaft with very dark cloudes, to the great joy of all, and credit of their Minifters, who did already promife themfelves the happy accomplifhment of their undertaking; expecting every moment, when the raine fhould fall. When behold, of a fudden there fel a furious ftorm of Haile, the stones were as big as eggs, and fome bigger, which did ruine, not only their fields, but their gardens and killed diverfe persons, that could not in them recover fome shelter. The Fathers have writ me from thence, that they thought the end of the world was come, fo great was the confufion and noife of the haile that fell. The Propehts, for having procured ftones in ftead of water, were all rewarded with ftore of Baftinadoes.[50]

Daoist masters were often asked to procure rain or to prevent it. Such requests were made by village headmen, wealthy landlords, and even the imperial bureaucracy. During the Qing dynasty, the Kangxi 康熙 emperor (r. 1661–1722, birth name Xuan Ye 玄燁) demonstrated the ongoing significance of this practice by inviting the fifty-fourth

145

Celestial Master Zhang Jizong (張繼宗, 1666–1715) to court to perform both rain making and flood control rituals, probably not unlike
those to which Semedo is referring.[51]

Semedo's chapter 19 is devoted to Chinese superstitions and sacrifices. In this chapter he, like Ricci, is very critical of the practices of
calendrics and the use of what he calls an "almanack" for determining
auspicious days and times. He enumerates among the Chinese superstitions the use of lots and divination slips and the "booke that explaineth
them" as well as the practice of *fengshui* (风水) and physiognomy. As for
the book that explains the lots, we cannot be sure whether Semedo is
referring to the sixty-four hexagrams and their explanations in the *Yijing*
(易經) or if he means to refer to divination instruments known as oracle
slips (*lingqian* 靈籤), wooden sticks with a number from a box containing the prediction. There were certainly books that were used to interpret these slips. The Daoist canon contains nine texts on oracle slips,
which usually consist of between forty and one hundred readings.[52]

The practice of physiognomy (*xiangshu* 相術) known to Semedo
derives from the belief that a person's abilities and destiny may be read
by paying attention to the subject's back, chest, eyebrows, eyes, cheek
bones, forehead, ears, and nose. Immortals were identifiable by their
possession of the particular skeletal sign of immortal's bones (*xiangu* 仙
骨). The work entitled *Physiognomic Methods of the Hempclad Daoist* (*Mayi
daozhe*) 《麻衣道者》 was well known in China of the late Ming and
early Qing. The physiognomic methods of this work figure in literary
novels of the Ming, such as *Plum in the Golden Vase* (*Jinping Mei*) 《金瓶
梅》, in which the Daoist master Spirit Immortal Wu (吳神仙) "reads"
the faces of the two protagonists of the novel, Ximen Qing (西門慶)
and Li Ping'er (李瓶兒). Semedo concludes that although these practices are widespread and persons give large sums of money to those who
are alleged to know these arts they are really "without any profit at all."[53]

In an effort to demonstrate what he considers the charlantry of
Daoist practices, Semedo reports an account of which he had personal
knowledge from his time in Nanjing:

[T]here was a man, who went to confult one of thefe about a dreme he
had, which was concerning an umbrella, or skreen to keep off the sunne

the profeffour asked him, if there were any plea or enditement againft him, in any Court of Juftice; he anfwered, there was: well faid the profeffour, then san fignifieth an umbrella, and san alfo fignifieth to vanifh; and the interpretation of your dreame is, that all that is againft you will vanifh and come to nothing. The poore man was very well plefed, but being afterwards arainged, he received thirty bastinados well fet on. The wretch being angrie at his punifhment, whereof he thought himfelfe fecure, went to quarrel with the profeffour, who anfwered him, Alas, I had forgot to aske thee, whether the umbrella, which thou faweft, were a new one, or an old one: it was a new one, anfwered the foole. Then faid the profeffour, make account, that thy forrowes do but now begin.[54]

Semedo is exposing Daoist practitioners in a way similar to that employed often in Chinese history, sometimes even by court Daoists, directing their disdain toward popular masters who practiced their arts among the common people.

Semedo reports also that Daoist masters consult with spirits (*shen* 神): "They fay alfo, that they have familiar fpirits, which they frequently confult: But of this I have not had any knowledge."[55] Talismans were Daoist instruments of communication with spirits, and some spirit mediums were also Daoist masters. It is probably to these two practices to which Semedo is referring. He reports personal knowledge of one family that still received a pension from the ruler originating several generations before, the chief of the family being known as "magitian or wizard major." The persons referenced are almost certainly Daoist masters (*daoshi* 道士) and not merely popular wizards (*wu* 巫), because Semedo says directly that the chief among these practitioners was sometimes summoned to the king. Of these practices as a whole, Semedo concludes, "I for my part believe, the devill hath more power over them, than they have over the devill."[56]

A growing consensus of reports on Daoist practice revealed itself in the hundreds of letters sent back from China to France by other Jesuit missionaries much less well known than Ricci and Semedo. In fact, the French Jesuit writer and scholar Charles Le Gobien (1653–1708) contributed to the editing of thirty-four volumes of materials from missionaries under the title *Edifying and Curious Letters of Foreign Missionaries*

(*Lettres edifiantes et curieuses ecrites des missions etrangeres*). Le Gobien's office served as the clearinghouse for correspondence, reports, and written journals from French missionaries in China and Gobien determined which of these pieces should be publicly circulated and in what form.[57] In large measure his work was to act as a public relations agent for the mission in China, presenting it in a favorable light.

Le Gobien gleaned through the vast letters and records at his disposal and published the work, *History of the Emperor of China's Edict Favoring the Christian Religion* (*Histoire de l'edit de 'lempereur de la Chine en faveur de la religion chrestienne*, 1698).[58] In this text, which was widely translated in Europe, Le Gobien categorizes Chinese religion into four sects: (1) the civil worship of Shangdi 上帝 (Lord of Heaven); (2) the li 理 principle school, by which he meant the Song Neo-Confucianism of Zhu Xi 朱喜 that was very influential in late Ming and early Qing politics; (3) Buddhism; and (4) Daoism. The version of Daoism Le Gobien describes is much more like the Quanzhen sect founded by Wang Chongyang (1113–1170)[59] than the much older and more deeply entrenched sect of the Celestial Masters or Zhengyi (a.k.a., *Tianshi*). Actually, this is not surprising. Quanzhen enjoyed a renaissance under the Qing dynasty imperial system. The Longmen (龍門) branch of Quanzhen was favored by the government. The masters of that lineage lived in monasteries and followed a well-regulated conduct not nearly so malleable and popular among the commoners as was Zhengyi.

Two of the most obvious evidences that Le Gobien is describing Quanzhen Daoism in his account of the tradition are that he says Daoists do not marry or raise families, and that he associates the pursuit of immortality with the achievement of a kind of meditative stillness by which we should understand what the Quanzhen masters call "inner alchemy" (*neidan* 內丹), rather than the never-ending longevity promised by the Zhengyi masters through elixirs of immortality in "external alchemy" (*waidan* 外丹).[60] In the 1650s, White Cloud Monastery (Baiyun Guan 白雲觀), founded in the Tang dynasty, became the training school for Daoist masters of the Quanzhen lineage under the abbot Wang Changyue (王常月, ?–1680). In his role as abbot, Wang was the "Master of Discipline" who transmitted the precepts of Daoist belief and practice (*chuanjie lushi* 傳戒律師). The discipleship program at the White Cloud Monastery did much to put into place exactly the two characteristics of practitioners that Le Gobien associates with Daoism.

However, Le Gobien does know of the more popular quest for immortality through the hundreds of different recipes of elixir alchemy, specifically referring to it as the effort to become an immortal (*shenxian* 神仙) and calling it "ridiculous." Alluding to the rituals and popular activities of Daoist masters among the common people, he says Daoism corrupts the spirit and morals of the people of China and accuses Daoists of poisoning the Chinese culture with a stream of "magicians, enchanters, and professional crooks."

Jean-Baptiste Du Halde (1674–1743) never visited China, but like Le Gobien, he collected letters and materials from Jesuit missionaries who had lived and worked there.[61] Du Halde edited these reports and letters while in his position as procurator of the Chinese Mission initially for the thirty-four volumes of materials from missionaries under the title *Edifying and Curious Letters of Foreign Missionaries* on which Le Gobien also worked. From these, Du Halde selected materials for his work, *The General History of China* (1736). Writing of this volume, he explains in his own words that his intention is to cover the large field of China's "character, manners, customs, government, and progress in the sciences."[62] He recapitulates essentially all of the basic arguments behind the China-as-a-model-for-Europe epoch of the eighteenth century in virtually all areas except religion.

When he departs from the historical narrative and comes into his own contemporary period, Du Halde offers the chapter, "On the Religion of the Chinese." In it, he follows the standard model used since Ricci for dividing Chinese religion into three sects: the Learned (Confucians), the disciples of Lao Kien (i.e., the Daoist Laozi 老子), and the idolaters who worship Fo (the Buddhists). For his description of Daoism, Du Halde insists he draws only on Chinese historical records and "the memoirs of perfons of judgment and sincerity, who have fpent the greteft part of the lives in the Empire of China, and who are become skilful in the language and learning of this nation."[63] Of the Daoists, Du Halde says their doctrines and practices are "nothing but a web of extravagance and impiety." They have "degenerated into a profeffion of magick and enchantment; for the difciples of this sect boaft of the secrets of making gold, and of rendring perfons immortal."[64]

In his account of "the sect of the Taossee," Du Halde begins with Lao Kiun (i.e., Laozi), its founder. He says Lao Kiun avoided desires and passions that might disturb the peace and tranquility of the soul. Of Daoist masters, he says that they boast of having invented a liquor that has the power to render them immortal, and that they are "fond of Magick" and seek the "affiftance of the demons" to help them succeed in their desires.[65] It seems clear that Du Halde may not be entirely clear on his understanding of what Daoists of the Qing period meant by "demons." The term gui 鬼 here being rendered as "demons" can also mean "ghosts," in which it refers to spirit beings that can possess bodily resemblance to humans, although not in flesh, but in some version of the substantive elements that make up all things (i.e., the five elements wuxing 五行). These gui did serve the court of the Great God of the Eastern Peak in the hells, and thereby came to be associated with demons. But they were not demons in the sense of Western ontology as a different category of being set in opposition to the supreme being or power of the universe. Du Halde's interpretation, however, shows that he does not so much mean to deny the practices of Daoist masters reported to him, as to align them with the powers of darkness and evil.

Du Halde provides what we may consider the first history of Daoism from the time of Laozi to his own era. Tracing the development of Daoist practice through the Tang and into the Song, Du Halde says, "it was chiefly under the government of the Song that the doctors of this sect were greatly ftrengthned."[66] In this, he is on solid ground, because the third Song emperor, Zhenzong 真宗 (r. 997–1022, birth name, Zhao Heng 趙恆), like a number of other Song emperors, stressed Daoism at court and issued the royal decree acknowledging the Jade Emperor as the highest ruler of Heaven, a fact that would remain deeply important throughout the Song when it would be revealed to Huizong 徽宗 (r. 1101–1125, birth name Zhao Ji 趙佶) that he was the incarnation of the eldest son of the Jade Emperor. Zhenzong also built a temple to the Daoist numinal being "The Dark Warrior" (Xuanwu 玄武) in the Song capital of Bianliang (current Kaifeng, Henan

Province), and in 1018 he gave Xuanwu the title "Perfected Warrior" (Zhenwu) and charged him with using his powers over the spirits to protect the Song state. Zhenwu was primarily associated with his place of manifestation in the Wudang mountain range (Wudang shan 武當山) of Hubei Province, a site listed in Du Guangting's "Seventy-two Blessed Plots" (*Qishier fudi* 七十二福地) and a sacred space on which the Song emperors built a massive temple complex to honor their patron and protecting spiritual power.[67] Of course, it was this same numinal entity that was believed by Ming emperors to be the protector of their dynasty. Du Halde's interpretation of this impact of Daoism on Chinese government is simply that the Song was "ridiculoufly" led away by tricks and forgeries.

Of the reported powers of Daoist masters, Du Halde writes, "The Compacts of the Minifters with demons, the lots which they caft, the furprifing effects of their magical arts infatuated the minds of the multitude, and they are ftill extremely prejudiced in their favour; thefe impoftors are generally called to heal difeafes, and drive away the demons." Du Halde laments Daoist masters' use of charms and talismans. He reports that Daoists practice the trade of divination, telling persons about their families and circumstances and surprising the "weak and credulous minds, fuch as the vulgar are among the Chinefe."[68]

He reports the activities of "conjurers" who make invocations and cause the figures of Laozi and other spirits to appear in the air and he says these Daoists make pencils write of themselves without anyone touching them. "In short, they pronounce myfterious words without any meaning, and place charms in houfes and on men's perfons: nothing being more common than to hear thefe fort of stories, it is very likely that the greteft part are only illufions, but it is not credible that all can be fo, for there are in realtiy many effects that ought to be attributed to the power of demons."[69] Du Halde here refers to one practice not mentioned by Ricci or Semedo, which he does not deny being performed, but attributes to the power of demons. I refer to the Daoist art of spirit writing (*fuji* 扶乩). This practice began in the Tang, became structurally organized in the Song, and was widely practiced in the Ming and Qing in every prefecture and county.[70] The most common ritual performance was by using a T-shaped frame to which was attached a sharp stick about two feet long, which had been extracted from the southeastern side of a tree auspiciously placed according to *fengshui*. A ritual of summons was performed to invite a numinal spirit to take possession of the stick and afterward it would move automatically. One master would recite the characters as they were written in the air and another would write them down. Beginning in the 1700s, some Daoist morality books were said to have been written by these means and attributed to various spirit immortals such as Lu Dongbin (呂洞賓), thereby adding to their authority.[71]

Although it cannot be certain that he believed the Chinese held to an original monotheism in the distant past, Du Halde does say that it was the followers of Daoism that introduced into China the multitude of gods (i.e., *shen*, spirits) which were previously unknown.[72] This is no passing remark. Du Halde is bearing witness to the expansions of the Daoist pantheon which occurred in the late Ming and extended into the Qing. As we have seen, Zhenwu was raised to veneration by the Yongle emperor and those who followed him. Zhenwu's status continued and even increased throughout the Ming. But there was a steady stream of new spirit beings into the Daoist belief system. Guandi 關帝 (a.k.a. Guan Yu關羽) sometimes mistakenly called the Daoist God of War because he was a well-known general from the Three Kingdoms period, actually defends and blesses those who observe the code of brotherhood and righteousness, not those who go to battle per se. The apotheosis of Guandi to the status of a "god" and his enrollment in the Daoist pantheon came in stages and some of the most important moves in this story took place in the Ming and Qing.[73] By the time of Ricci's death, Guandi had over fifty sanctuaries in Beijing alone and in 1614 he was given the title Wusheng (武聖) or "The Warrior Sage." Likewise, Chenghuang (城皇) the "City God" who acted as the spirit representative of any locality or city was brought into the Daoist circle of divinities as an emissary of Lord Lao (i.e., the divine Laozi).[74] Additionally, Daoists in the late Ming adopted Mazu媽祖, the goddess of merchants and fishermen and the extraordinarily mysterious Zhang Sanfeng 張三豐. An extensive hagiography developed around Zhang, including

stories of his resurrection, mastery of martial arts, and his appari-
tional manifestations on Mt. Wudang. It is probably these shifts that
Du Halde is reporting.

In Description, Neither Stupid nor Lying; In Interpretation, Advocates of Another Gospel

By the end of the eighteenth century, then, the lens through which
Europe was to view Daoism had been fully carved by the Jesuits and
virtually all Western intellectuals viewed the tradition through it.
Having said this, we may now return to our original questions. Is it the
case, based on what the Jesuits reported and what we now know about
Ming and Qing dynasty Daoism that these descriptions were only the
testimonies of "stupid and lying missionaries?" Did they, in fact, pass to
Europe a lens for viewing Chinese Daoism that could only yield "variance with the facts?"

Actually, I wish to leave the answers to these questions up to the
final interpretive moves of the reader. I have explained briefly but substantively what the most relevant beliefs and practices of Daoism in the
Ming and Qing looked like and I have drawn them into the reports of
the most important Jesuits writing on China in the early modern period.
For myself, I must admit that I do not find the Jesuit reports in themselves to be the work of lying missionaries. Nor do I think that they are
substantially at variance with the facts.

I do believe that what we must do is separate the actual descriptions
of Daoist activities and practices in the journals and letters we have identified in our survey from the interpretations placed on them. It is one thing
to report that Daoists practiced spirit writing, wrote talismans, mixed
elixirs, and used divination, but quite another to interpret these activities
as "perversions" and "superstitions," and to call the Daoist masters who
employed them "charlatans" and "crooks." If this separation of report and
interpretation can be maintained, then my own view is that the travel
journals and letters of the Jesuits are, on the whole, largely accurate and
revealing. After all, travel writing should not be treated as providing an
infallible window on a particular time and culture, but rather, as opening
a space in its textual reality in which disparate cultures and worldviews
meet, clash, and grapple with one another.[75]

Notes

1. T. H. Barrett, "Chinese Religion in English Guise: The History of an Illusion," *Modern Asian Studies* 39 (2005): 509. Several recent projects have been devoted to studies of this "variance with the facts" in constructions of Chinese religions including those of Benjamin Penny, "Meeting the Celestial Master," *East Asian History* 15/16: 53–66; and Norman Girardot, "'Finding the Way': James Legge and the Victorian Invention of Taoism," *Religion* 29 (1999): 107–21; and *The Victorian Translation of China: James Legge's Oriental Pilgrimage* (Berkeley: University of California Press, 2002) on Daoism, those attending to how Buddhism was understood such as Jonathan Silk, "The Victorian Creation of Buddhism," *Journal of Indian Philosophy* 22: 171–96, and more recently Francesca Tarocco, *The Cultural Practices of Modern Chinese Buddhism: Attuning the Dharma* (London: Routledge, 2008), and the one on Confucianism by Anna Xiaodong Sun, *Confusions over Confucianism: Controversies over the Religious Nature of Confucianism, 1870–2007*, PhD diss., Princeton University, 2008. ProQuest (AAT 3305310).

2. David Mungello, *Curious Land: Jesuit Accommodation and the Origins of Sinology* (Honolulu: University of Hawai'i Press, 1989), 169–71. Also the Spanish Dominican Domingo Navarrete accused the Jesuits of misrepresenting the Chinese rites in his *Tratados historicos, politicos, ethicos, y religiosos de la monarchia de China* (Madrid, 1676). See J. S. Cummins, *A Question of Rites: Friar Domingo Navarrete and the Jesuits in China* (Cambridge, England: Scolar Press, 1993).

3. Richard Smith, "Ritual in Ch'ing Culture," in *Orthodoxy in Late Imperial China*, ed. Liu Kwang-Ching (Berkeley: University of California Press), 1:565. For Adam Smith on "stupid and lying missionaries," see David Martin Jones, *The Image of China in Western Social and Political Thought* (New York: Palgrave, 2001), 32.

4. I am certainly not claiming that the Jesuit order alone was responsible for shaping the broad understandings of early modern image of China in Europe. Colin Mackerras identifies several other important works on China published by non-Jesuits in the early sixteenth century in *Western Images of China* (New York: Oxford University Press, 1989), 22.

5. This still seems to be the case. Consider Kenneth Winston and Mary Jo Bane, "Reflections on the Jesuit Mission to China," Faculty Working Paper Series, RWP10-004 (Cambridge, MA: Harvard Kennedy School, 2010). This paper undertakes to study the ethics of the Jesuit mission in China, especially with respect to Confucianism, but does not mention Daoism.

6. J. J. Clarke, *The Tao of the West: Western Transformations of Taoist Thought* (London: Routledge, 2000), 40. See also Jonathan Spence, *The Chan's Great Continent: China in Western Minds* (New York: W.W. Norton), 81–101.

7. Daniel Cook and Henry Rosemont, eds., *G.W. Leibniz: Writings on China* (La Salle, IL: Open Court, 1994).

8. Helmuth Von Glasenapp, *Kant und die Religiomen des Osten* (Kitzingen-Main: Holzner Verlag Press, 1954), 104. This is, of course, Kant's misunderstanding of the Daoist notion of *wu-wei* 無為 which certainly does not mean nonacton or inaction, but effortless action in a spontaneous and nonintentional manner. See Edward Slingerland, *Effortless Action: Wu-wei as Conceptual Metaphor and Spiritual Ideal in Early China* (Oxford: Oxford University Press, 2003).

9. Clarke, *Tao of the West*, 41.

10. There are many studies now of Ming and Qing Daoism. In addition to those specifically cited in the course of our overview, I mention as well Judith Berling, "Taoism in Ming Culture," in *Cambridge History of China. Vol. 8. The Ming Dynasty*, ed., Denis Twitchett (Cambridge: Cambridge University Press, 1998), 953–85, Chen Bing, "Ming-Qing Daojiao," in *Daojiao tonglun*, ed., Mou

Zhongjian (Jinan, Shandong: Wenlu Press, 1991), 551–79, and Richard Smith, "Ritual in Ch'ing Culture," in *Orthodoxy in Late Imperial China*, ed., Liu Kwang-Ching (Berkeley: University of California Press, 1990), 281–310.

11. Anthony Padgen, "The Immobility of China: Orientalism and Occidentalism in the Enlightenment," in *The Anthropology of the Enlightenment*, eds. Larry Wolff and Marco Cipolloni (Stanford, CA: Stanford University Press, 2007), 57–78. The relevance of Ricci for twentieth-century scholarship on Chinese religion is discussed in Jordan Paper, *The Spirits Are Drunk: Comparative Approaches to Chinese Religion* (Albany: State University of New York Press, 1995), 4–12, and Otto Van der Sprenkel, "Western Sources," in *Essays on the Sources for Chinese History*, eds. Donald Leslie, Colin Mackerras, and Wang Gungwu (Canberra: Australian National University Press, 1973). Jonathan Spence's, *The Memory Palace of Matteo Ricci* (1984) is also a work well worth reading on Ricci.

12. Penny, "Meeting the Celestial Master," 58.

13. Mackerras, *Western Images*, 35–37.

14. David Mungello, *Curious Land: Jesuit Accommodation and the Origins of Sinology* (Honolulu: University of Hawai'i Press, 1989) is an excellent starting place for identifying the key players in the formation of the Jesuit understanding of Chinese religions. However, in my construction of Daoism in Jesuit travel narratives, I weave my way through primary materials for myself, rather than following the course set out either by Mungello or Joseph Dehergne, "Les Hisotiens Jesuites du Taoisme," in *Actes du Collque International de Sinologie. La Mission Francaise de Pekin aux XVII et XVIII siecles* (History of Christianity Collection. The Beijing Center for Chinese Studies, 1976), 59–67. Some comments about my choice of various source materials in the following exposition of Jesuit interpretations of Daoism are in order. For example, I exclude from my survey the German Jesuit Athanasius Kircher and his work, *China Illustrata* published in 1667. Kircher follows the published version of Ricci's work very closely but departs radically from Ricci in constructing a theory of China's dependence on pagan Egyptian religion. Kircher claimed that the Chinese were descended from the sons of the biblical figure Ham and that Chinese characters were corrupted hieroglyphs. He ratcheted up Ricci's rejection of Daoism saying it was filled with "abominable falsehoods" and portrayed it as a form of idolatry originating in Egypt. Since his construction of Daoism is heavily dyed with his theory of their Egyptian derivation, I have decided to bypass him in this study.

15. This work is in the Daoist Canon as CT 958, Kristofer Schipper and Franciscus Verellen, eds., *The Taoist Canon: A Historical Companion to the Daozang*, 2 vols, (Chicago: University of Chicago Press, 2004)..

16. The *Illustrated Album on the Auspicious Miracles Performed by the Supreme Emperor of the Dark Heaven* (DZ 659) (*Da Ming xuantian shangdi ruiying tulu*) 《明玄天上帝瑞應圖錄》 reproduces the decrees ordering the rebuilding of sanctuaries on Wudang and records a number of apparitions and manifestations of Zhenwu on the mountain between 1412 and 1413. There is a 1598 Ming dynasty reprint of one of these apparitions in the Bibliotheque nationale de France and a printed version of it in Schipper and Verellen, *Taoist Canon*, 1201.

17. The *Daoist Canon of the Zhengtong Era* (*Zhengtong daozang*) 《正統道藏》 was printed during the reign of Zhu Qizhen 朱祁鎮 (r. 1435–1449, a.k.a., Zhengtong正統). It was one of the greatest achievements of Ming dynasty woodblock printing. The canon divides its materials into Three Caverns and Four Supplements. The texts largely represent the lineages of Highest Clarity (Shangqing上清), Numinous Treasure (Lingbao 靈寶), Three Sovereigns, and Orthodox Unity (Zhengyi). Within each of the groups, there are subdivisions according to twelve categories: Fundamental Texts, Divine Talismans, Secret Instructions, Numinous Charts, Genealogies and Registers, Precepts and Regulations, Rituals and Observances, Techniques and Methods,

Various Arts, Records and Biographies, Eulogies and Encomia, and Lists and Memoranda. See Pierre-Henry DeBruyn, "Daoism in the Ming," in *Daoism Handbook*, ed., Livia Kohn (Boston: Brill, 2004), 604.

18. See Richard Barnhart, *Painters of the Great Mind: The Imperial Court and the Zhe School* (Dallas: Dallas Museum of Art, 1993).

19. In this paper, I use the English translation of Ricci's journals by Louis Gallagher, *China in the Sixteenth Century: The Journals of Matthew Ricci: 1583–1610* (New York: Random House, 1953) made from Nicolas Trigault's 1615 Latin edition. This was the first English translation of the Trigault's edition of the *Journals*. Ricci's diary was found among his papers at his death. It was written in Italian and very probably with no thought of publication. It was brought from Macao to Rome in 1614 by Father Trigault who edited it and translated it into Latin in 1615 and then into French in 1616. A reading of Trigault's edition makes it clear that some material seems consistent with what we may surely take to be directly from Ricci's diary the veracity of which may be ascertained by a comparison with Pasquale M. d'Elia's three-volume Italian edition of Ricci's original. However, other accounts in the "third person" about events which happened to Ricci just as certainly are Trigault's interpretation and faith-based responses. A fruitful study of the comments I make in this paper, which are depended on the English translation of Trigault's edition would be to compare the passages I mention with those in Ricci's original and available in d'Elia. Trigault admits freely to alterations of the original in his preface to the reader and says, "As for myself, I can assure you that what I have added, I have seen with my own eyes, or have obtained it form the true report of other Fathers, who either witnessed it themselves, or approved of it for the annals of the Mission" (Ricci, *Journals*, xiv).

20. Ibid., 83.

21. Sakade Yoshinobu, "Divination as Daoist Practice," in *Daoism Handbook*, ed. Livia Kohn (Boston: Brill, 2004), 541–56.

22. Ricci, *Journals*, 83–84.

23. I will mention only a few examples of such texts. The *jianchu* method is described in chapter three of the *Writings of the Masters of Huainan (Huainanzi)* 《淮南子》. Two texts in the Daoist canon discuss the *liuren* method: *The Yellow Emperor's Perfect Scripture of the Dragon Head, (Huangdi longshou zhenjing)* 《皇帝龙首真經》, CT 283 and *The Yellow Emperor's Scripture of the Gold Casket and Jade Equalizer (Huangdi jinkui yuhengjing)* 《皇帝金匮玉衡經》, CT 284. In the canon, the text that most clearly sets out the *dunjia* method is the *Perfect Scripture of the Six Yin as Applied in Dunjia Calculation (Liuyin dunjia zhenjing)* 《六陰通甲真經》, CT 857.

24. Ricci, *Journals*, 84.

25. This work is in the Daoist Canon as DZ 1281 (*Wuyue zhenxing tu*) 《五嶽真形圖》.

26. See Catherine Despeux, "Talismans and Diagrams," in *Daoism Handbook*, ed. Livia Kohn (Boston: Brill, 2004), 498–540.

27. The work is *Record of Complete Filiality through Proper Place Selection (Kanyu wanxiao lu* 堪輿完孝錄), CT 1471, 8j.

28. Ricci, *Journals*, 85.

29. Ibid., 90.

30. Ibid., 91.

31. Ibid., 104.

32. Ibid., 103. Ricci's negative appraisals of alchemy are traceable, in part, to his belief that this practice would serve as an obstacle to the Confucian-Christian synthesis he was trying to create, and because it was a competing belief with the Christian teaching about future life. Mungello, *Curious Land*, reports the rumor current during Ricci's days in Beijing and mentioned by him in his *Journal* that the Jesuits possessed a secret alchemical formula for converting base metals into silver, but not that they had the secret elixir to immortality, although this may well have been part of the belief. It was easier to believe that the Jesuits had an elixir to immortality than the actual Christian message! This may well explain what Ricci does record: that many Chinese lost interest in the Jesuits and their message when they learned that they did not possess such an alchemical mystery.

33. Ricci, *Journals*, 345–46.

34. Ibid., 347.

35. Ibid., 348.

36. Ibid., 103, 104.

37. Tang Xianzu, *The Peony Pavilion (Mudan Ting)* 《牡丹亭》, trans. Cyril Birch (Bloomington: Indiana University Press, 2002), 94.

38. For a detailed discussion of the Ming dynasty Daoist rituals and techniques attributed to Shi Daogu see Ronnie Littlejohn, "The Daogu 道姑 of *The Peony Pavilion*," presented at the *National ASIANetwork/ASDP Conference*, Whittier, CA, April 2005.

39. Actually, it was Song Huizong 徽宗 (r. 1100–1126) who created a network of state sponsored temples called Temples of the Eastern Peak. These were temples dedicated to the numinal spirit of Mt. Tai, the Eastern Peak of Daoism's five sacred mountains.

40. Wenbi Gu 文壁 顧, "Mingdai wudang shan de xingsheng han Suzhou ren de da guimo Wudang jinxiang luxing," *Jianghan kaogu* (1989): 71–75.

41. See John Lagerwey, "The Pilgrimage to Wu-tang Shan," in *Pilgrims and Sacred Sites in China*, eds Susan Naquin and Chun-fang Yu (Berkeley: University of California Press, 1992).

42. Susan Naquin, "The Peking Pilgrimage to Miao-feng Shan: Religious Organizations and Sacred Sites," in *Pilgrims and Sacred Sites in China*, ed. Susan Naquin and Chun-fang Yu (Berkeley: University of California Press, 1992), 335.

43. Ricci, *Journals*, 589–91. See also Alvarez Semedo, *The History of that Great and Renowned Monarchy of China* (London: E. Tyler, 1655), 202. E Books and Internet Archive. American Libraries, http://www.archive.org/stream/historyofthatgre00seme#page/n1/mode/2up.

44. Daniel L. Overmyer, "Protestant Christianity in China: Perspectives from the History of Chinese Religions and Early Christianity in the Roman World," *China Review* 9 (2009): 41.

45. Semedo, *Renowned Monarchy of China*, 86.

46. DeBruyn, "Daoism in the Ming," 604.

47. Overmyer, "Protestant Christianity," 45.

48. Naquin, "The Peking Pilgrimage to Miao-feng Shan: 333–77.

49. Semedo, *Renowned Monarchy of China*, 86.

50. Ibid., 86–87. "Baftinadoes" means beatings with a stick or rod, usually on the soles of the feet.

51. Daoist rituals of many sorts continued in the imperial courts well into the Qing dynasty. A large hanging scroll in the Arthur M. Sackler Gallery in Washington, D.C., provides visual evidence for the presence of Daoist rituals in Qing court life. See Stephen Little, "Daoist Art," in *Daoism Handbook*, ed. Livia Kohn (Boston: Brill, 2004), 739.

52. Sakade Yoshinobu. "Divination as Daoist Practice," in *Daoism Handbook*, ed. Livia Kohn (Boston: Brill, 2004), 555.

53. Semedo, *Renowned Monarchy of China*, 94.

54. Ibid.

55. Ibid.

56. Ibid., 95.

57. Mungello, *Curious Land*, 343.

58. The edict to which Le Gobien refers in his title was made in 1692 by the Kangxi Emperor in order to put to an end the persecution of Christians that took place in Nanjing from 1617–1621, and flared up again in 1664.

59. While some Quanzhen beliefs and rituals are similar to those of other Daoists, it is based on celibate lineages of masters and disciples who live in monasteries and follow ordination rituals that are closely related to Buddhist ones. By the mid-eighteenth century there were about 20,000 Quanzhen masters and about 12,000 temples.

60. See Vincent Goossaert, "The Quanzhen Clergy, 1750–1950," in *Religion and Chinese Society*. Vol. 2, ed. John Lagerwey (Hong Kong: Chinese University Press, 2004), 699–771.

61. Du Halde seems likewise to have been influenced by the work of Martino Martini (1614–1661, Wei Kuangguo 卫匡国). Martini, who spent about half of his life in China, had planned a grand history of the culture, but completed only the story through the ancient period, up to the demarcation most important to Westerners, the birth of Jesus.

62. Jean-Baptiste Du Halde, *The General History of China*, 4 vols., trans. Richard Brookes (London: John Watts, 1736), 1.11, accessible through Gale CENGAGE Learning.com "Eighteenth Century Collections Online."

63. Ibid., 4.15.

64. Ibid., 4.14.

65. Ibid., 4.30, 31.

66. Ibid., 4.33.

67. Lagerwey, "Pilgrimage to Wu-tang Shan," 293–95.

68. Du Halde, *General History of China*, 4.33, 34.

69. Ibid., 4.34.

70. Monica Esposito, "Daoism in the Qing (1644-1911)," in *Daoism Handbook*, ed. Livia Kohn (Boston: Brill, 2004), 648.

71. Paul Katz, "Enlightened Alchemist or Immoral Immortal? The Growth of Lu Dongbin's Cult in Late Imperial China," in *Unruly Gods: Divinity and Society in China*, eds Meir Shahar and Robert Weller (Honolulu: University of Hawai'i Press, 1996), 76.

72. The position that the Chinese were originally monotheists worshipping the high god *Shangdi* 上帝 and that they fell into polytheism only as a result of the Daoist influence in the sixth century BCE is generally first associated with the views of James Legge, *The Notions of the Chinese Concerning God and Spirits* (Hong Kong: Hong Kong Register Office, 1852), 30, 31; and *The Religions of China: Confucianism and Taoism Described and Compared with Christianity* (London: Hodder and Stoughton, 1880). See also Norman J. Girardot, *The Victorian Translation of China: James Legge's Oriental Pilgrimage* (Berkeley: University of California Press, 2002).

73. See Duara Prasanjit, "Superscribing Symbols: The Myth of Guandi, Chinese God of War." *Journal of Asian Studies* 47 (1988): 778–95.

74. Kahn, Livia. "The Taoist Adoption of the City of God." *Ming Qing Yanjiu* 5 (1996): 69–108.

75. I was introduced to this understanding of travel narrative writing by Li Qingjun. See her paper, "Of Golden Lilies and Gentlewomen: Women's World in Early Modern Literature and Travel Narratives," presented at the National Conference of ASIANetwork, Emory University Conference Center, Atlanta, GA, April 10, 2010.

| Terry Logan Mazurak, College of Idaho

*B*uddhism and Idolatry

PHILOSOPHICAL ANALYSIS OFTEN FOCUSES UPON TERMS and concepts, some would say obsessively so. However, in assessing the influence Chinese Buddhism had upon early modern Europe, it is instructive, I believe, to bear in mind a terminological and conceptual point that apparently has been almost universally overlooked: in all his years in China, Matteo Ricci never knowingly encountered a Buddhist; nor did he ever express contempt for Buddhism, nor appreciation of it, nor even curiosity about it.[1] The same may be said of those Europeans who traveled in China before him, such as Marco Polo, and those early modern Europeans who were so influenced by Ricci's reports. We may be quite certain of these probably surprising facts because, according to the *Oxford English Dictionary*, the terms Buddhist and Buddhism first appeared only at the beginning of the nineteenth century.

Let me immediately say that I am not of the intellectual tribe that holds that the facts that oxygen was not discovered until the 1770s and the term "oxygen" was not accepted as its name until the beginning of the next century (again, according to the OED) are reasons to believe Ricci could not have breathed it. My point is epistemological or cognitive, not metaphysical: in the early modern European encounters, expressions, condemnations, appreciations, and inquires, the ideas or meanings we intend when we speak of Buddhism and Buddhists played no role. And they played no role in the reception of their reports in early modern Europe. Those terms were coined, and the concepts they labeled constructed, by a later, very different system of thought and discourse with very different methods and very different goals than those of Ricci. To anticipate, "Buddhism" is the name coined in nineteenth century Europe for what was claimed to have been a movement that originated in India in the sixth century BCE as a humanistic philosophy in opposition to Brahmanic religion, but that as it spread through Asia it degenerated into religious superstition to the extent that its originating, essential message is now only accessible through the "scientific," that is to say, the European, study of ancient texts. In the first section of this essay we will look more closely at the dimensions of this concept by reviewing its construction in one of the seminal works of modern Buddhist studies, Eugene Burnouf's *Introduction to the History of Indian Buddhism*.[2]

Early modern Europeans knew nothing of Buddhism. Prior to roughly the beginning of the nineteenth century Europeans sorted religions into four categories: Christianity, Judaism, Mohammedanism (as Islam was then called), and heathenism/paganism/idolatry. The last category was huge, including by one estimate two-thirds of the world's population and also very diverse, with each country seeming to have its own variants.[3] What united that incredible diversity for Europeans was the belief that whereas the first three religions worshiped the one True God (though Judaism was deficient in not accepting Jesus as His Son, and Mohammedanism deficient in accepting the false prophet Mohamed), the heathen or pagans or idolaters did not. To put their error, or rather sin, positively, they substituted a part of God's creation for God Himself in religious practice and belief. That sin, which we will refer to as "idolatry," has always been a singular concern to Christianity and the other two great Abrahamic religions. Indeed, it is not an exaggeration to suggest that for them it is precisely the rejection of the idol worship for the worship of the True God that essentially defines them, at least for the believers themselves. From the Second Commandment and the Prophets to Paul's letters; from Tertullian and Augustine to Mohamed, idolatry whether in the form of the worship of false gods or the idolatrous worship of the True God is a major sin, one that is often said to encompass all other sins.[4]

In general, then, in early modern Europe, "idolatry" was less the name of a religion than a catch-all condemnation of those who do not worship the God of the Bible, that is, of course, Europe's God. However, in the early modern European perception of China matters were more complex, as the second part of this chapter will show. In the late sixteenth century, Europe's information about China came from two main sources: the letters of Jesuit missionaries and a compilation of travel accounts written by an Augustinian monk Juan Gonzales de Mendoza (who never visited China himself). That work was translated into English in 1588 as *The Historie of the Great and Mightie Kingdom of China, and the Situation Therof*. As we shall see, Mendoza's presentation of Chinese religion is largely controlled by the traditional schema of idolatry, even though Mendoza expresses a surprising degree of sympathy for its priests and practitioners. However, in the early seventeenth centuries this picture was radically altered by the publication in 1615 of the Latin translation of Matteo Ricci's diaries.

Ricci altered Europe's view of Chinese religion in two ways. First, following his Ming informants, Ricci articulated Chinese religion into three distinct traditions: the Literati who regarded Confucius as the prince of philosophers; the cult of Sciequia (from the Chinese rendering of "Shakyamuni"); and the Lacau or the followers of Lauzu.[5] Second, he used the traditional schema of "idolatry" to both elevate the tradition of the Literati to respectability and denigrate the cult of Sciequia with both representations being fundamental to the new, Enlightenment understanding of China. While it is well known that Ricci elevated the Literati to a level that would make them ideals in Europe in the seventeenth and eighteenth centuries, and Confucius a popular emblem of the Enlightenment, it is much less widely appreciated that he maintained that the cult of Sciequia was just "the cult of the idols," with all the old connotations of that evaluation. Nor is it adequately appreciated that both evaluations were based at least in part upon the same logic, which should now be familiar. Again to anticipate, Ricci argued that one of the main reasons to respect the Literati, if not the main reason, was that their tradition was founded upon the belief in the True God, the Creator utterly transcendent to and independent of His creation, a fact he believed was demonstrated by his own careful reading of its founding texts. Likewise, based upon his experience with the practices of the followers of the cult of Sciequa, most especially his debates with the priests of the cult, Ricci believed he demonstrated it essentially involved the sin of substituting a created thing for the Creator. Thus, its followers were only to be despised or pitied. The sin occurred at two levels. First, at the level of practice by the people who worshiped idols; but, second, by their educated priests who denied the transcendence of God, His independence and creative power by maintaining that all beings were metaphysically equal.

Now there is no doubt that each evaluation played a crucial role in the Jesuit missionary strategy of "top down" conversion. The importance of the conversion of the Literati elite in Ricci's thinking and writing can never be underestimated. However, Ricci was neither insincere nor blind in his evaluations, as we shall see in the second section of this chapter, though he may have deceived himself, as we shall suggest in the third part of this chapter.

Over the course of the first two sections of this chapter, there emerges remarkably little overlap between Buddhism as constructed in the nineteenth century and Mendoza's reports or Ricci's analysis of the cult of Sciequa, either in terms of content, method of construction, or aim. Two very different conceptual networks are in operation. Buddhism is, of course, triumphant in contemporary Western religious imagination not only among academics but also among those Westerners who think of themselves as Buddhists. Mendoza and Ricci's presentations of the cult of Sciequia, when attended to at all, are regarded as embarrassments. There is, however, one very important point of contact between Buddhism and the cult of Sciequa: while Buddhism has no proper place for the worship of idols, either denying it outright or marginalizing it, the worship of idols is the essence of the cult of Sciequa. In the third section of this chapter we will consider the possibilities inherent in this nearly perfect contradiction and what might be gained by taking the early modern view much more seriously.

The Invention of Buddhism

The story of the creation of Buddhism has already been told by Stephen Batchelor, Donald S. Lopez Jr., and Tomoko Masuzawa.[6] However, it is worth reviewing a few points in that story to justify the perhaps still relatively unfamiliar point that Buddhism is a Western construction and to emphasize certain points about that construction.

Unlike "Buddha" which attempts to transliterate a Sanskrit word, "Buddhism" corresponds to no term in any premodern Asian language. The term was invented by a Westerner working in Sri Lanka, first appearing in 1801 in *Asiatick Researches*, one of the journals produced by the Asiatick Society of Bengal, a group of amateur students of South Asia most of whom were officers in the East India Company. The members of the Asiatick Society and other amateur academic groups of Westerners working and ruling in Asia did much to supply the material for the creation of the concept of Buddhism, but the formulation of the concept itself was the work of professional academics working in Europe in the mid- and late nineteenth century. Among those professors, one name stands out: Eugene Burnouf, linguist and second holder of the chair in Sanskrit at the Sorbonne. To be more precise, Burnouf's *Introduction to the History of Indian Buddhism*, published in 1844, is a work of unparalleled importance in the formation of Buddhism and the correlative "scientific" understanding of it. On one hand, it was immensely important in forming the cultural elite's understanding of the subject, embraced by Schelling, Schopenhauer, Nietzsche, and Wagner on the continent, and Emerson and Thoreau in America, to name only a few. On the other hand, it was instrumental in laying the conceptual and methodological foundations of a new academic discipline ultimately called "Buddhist studies." Burnouf's direct students included some of the most prominent figures in that new field, most notably F. Max Muller. While seldom read today, *Introduction*'s influence remains so fundamental to the field that it is hardly even recognized as an influence.[7]

It is of major importance for us that *Introduction* was based completely upon the examination of old texts. Burnouf never left France and never met a living follower of the Buddha. Though he occasionally made reference to reports about practices by Europeans in Asia in *Introduction*, these were used merely as illustrations of, or deviations from, what he found in the texts.[8] It never occurred to him that restricting himself to reading old texts to grasp the essence of the movement might be methodologically problematic. In fact, one of the most important effects of *Introduction* is that, until quite recently, it would not occur to most academics studying Buddhism that there is a problem here. Gregory Schopen in an important essay on this matter has identified this as part of the "Protestant assumptions" governing Buddhist studies.[9]

To insist upon, or rather assume, the sole legitimacy of old texts in understanding a movement is not enough, of course. While access to Buddhist texts had been limited in Europe until the first third of the nineteenth century, that changed as Burnouf began his work on *Introduction*. Pali texts, in which Burnouf was an early expert, had become available, as had Tibetan, Mongolian, and a few Chinese ones. However, the breakthrough for Burnouf came in 1837 when Brian Houghton Hodgson an officer in the East India Company working in Kathmandu sent copies of eighty-five Sanskrit manuscripts to various libraries in India and Europe. These were the first Buddhist works in Sanskrit available to the West and Burnouf immediately recognized their importance. Hodgson would ultimately send Burnouf 150 Sanskrit manuscripts.[10]

In *Introduction*, Burnouf sets out four principles for organizing the now fairly sizeable body of Buddhist texts, principles that still govern much of the Western academic study of the texts of Buddhism. First, he argueds, for the first time, that all Buddhist texts in Chinese, Tibetan, and Mongol originated as translations from either his Nepalese Sanskrit "originals" or Pali ones. The precise relation of the Pali texts to the Sanskrit remained to be resolved in the never completed volumes two and three of his projected work, but he believed it was likely they represented a parallel, roughly contemporaneous textual tradition. He thus introduced a second notion to organize the texts, that of a Northern school and a Southern school of the movement, the precursor to the more familiar notion of Theravada and Mahayana "branches." (The crucial task of understanding the relation between the originating messages of these two schools was also deferred to the never completed second and third volumes of the work.)[11] Third, following one set of categories found within the texts themselves, Burnouf divided the texts into genres, the most important being *sutras* (roughly, sermons), *vinaya* (the rules of the monastic orders), *abhidharma* (philosophical commentaries), *tantra* (esoteric extensions of the teachings), and literary commentaries.[12] Fourth, however, he deploys another new distinction found nowhere in the texts themselves, that of two basic strata of texts: "simple" ones which were the earliest and closest to the words of the founder of the movement and his immediate followers; and "complex" ones which were later embellishments of the original core. According to Burnouf, all of the *tantra, abhidharma,* and commentaries fell into the second category. Only some of the sutras and some of the vinayas, or sections of them, the most simple of course, are in the first.[13]

We thus arrive at the fundamental framework controlling the conception of Buddhism with which Westerners are familiar: there was an original message of the founder, a system or at least cluster of core beliefs ("What the Buddha taught" in the well-known phrase) which, given the Protestant model, is the true essence of the movement, an essence to be found in only certain Sanskrit and Pali texts; that message was later embellished by others in the complex texts and then translated by still others into foreign tongues and concepts. Lopez correctly suggests that the following sentence is the most important in Burnouf's *Introduction:* "The belief to which the name Buddhism was given, after that of its founder, is entirely Indian."[14] We should also note an important corollary to this claim: the essence of Buddhism, its genuine message, can only be discovered by, and remains forever in the sole custody of, a group of highly trained academics who alone are capable of reading and understanding the old texts. Genuine Buddhism belongs to Buddhist studies alone. The rest of Buddhism whether ancient or modern, whether Western or Asian, is at best elaboration and, more often, distortion by the unlearned.

The content of that originating and genuine message as Burnouf filled it out will also be familiar to contemporary Westerners. At its core is the notion that Buddhism was not originally essentially a religion, but a "belief." This is a perspective to which Burnouf constantly returned, elaborating on the notion that the Buddha (or as Burnouf prefers to refer to him, "Shakya," using his given clan name, not his spiritual title) was a "humanistic" philosopher, concerned mainly with morality, and, in fact, disdaining religion and speculation of any kind, including abstruse philosophy. So, for instance, in commenting upon a notion ascribed to Shakya in a story of his life, Burnouf maintains we see evidence Shakya claimed "an independence of morality with regard to religion" and "did not have the thought" of creating a new religion.[15] Rather, he "lived, he taught, and he died as a philosopher."[16]

To amplify a bit, Burnouf readily admitted that "Buddhism" is now used to designate an Asian religion, replete with divinities, miracles, supernatural forces, and objects of worship, and that it had this meaning for most of its history. But one of the most seminal discoveries of *Introduction* is that *that* Buddhism is the Buddhism of the later, complex texts; the Buddhism of "development" in India and the "transportation" to alien soils.[17] Burnouf believed his analysis of the texts demonstrated that Shakya himself and his earliest followers taught a simple moral doctrine emphasizing karmic cause and effect, and nonharm, with a realistic way to end suffering. His teaching was simple and nonspeculative, the complex philosophical system of the *abhidharma*, to say nothing of the work of Nagarjuna's and other philosophers Burnouf had read among the Nepalese manuscripts, were later elaborations found only in the complex texts.[18] Similarly, the moral code Shakya taught was simple and straightforward, in stark contrast to the elaborate rules of the later monastic order.[19] Finally, Shakya resisted all attempts of his lay followers to divinize him, and the early movement did not do so. While Burnouf allows that Shakya employed magic tricks to win over the populace to his message, including the creation of talking statues of himself,[20] the understanding of him as a semi-divine being with supernatural powers, much less the concepts of the celestial Buddhas and Bodhisattvas such as Amida and Kuan Yin were all the products of later development and degeneration.

Of special importance for the formation of "Buddhism" was Burnouf's claims that Shakya's original message left little room for anything resembling religious worship: "It is obvious *a priori* that worship must have been an object of small importance for Shakya; the sutras even give us direct proof that he placed the accomplishment of moral duties far above the practice of religious ceremonies."[21] Burnouf claimed that while Shakya's early followers did make use of representations of him, they were merely aids to remembering his message. Even the *stupas* which were burial mounds or buildings containing an alleged relic of Shakya or one of his prominent disciples served no other purpose. According to him, the cults involving statues and *stupas* which would later arise bespoke only the influences of ideas foreign to the original works.[22] In fact, the main polemical thrust of Shakya's message, according to Burnouf, was precisely against the supernatural religions of the Brahmans, his mortal enemies who ultimately drove Buddhism from India. While Shakya's original movement shared the Brahman's world view of karma-samsara and rebirth, his revolution consisted of redirecting salvation from the gods' grace to human effort.[23] Burnouf did admit some misgivings with Shakya's ultimate goal of Nirvana—he understands it to be a kind of complete negation.[24] However, by and large the original message he had unearthed, in stark contrast to its developed and degenerate mutations, was one with which an educated, post-religious European, albeit of a certain sensitivity and temperament, could be comfortable, as Burnouf clearly was. It was in that sense, a universal message, not a regional or ethnic religion.[25]

This picture no doubt sounds quite familiar to Westerners conversant with Buddhism. If it is incomplete in important ways and differing slightly in emphasis from the familiar, it is because others also contributed to the contemporary sense designated with the term Buddhism. I will note only three of the most important. F. Max Muller, one of Burnouf's closest students, edited *The Sacred Books of the East* which was foundational not only to the Western view of Buddhism, but Asian religion in general. Of special importance to contemporary Americans is the work of D. T. Suzuki. The emphasis upon meditation in Western conceptions of Buddhism is in large part due to his radically modernized version of Zen as the core of Buddhism and meditation as the core of Zen. More recently the Dalai Lama has contributed an insistence upon an ecumenical and ethically engaged Buddhism.[26] However, it is difficult to imagine any of these messages without the framework provided by Burnouf.

The Cult of Sciequia

In Tomoko Masuzawa's felicitous formulation, "The discovery of Buddhism was . . . from the beginning, in a somewhat literal and nontrivial sense, a textual construction; it was a project that put a premium on the supposed thoughts and deeds of the reputed founder and on a certain body of writing that was perceived to authorize, and in turn was authorized by, the founder figure"[27]; however, the early modern European sense of the cult of Sciequia grew out of travelers' tales of China and was authorized only by the acceptance of the veracity of their reports concerning the living religious practices, the daily customs and special rituals, the dress, the demeanor and the beliefs of the Chinese in all its peculiarity. We will consider two of the most important of such early modern accounts, those of Juan Gonzalez de Mendoza from the late sixteenth century and Matteo Ricci's from the early seventeenth.

The Historie of the Great and Mightie Kingdom of China

In the judgment of Donald Lach, Mendoza's The Historie of the Great and Mightie Kingdom of China was "the most influential and detailed work on China prepared in the sixteenth century."[28] In its English translation Historie is in two volumes. The first is a kind of topical encyclopedia divided into three parts in which Mendoza presents what he culled from various sources; the second is an anthology of three travel accounts as edited by him. The rather short second part of the first volume (31 pages out of 172 in the first volume) is of most interest to us. Its title would seem to indicate there was considerable continuity in the late sixteenth century accounts of Chinese religion with what we have seen was the standard European view of non-European religions: Wherein shalbe declared, of the religion that is amongst the people, and of their idols that they do worship, and of other things touching that they do use above nature.[29] In fact, however, while the category of idolatry remains central in this account, Mendoza's picture of Chinese religion is perhaps surprisingly sensitive to a wide variety of beliefs, practices, and institutions

From his sources Mendoza was able to piece together a rough hierarchy among the Chinese "gods": "spirits," who were believed to be eternal and have no bodies; "saints," who were people who had lived lives of great wisdom or virtue or valor and after death went to heaven; "the devil," who they knew to be evil, but made offering to out of fear; and many other strange gods too numerous to name. The principal spirits were "Laocon Izautey," the principal governor of the universe; "Causey," who ruled the lower heaven and the life and death of men; and Causey's three subordinates who ruled the waters. The Chinese made offerings to all these spirits with food and incense, entertained them with plays, and took vows before them.[30] (Interestingly enough, though quite characteristically, Mendoza later offers an account of the creation of the world and humans in which these spirits have no place, but only "one who resides in heaven" named Tayne.[31]) Of the many saints he names only the three most revered: "Sichia," who came from the west and was the founder of a religious order of men and women; "Quanina," a virtuous young woman to whom the people pray to be forgiven of sins; and "Neoma" another virtuous young women whose image is on the deck of all ships, since she is especially effective in protecting those who sail. Mendoza apparently believed all of these gods were represented in the idols, though this is not completely clear. Nor is it clear exactly which were among the great number of carved idols his informants said were placed upon alters in the temples (as many as 120 in one temple alone), at crossroads and on the city gates.[32]

Mendoza immediately goes on to say that the Chinese in fact had little "esteeme" for their idols. First, he says it is remarkably easy to persuade them that their idols are merely wood and stone and not worthy of sacrifice, but that He who is the true Creator of the universe alone deserves worship. This was demonstrated according to Mendoza by the example of Friar Geronimo Martin in Canton, who having knocked over an idol out of righteous indignation with the Chinese worship of it, was able to quickly convince the mob that was about to kill him that it was he, not them, who was the more rational.[33] Second, according to Mendoza, the Chinese themselves in ordinary life did not really have much regard for their idols, much less hold them in awe. One of the chief functions of the idols was fortune telling. The Chinese regularly asked favors of their idols or question them about the future. They begin by flattering the idols with gentle words and offering them great rewards if they grant good fortune. Then throwing up sticks that are round on one side and flat on the other, they determine the idol's answer. If the idols refuse to grant them their desires, they roundly abuse them, even throwing them to the ground. They then try again. If the idols continue to refuse to give the desired answer, they are thrown into a fire or the sea.[34]

The claim that the Chinese have no great regard for their idols, either intellectually or practically, is a piece of the much more important message that Mendoza comes back to again and again throughout his work: converting the Chinese to Catholicism would be relatively easy, if enough members of the religious orders would begin missionary work there. The Chinese are reasonable, easily educated, and docile. They are very well governed and, thus, fundamentally very virtuous. All they are lacking is "the cleere light of the true Christian religion."[35] As important, the ground has long since been prepared for this harvesting of souls, for Saint Thomas the Apostle preached in China on his way to the Indies after the crucifixion. While the Chinese were not completely converted, his preaching left an obscured foundation for future work. Images of the Trinity, the Twelve Apostles, and the Blessed Virgin remain in China, though they are not clearly understood by the Chinese.[36] More importantly, the Chinese do recollect several important points which can only have come from someone with knowledge of God's revealed religion. They understand that each person has a soul that was created in heaven and is immortal. They also know that one's deeds in this lifetime determine one's eternal fate after death: the good become angels in heaven; the evil, "shall go with the devils into dark dungeons and prisons, whereas they shall suffer with them torments which never shall have end."[37] Finally, we know Saint Thomas preached in China, preparing the way, because of the existence of those religious orders mentioned previously.

172

Mendoza is especially interested in the Chinese monastics, about whom he writes quite sympathetically. For Mendoza the fact that the Chinese have monastics, both monks and nuns, and so many of them in their villages, cities and forests, all living in close order and following carefully their rules, indicates the great virtue of the Chinese and, of course, the influence of Saint Thomas. The Chinese themselves take the founder of this religious life to be "Sinquian" apparently a variant of the previous "Sichia" whom they worship like a god.[38] Any male may join the monastic orders except the eldest son who, since the monastics cannot marry, would violate his special responsibilities to carry on his family. (Mendoza does not mention any restrictions for women.) Mendoza explains that there are four orders of monastics. Though he does not name them, he does indicate they have independent organizations each with its own hierarchy with a general appointed by the king of

China and "provincials" who visit and supervise the "convents" in each province. Each order has its own color of robe from among black, yellow, white, or russet. Beyond those differences, the monastics are not distinguished as to beliefs or practices. The convents and their hierarchies are supported by great "rents" from the King and the charity of the people; but the monastics also ask for charity going door to door on the streets. In return for their charity the people believe the monastics are able to cleanse them of sin. The monastics' heads are shaven and they wear simple robes of serge (in one of the four colors). They eat together in the convent, but have their own cells. They arise two hours before dawn to chant and prey to heaven and Sinquian. They do so by singing together as one, and ringing bells which are the best in the world because they are steel. They pray using beads ("as our papists use" the editor helpfully adds in the English translation). Every morning and evening they make offerings to their idols. Besides their begging rounds, the monks are involved with the wider society at funerals, festivals, and when launching ships. In all these cases, they offer sacrifices to the idols for blessings and protection, in exchange for charity.[39]

Matteo Ricci's Journals as Translated and Edited by Nicola Trigault

While Mendoza's *Historie* had a good deal of influence in shaping the early modern European view of China, it would soon be eclipsed by the reports of Ricci. The special authority the reports of Matteo Ricci were accorded in early modern Europe stemmed from his long residence and wide travel in China (nearly thirty years), his fluency in Chinese (he not only spoke it, but debated in it and wrote books in it), and his apparently close relationship with many Chinese elites. His was as close to an "insider's" view as was then possible for a European. While today we are suspicious of the effect on his accounts of what we regard as missionary obsession and Catholic prejudice, his contemporaries were much less concerned, since neither was particularly extreme by their standard and even buttressed his sincerity. Ricci was, of course, a religious outsider in China, an outsider bent on converting the Chinese, but for his contemporaries this was hardly a perspective that obscured his vision but rather anchored it firmly in the only manner possible. We will need to compensate for his religious perspective, but that is no reason to disregard what he says. He was no narrow-minded fanatic, but rather widely and well educated, a student not only of theology and philosophy, but mathematics, astronomy, and geography.

In 1541 Francis Xavier of the newly formed Society of Jesus sailed to the East Indies. After great success in converting indigenous people in India to Catholicism he moved on to Japan, arriving in 1549. Again he had remarkable success (though this would be brutally rolled back within a century after the Tokugawa shogunate had united the country). However, he also learned there was a far more important field for missionary work in China. He died in 1552 seeking entrance to the mainland of Ming China. It would take the Jesuits thirty-one years to gain permission to settle on the mainland, another twelve to be allowed to settle in Nanjing and another six to finally settle in the imperial capital of Beijing. The Jesuit most responsible for this progress was Matteo Ricci.

Ricci had joined the Society of Jesus in 1571, sailing to Asia as a missionary in 1578. After four years teaching in Jesuit mission in India, he was sent to China where he lived until his death in 1610 in Beijing. His missionary activity was quite controversial among the Chinese, and he was sometimes in real peril; but in the end he was respected enough by the Chinese that the Emperor granted his request to be buried in China.

One particular genius of the Society of Jesus, and there were many, was its system of international intelligence. The main conduit for this through the first three decades of the seventeenth century were the regular letters missionaries were required to write back to Rome reporting upon local conditions and success in mission work.[40] These were edited, censored, and compiled in "letterbooks" to be re-circulated to other missions across the world. The Jesuits quickly discovered these letterbooks were also valuable tools for propaganda and raising money especially in a Europe hungry for news of the exotic East. The first such public letterbooks appeared in 1552. Initially they centered on the mission work in India and then Japan; but the edition of 1586 included excerpts of six letters from China, including one from Ricci. Though very brief it is important, announcing the publication of a Catechism in Chinese (the first European book printed in China) in the form of a dialogue between a "Gentile" and a priest from Europe in which the principle sects of China are refuted.[41] A few other letters of Ricci's appeared in the sixteenth century and some of his letters influenced the publications of other Jesuits, but his major impact upon Europe's understanding of China came only after his death in 1610 when commentaries concerning the history of Jesuit mission to China he had composed toward the end of his life were edited and translated into Latin by Father Nicola Trigault who also added additional material based on his own experiences in China.[42] Trigault's version of the commentaries, referred to as "Ricci-Trigault," would be supplanted in the 1940s when the complete commentaries in their original form and language were finally published in Italian[43]; but prior to that, Ricci's writings were just Ricci-Trigault. In that form, the work had substantial impact. In the seventeenth century alone it had five Latin editions, three French editions, as well as editions in German, Spanish, and Italian, and was excerpted in English.[44]

Trigault organized the commentaries in a manner similar to, and 175 perhaps in imitation of, Mendoza's *Historie*: "Book One" was a topical overview of Chinese culture close followed by four books that documented in travelogue form the Jesuit penetration of China with special emphasis on Ricci's role. Several chapters of Books 1, 4, and 5 are of special interest to us.

In chapters 9 and 10 of Book 1, Ricci-Trigault catalogs some common and widespread features of Chinese "superstition," several of which were mentioned by Mendoza, and then turned to closer examination of the religious sects proper. The most widespread of these superstitions were: the belief in lucky and unlucky days as set out in special calendars, which governed all important aspects of life; consultation with demons "or the family spirits, as the Chinese call them"; the practice of "geologists" who chart the forces of the landscape and provide advice on orienting buildings and graves; astrology, divination, and fortune telling. The full dimensions of Chinese ignorance were only revealed, however, when the ethical horrors of the culture were listed, beginning with polygamy and moving on though slavery, female infanticide, frequent suicides, castrating male children to serve as eunuchs for the court, magistrates who terribly abused their power, a bloated royal class, xenophobia, and a military made up not of brave men striving for glory, but unwilling conscripts. (All of these are recounted along with the earnest wish that readers not despise the Chinese but pray for them.) The chapter ends with a discussion of two kinds of "insanity" prevalent among the elites. The first is the attempt to produce silver from other metals; the second the pursuit of the secret of immortality. These quests, often interlinked, not only preoccupied the elites, but led to financial ruin for many of them.[45]

Against this background, Ricci-Trigault turns to the religious sects proper. Guided by the four traditional categories of religion he separates discussion of the traces of the three Abrahamic found in China from his discussion of the indigenous religions; but, as we have already noted, unlike any previous Westerner he follows his Ming informants and distinguishes three separate, but interconnected "cults": the "Literati" who are said to rule the country and look to Confucius as "the prince of philosophers"; the "Sciequia" or "Omitose" (again, the Chinese renderings of "Shakyamuni" and "Amida") who are those to whom Ricci-Trigault refers as idolaters; and the "Laucu" who follow a contemporary of Confucius, Lauzu.[46] The cults were said by the Chinese to be interconnected in several ways. First, the Literati themselves denied that they actually belonged to a cult because they put forth no views concerning life after death and individuals do not choose Confucianism, but "imbibe the doctrine of it in the study of letters." Rather, they see theirs as a society for the purpose of providing good government. For anything more, the Literati turn to one of the other two cults, most often that of the idolaters.[47] Second, the founder of the Ming dynasty proclaimed that all three cults should be preserved, and since his time Kings have not only forbidden any attempt by one to destroy the other, but have supported all three.[48] Finally, most of the educated in China believe that these cults "coalesce into one creed, and that all of them can and should be believed."[49]

Ricci-Trigault simply catalogues the "superstitions" of what we might call popular religion, presumably for the edification (and entertainment[50]) of its European audience, and dismisses them. The cults proper are, however, seriously intellectually engaged as part of the missionary strategy to the Literati elites that included, among other things, imitation of their dress and the adoption of vegetarianism to demonstrate a level of piety equal to any priest of Sciequa. Viewed as an argument, that engagement had two main steps: first, persuade the Literati that distinguishing among the three cults was necessary; second, persuade them that Christianity is not only compatible with their own most fundamental beliefs as followers of Confucius, but actually "completes" those, while simultaneously demonstrating that the cult of Sciequa contradicts those beliefs.

In the first step, Ricci attempted to demonstrate to the Literati that the notion of a "triple cult" or as it was also known "the Religion of Three in One" was not only intellectually confused but also dangerous for the society. For Ricci-Trigault it was *a priori* obvious that one cannot honor all three cults at the same time, since if one attempts that, one will not be able to honor any of them with sincerity. In pretending to honor all, one thus in fact ends honoring nothing, thus risking becoming an atheist, as many Literati admitted they were according to Ricci-Trigault. And thus, it is simply not true, again *a priori*, that as the Chinese aver | 177 | "the more different ways there are of talking about religious questions, the more beneficial it will be for the public good."[51] To put the point from another direction, just as there is only one truth concerning each matter in the world and many falsehoods, there is and can be only one genuine, that is, true religion. Since true religion is the foundation of a good society in providing ethical and other kinds of order, accepting multiple religions courts anarchy.[52]

There was, of course, no doubt in the Jesuits' minds as to what the true religion was and it was not any of the three cults. This brings us to the second step of the overall argument. What most famously distinguished Ricci's view of Chinese religion from that of all previous Westerners, and most who were to follow, was his claim that the beliefs of the Literati were completely compatible with Christianity; more precisely, Roman Catholicism completed and perfected that tradition.[53] Ricci believed this would be clear to any European impartially reading Confucius's works (the translation of which became a major project for the Jesuits). It would only be clear to the Literati themselves if they stopped polluting the original teaching of Confucius as found in the ancient texts of his teaching with the views of the other two cults, especially the cult of the idols, a tendency that had begun five centuries previous.[54] In fact the ancient texts of Confucius taught that the world was created by and remains governed and sustained by a supreme deity, the Lord of Heaven. They also taught that human souls are immortal and established a code of virtue that in no way contradicts Christianity's. Convincing the Literati of this became a main focus of Ricci's life work.

Ricci's well-known attempt to carry out this program of theological "accommodation" between Confucianism and Christianity is one of the most intellectually interesting in the history of the relations of Europe and Asia. However, it was only one aspect of the mission Ricci-Trigault calls "the spread of the Christian law." The full strategy of the second step had two wings, succinctly formulated in four words by one of Ricci's Chinese converts: *Ciue, Fo, Pu, Giu,* "do away with *Fo,* complete the law of the Literati," where "*Fo*" is the Chinese transliteration of the Sanskrit "Buddha."[55] Let us turn then to what was, at least in this formulation, the first priority for the spreading of the Christian law.[56]

178

Ricci-Trigault point of attack on the cult of Sciequia is, of course, its idolatry. We may distinguish two levels of idolatry in this attack: an "empirical" level of practices and behavior witnessed by Ricci and presumably Trigault, and, much more important, a "theoretical" or "philosophical" level discovered by Ricci in his debates with priests of the cult.

Like many previous European reports on China such as Mendoza's, Ricci-Trigault is astonished by the number and pervasion of the idols through China. Their number was "simply incredible" and they were found not only in temples (often thousands at a time), but in nearly every private dwelling (where they had a special assigned place), in public squares, throughout public buildings and even on boats. Indeed, "this common abomination is the first thing to strike the attention of the visitor."[57] Like Mendoza, Ricci-Trigault maintains that few have real faith in the idols, and only believe that "if their external devotion to idols brings them no good, at least it can do them no harm."[58] Unlike Mendoza's *Historie,* Ricci-Trigault is unyielding in its condemnation of the cult and those who practice it.[59] However, Ricci-Trigault's attitude toward the cult did not prevent it from describing some of the cult's most important institutions and practices, or uncovering important details about its history in China.

In recounting the history of the cult of idols in China, Ricci-Trigault adds several important details to Mendoza's account, most importantly correcting his notion that it was a degenerate variant of early Christianity. Ricci-Trigault discusses the remnants of Christianity in China in a later chapter, but makes clear that the cult of Sciequia is not part of that heritage. It adds the story that the cult came to China because the king of China had a dream and sent to the West for the true law. However, according to Ricci-Trigault Saint Thomas did not teach in northern India, but in the south, and Saint Bartholomew in northern India. While the Chinese king might have been inspired to seek that Gospel, what he received was something altogether different. Ricci-Trigault characterizes it in one place as a mish-mash of ideas drawn from a poor understanding of Democritus and Pythagoras, while allowing that perhaps it does contain a glimpse of Bartholomew's teachings "unfortunately obscured by clouds of noisome mendacity." The cult does have a trinity, teaches reward in Heaven and punishment in Hell, prizes celibacy and pilgrimage, and has rites and even vestments resembling those of the True Church. However, those glimpses are obscured by egregious errors including that souls are reborn and may be ransomed from Hell.[60] Later in the work, there is a harsher assessment: these very similarities with the True Religion indicate nothing less than the attempt by the Prince of Liars to craft a doctrine resembling Christianity, presumably to make his own harvest of souls easier.[61] In either case, the Chinese king's initial adoption of the cult led to disaster for him, his nobles and the country, at least according to the Literati. Nonetheless, it grew in popularity, fueled in part by new texts that continued to be created, its popularity attested to by the great number of monasteries.[62]

179

Ricci-Trigault calls the priests of one sect of the cult "Osciami" and estimates that there are between 2 and 3 million of them, some on constant pilgrimage, some living in cloisters of temples. They are supported by alms, revenues, and personal labor. There is not a hint of respect for the Osciami, ethical or otherwise in the work. Ricci-Trigault claims they are mostly drawn from the dregs of society, sold into slavery to the monasteries when boys, and when they grow up, are ignorant and inexperienced. They are remarkable only for "their natural bent to evil [that] becomes worse with the lapse of time" and that, while celibate, "they are so given to sexual indulgence that only the heaviest penalties can deter them from promiscuous living."[63] One may also add disorder to the list of their faults since members of the sect live in monasteries without any hierarchy. Nonetheless, "as vile and abject as they are known to be" the Osciami are called to take part in funerals and other rituals such as freeing animals.[64] There is a second sect, called Ciaicum or "observers of the fast," who were growing in popularity in Ricci's time, but who were apparently no better than the Osciami, being popular only with "women, eunuchs and the common horde."[65]

As scathing as these assessments are, they are only the surface. When we move down to the level of Ricci's theological or philosophical account of the cult, we can see how desperate the situation of the idolaters really was from his perspective. In its initial description of the idolaters' fundamental beliefs, Ricci-Trigault claims that its doctrines include that: "the entire universe is composed of a common substance; that the creator of the universe is one in a continuous body, a corpus continuum as it were, together with heaven and earth, men and beasts, trees and plants, and the four elements, and that each individual thing is a member of this body. From this unity of substance they reason to the love that should unite the individual constituents and also that man can become like unto God because he is created one with God."[66] Some contemporary readers may find these ideas insightful and comforting. Some others may find them harmless, if muddle-headed. What is not explicit in Ricci-Trigault since its author and editor knew it would be assumed by its educated, Western readers was that these beliefs were, if not the source of all evil, at the very least the Devil's own catechism. Ricci did make this explicit in his works written for a Chinese audience, for instance, *The True Meaning of the Lord of Heaven*.[67] Since so many of our contemporaries are either bereft of a sound theological education or mired in latitudinarianism, let us briefly explain.

For those of Ricci's and Trigault's theological perspective—a perspective shared by nearly all post-Platonic Jewish, Christian and Islamic theologians[68]—what is rehearsed is the metaphysical expression of the pride of Lucifer. Lucifer fell because he rebelled against God, precisely because he believed he was God's equal. Similarly, human sin originates from and is largely a matter of one placing oneself on an equal plane with

God, or placing some other thing, rightly merely a part of His creation, on His level. Correlatively, true holiness, righteousness, and piety begin and end with a terrible awe, a fear and trembling, in the face of God's "otherness" and "transcendence." In this perspective, true faith is the humble acknowledgment of His miraculous creation of the world and everything in it out of nothing, including first of all oneself, and also of His complete domination of it at every instant. To deny the infinite gap between God and His creation including every demon, every human, and every piece of wood or stone, in terms of majesty, wisdom, goodness, and all other powers, is to forget who we are and what we must do. If a man believes he is God's metaphysical equal, or rather believes he is metaphysically identical to Him in substance and creative order, he denies the infinite gap between man and God and the transcendence of God as did Lucifer. If a person believes a piece of stone or wood is divine, he or she commits exactly the same error. The cult of Sciequia is precisely the cult of the Devil.

In Ricci-Trigault, the philosophical or theological conflict between Christianity and the cult of Sciequia is most fully set out in one of the most remarkable episodes in the second part of the book: the debate between Ricci and the monk Sanhoi.[69] Ricci is said to have refused to read the works of the idolaters,[70] and according to Ricci-Trigault he had declined to debate a priest of the idols on the grounds that he had nothing to learn from them.[71] However, in Nanjin a certain unnamed city judge who had abandoned the teachings of the Literati for that of the idolaters learned of Ricci's prowess in criticizing the cult bombarded him with dinner invitations until he could no longer refuse to accept one. He also invited Sanhoi who, unlike most monks "whose supine ignorance renders them infamous," was an accomplished literary man and orator.

According to Ricci-Trigault, the ensuing dinner conversation dramatically swirled around the arguments between Ricci and Sanhoi. It records only two of the arguments in any detail, or rather a single argument in two acts. The first took the form of a classical "disputation" over the nature of the Creator of the universe. When asked by Ricci about "the first principle of heaven and earth and the Creator of all things whom we call the God of Heaven," Sanhoi only accepted that there was a "moderator" of heaven and earth, but that we are his equals and owe him no particular respect (this all said with disdain according to Ricci-Trigault). Ricci then asserted that if that was Sanhoi's position he must maintain that he, Sanhoi, had the power to do whatever the creator of the world could do, and Sanhoi agreed he could. Ricci then asked him to create a fireplace such as the one in the room. Bedlam ensued as Sanhoi protested in a high voice that such a request was unfitting, and Ricci replied in kind. When order was restored by the host, Sanhoi (rather than pointing out Ricci's conceptual slide from "moderator" to "creator") defended his notion that we are creators of the universe on an equal footing with God. Knowing that Ricci was an astronomer, Sanhoi asked him if when he saw the moon, he went up to it or if it came down to him. Ricci, of course, replied that neither was the case but rather that when we see something we form an image of it. Sanhoi, standing to indicate his victory, then averred that Ricci thus admitted that he could create a new moon "and in the same way anything else can be created." Ricci replied by insisting that the great difference between a thing and its image should be clear to everyone since, first, one could not have an image of the moon without having seen it, and, second, no one believes a mirror with the image of the moon in it created the moon. Of course, the rest of the group found Ricci's position more convincing, at least according to Ricci-Trigault; and, of course, again "the disputatious templer" refused to concede and created such a stir that the host was forced to take him aside and ask him not to debate again.[72]

182

The second phase of the discussion concerned a much more traditional Chinese question, especially prominent among the Literati, regarding human nature: is it good or bad or neither? It began with the other guests stating their position, while Ricci remained silent. When finally pressed into giving his view, Ricci demonstrated his famous memory by summarizing all that had been said, and then set forth his position in the form of an argument aimed at Sanhoi that was linked back to the previous argument. It began with Ricci's claim that "there is no room for doubt that the God of heaven and earth must be considered infinitely good." Ricci went on to maintain that that obvious claim was contradicted by Sanhoi's position that man as well as God is creator of the universe, since, as the discussion had shown, there is considerable doubt about whether man's nature is good or bad. Sanhoi first replied only with a supercilious grin, and then, when forced by the others to reply, resorted to quoting his scriptures, which was, of course, disallowed by Ricci. Finally, Sanhoi "rambled on slyly . . . pretending to prove that he who was good could also be bad." Ricci replied by first invoking the traditional Western metaphysical distinction between substance and accident, then pointing to the example of the sun. In Ricci's metaphysics only the accidental characteristics of an entity can change. Since the sun is bright because of its natural, innate brightness, that is, its substantial nature is brightness, it could never be otherwise. The audience was left to apply the principle to God and His goodness, and the argument ended.[73]

Throughout its account, Ricci-Trigault comments that the Chinese even though they are highly educated have "no logic" and do not understand the difference between substance and accident, or innate and accidental properties.[74] However, the "great error" in the discussion here and with the idolaters in general is the notion "that God and all things material are one and the same," the error that is "fatal to the idea of divinity."[75]

Buddhism and the Return of Idolatry

"Buddhism" names a humanistic philosophy which is said to have originated in sixth century BCE India. At its center is its founder Siddhartha Gautama, the sage of the Shakya clan, and his message showing how to end human suffering without the aid of divinities, ritual, magic, or resort to any religious paraphernalia, such as idols. That message in its purest form is completely contained in certain ancient Pali and Sanskrit texts, the sacred books of Buddhism. More precisely, it constitutes the earliest stratum of some of these texts, a stratum that can only be uncovered by the painstaking historical-critical work of highly trained Western or Westernized scholars. What they have uncovered in this original and originating message is only accidentally Asian and ancient. Buddhism in its genuine sense is a humanistic message regarding how to end suffering for oneself and others without appealing to God, gods, or superstitious practices. It is universal in its appeal and application, as the intellectual and religious history of twentieth century Europe and America testifies. While it is true that "Buddhism" can also be used to name a large family of practices, beliefs, and institutions found in modern and contemporary Asia, that family is, as European scholarship has also shown, actually a hodgepodge of folk superstition, native practices, and non-Indian ways of life that either completely conceals or simply replaces Shakyamuni's original message. That mutation came about as Shakyamuni's message moved from India into other cultures. Careful students of Asia will want to distinguish "genuine" or "pure" Buddhism, a movement to be accorded respect, from "folk" or "popular" Buddhism, which deserves condescension at best.

The "cult of Sciequia," on the other hand, is a much earlier phrase which refers to a certain religious group observed by early modern European missionaries in China. In Mendoza's *Historie* the cult is portrayed as part of the wider pattern of Chinese idolatry and "spirit" worship, an especially important part because it included the religious orders brought from the West by "Sinquian" or "Sichia." Mendoza regarded the idolatry of the Chinese as rather fragile and not a real obstacle to the missionaries' goal of conversion, and even showed a certain amount of respect for the Chinese monastics in their kinship with Western monks and nuns. That attitude was not shared by Matteo Ricci, at least as he was presented to early modern Europe in Ricci-Trigault. His Chinese informants told him the cult had been brought to China from India and he believed it arose out of a distortion of Western philosophical ideas by Satan himself in the hope of winning souls from the true religion. Its essence was idolatry, not only in its practices of idol worshipping, but more profoundly in its philosophical belief in the metaphysical equality of all beings, as verified by Ricci when he debated its priests. It was opposed to the true religion not simply in failing to recognize and worship the True God, but by accepting a conceptual framework that makes the idea of genuine divinity impossible. It thus emerged in Ricci's mind as the chief obstacle to the successful conversion of the Chinese.

The conceptual web that includes "Buddhism" and the one that focuses upon the "cult of Sciequia" as idolatry have very little in common beyond a shared sense of an origin in India, a name of a founder (variously transliterated) and the importance for each of the monastic system he founded. They are derived from different sources and different modes of validation, and have very different aims and uses. So for instance, while the story of Shakya's life, especially his spiritual struggle and attainment of enlightenment, is central to Buddhism, the human Shakya is of little importance in the constellation of ideas that is the cult of Sciequia.

Buddhism so completely dominates the contemporary Western imagining of Asian religion that Mendoza's and Ricci's account of the cult of Sciequia has been relegated to the status of embarrassing reminders of missionary zealotry. Idolatry has, until very recently, almost completely vanished from Western accounts of Buddhism. However, the idolatry of the cult in the early modern accounts vanished only from the classrooms of the West and its academic journals, never from Asian reality or from the experiences of Westerners who actually traveled there (as many nineteenth and twentieth century scholars of Buddhism never did). Indeed, contemporary Westerners who have learned about Buddhism from popular sources or college courses are generally surprised and sometimes shocked by what they find when visiting Asia for the first time. If one goes to virtually any Buddhist temple in any city in China or the rest of Asia, one finds nothing like "Buddhism." One finds no meditation and no humanistic message. What one finds are statues, many statues, mostly gaudy, often enormous. Shakyamuni may well be among them, but he seldom has pride of place except in South East Asia where he is usually depicted less as a man than a god. In front of these statues we observe ordinary Asian men and women offering chants, bows, incense, fruit, flowers, and money. If one asks through one's interpreter what these people seek by these acts, there likely will be no mention of Enlightenment or Nirvana. One will be told they are asking Lord Buddha (or a powerful Bodhisattva such as Kuan Yin) for a male child, or to pass an important exam, or to protect their dead parents. One may buy a statue of the Buddha for oneself from any of the numerous shops surrounding the temple or even within it (the fact that ways into the temples are always lined with shops is another jolt to Westerners schooled in Buddhism). The careful observer will also note that many Asians make offerings to a monk so he will perform ceremonies over their statues. If one investigates further, one may learn the monk is sometimes not merely blessing the statue, but empowering it.[76] If one wishes to see the Buddhism of the popular books and the college courses, the living out of the supposed message of Shakyamuni's original teaching, one needs to go to San Francisco or New York and visit an assembly of Western converts.

It ought to be intellectually disturbing to our academics that Westerners in Asia have been reporting these same observations for at least seven hundred years since Marco Polo's *Travels*, and reporting very little else about "Buddhism." In fact, academics studying Buddhism, beginning with Burnouf himself, have long acknowledged the reality of what seems best described as idolatry in Buddhism (and other Asian religions such as Hinduism and Taoism). We recollect, for instance, the sutra containing the story of the Buddha creating a talking statue Burnouf included in his work. However, they acknowledge it only to marginalize it in the next moment as "degenerate," or "peasant practice," or "external and secondary." Only quite recently have some Western scholars begun pushing the observed practices toward the center of their view of Buddhism as a very old and very central part of that path. For instance, Donald K. Swearer has demonstrated that the empowerment and animation of images of Shakyamuni by monks is the axis around which the Buddhism of Northern Thailand revolves.[77] Robert H. Sharf has pointed out that among the first Buddhist works translated into Chinese was one concerned with producing images of the Buddha and the merit generated by doing so.[78] There is little evidence that "idol worship" was ever absent from elite practice; quite the contrary, there are countless stories, from at least the time of the Emperor Ashoka in India, of royalty and other powerful elites venerating statues and relics, and going to considerable trouble to produce or acquire them. There is equally as little reason to believe that the "interior" practices of monastic "virtuosi" did not include worship idols; again, the contrary seems to be the case. Are these practices "degenerate," or more neutrally, not part of Shakyamuni's original message, but a practice and borrowed from non-Buddhist sources as Burnouf claimed? The consensus among academics is still that images of the Buddha and the worship of them were not part of the earliest strata of the tradition, though there are dissenters. Interestingly enough, however, there is little doubt among these same experts that the closely related practice of worshipping the relics of the Buddha in burial shrines called "stupas" goes back to Shakyamuni himself.[79]

Again, even Burnouf acknowledged the importance of images and stupa worship in the texts he studied.

Beyond the "empirical" question of what the vast majority of those in Asia the West has taught the world to call "Buddhists" actually do and may have always done, there is the "philosophical" aspect of Ricci's account. Here it must simply be conceded that he was right in claiming that the cult of Sciequia was idolatrous in that it denied the absolute transcendence of God and, thus, for traditional, post-Platonic Abrahamic theologians, the very possibility of divinity, by maintaining the metaphysical equality or identity of all beings. The learned members of the cult, such as Sanhoi, drew their ideas from a variety of Indian, Chinese, and Tibetan philosophical traditions, none of which countenanced transcendence in Ricci's sense. Madhyamika philosophy, one of the two main traditions of Mahayana philosophy imported into China is founded upon the principle that the Buddha taught that all beings are equal in being completely "empty" (*sunyata*). Humans are empty, demons are empty, stones are empty, and the Buddha is empty, as is Nirvana. Even emptiness is empty.[80] Yogacara, the other main Indian Mahayana school, maintains that an understanding of the Buddha's words more advanced than Madhyamika's realizes that all beings are metaphysically equal in being "mind" or the effect of "mind," not the ordinary consciousness of individuals, but the "deep mind" of the "storehouse consciousness." Tientai and Huayan, generally regarded as China's most important indigenous "Buddhist" philosophical schools, find new ways to express this Mahayana metaphysical principle. Huayan conceives of the universe as a vast web in which all beings and events are always interpenetrating all other beings and events, and, in turn, being interpenetrated by them. Tientai maintains that the contraries that structure ordinary thought and experience (true/false, good/evil, self/other, etc.) and those at the heart of the Buddha's message (bliss/sorrow, Nirvana/ samsara, wisdom/delusion, etc.) are in fact pairs which require and envelop each other. Which specific school or which specific mixture of schools Sanhoi was invoking in his debate with Ricci is not clear, perhaps a variant of Yogacara. However, that question is really unimportant for our purposes since none of these schools recognized the kind of transcendence Ricci believed divinity must have. While it is often and

187

somewhat misleadingly noted that the Buddha's way did not depend on gods or God, it is much more important to appreciate that Mahayana Buddhist philosophy has no metaphysical space for a transcendent deity in the traditional Abrahamic sense.[81] It is not without reason that the Dalai Lama in writing about the Mahayana doctrine of emptiness warns, "perhaps a deeply committed Christian practitioner might be wise not to delve too deeply into this aspect of Buddhist teaching."[82]

But was the denial of transcendence in Ricci's sense a part of the Shakyamuni's original teachings? It is difficult to know for sure anything about Shakyamuni's original message, much more difficult than Burnouf and his heirs believed; but the earliest strata of Buddhist philosophy while not claiming everything is empty or mind (there are nonempty, nonmind atoms that are, however, momentary and transcendent) has no very obvious place for a transcendent being or transcendence as a notion. The only plausible candidate would seem to be Nirvana. However, while Nirvana is perhaps "completely other" to ordinary experience and ordinary life, it seems not beyond the ordinary, natural world in being a possibility, however remote, of natural human life. It does not seem to be "transcendent" in the deep Abrahamic sense, and clearly is not substitutable for the Abrahamic God.

"What did the Buddha really teach?" is a question whose importance depends almost solely upon the degree to which one subscribes to the "Protestant" model of religion and a religion's "essence." I find it much more interesting to take Mendoza's and Ricci's reports in a different direction. Those accounts are derided at least in part because they took idolatry seriously both at the empirical level and, in Ricci's case at least, the philosophical. That is, he believed the Chinese really were worshiping idols and some of their priests at least were doing so because they embraced a principle of the metaphysical equality of all things. One interesting feature of contemporary thinking in this area is that while in these post-Nietzschean times many embrace something like the latter principle (God is dead, after all), few are comfortable with the possibility it opens up for religious practice and would insist out of respect for the Chinese that Ricci must have misunderstood what he observed.[83]

What have we moderns and postmoderns lost in refusing to consider the possibility that the worship of material objects is a legitimate human response to the world and that the belief that a god or a demon could animate a material representation of itself is not *a priori* primitive and irrational?[84] I believe we can now see that we miss an important aspect of Asian cultural reality at the very least. However, do we not also miss a good deal of contemporary Western reality as well? Does anyone doubt that the impact of a sculpture by Henry Moore cannot be explained by analyzing its chemical composition? Is not even the most literal-minded scientist moved by some special token, perhaps a treasured photo? Is our recognition of the ability of a great artist to infuse life and meaning into brute matter any less implausible than the belief that a congregation of holy monks chanting in unison can invest a sacred personality in bronze? Is the picture of a lost love inhabited merely by memory?

There are even deeper possibilities to consider as we move to the philosophical level of idolatry. Ricci believed idolatry was "fatal to the idea of divinity itself" since it contradicted the traditional Abrahamic notion of divinity as the absolute transcendence of the material. He believed if, as the idolaters believed, divinity exists in inhabiting and animating material things, and created things are in this sense equal to their creator, then not only would Christianity collapse, but so too would the very idea of religion. For Ricci, transcendence was the space that makes the divine possible. Of course, Ricci thought he knew that transcendence was God's essence and substance, just as were goodness and wisdom and power. He thought it made no more sense to deny that transcendence then to consider the possibility that the sun could one day cease to be bright.

Science has taught us much about the sun since Ricci's time, including, of course, that being bright is not its essence and that one day it will cease to be bright. Perhaps then we ought to also consider alternatives to his belief that the essence of divinity is its transcendence, that the holy must be our absolute other. Perhaps we might do this by reconsidering Buddhism in light of the fact that, as the early modern Europeans saw, it permits, and even enjoins idolatry, not just in practice but in theory. Perhaps Ricci's real error was not that he saw idolatry as the main feature of what we now call "Buddhism," but that was unable to fathom the possibility of idolatry's truth. Perhaps the most important message of Buddhism for our times is actually that there is a possibility for deep, meaningful human concern and comportment in a way of life radically distinct from both humanism and Abrahamic religion. Perhaps if we follow Shakyamuni's path we will discover that the death of the Abrahamic God does not necessitate the end of religion and the annihilation of meaning and purpose in life; but opens up the possibility of discovering them in every rock, tree, animal, and person.

Notes

1. To allow some linguistic variation, I shall use "Europe" and "the West," and "European" and "Western" interchangeably. The pairs are not, of course, synonyms; but in our context I do not believe this imprecision is problematic.

2. Eugene Burnouf, *Introduction to the History of Indian Buddhism*, trans. Katia Buffetrille and Donald Lopez, Jr. (Chicago and London: University of Chicago Press, 2010) The case of Buddhism is very much a part of the much wider nineteenth century European trend in the understanding of religion so trenchantly analyzed by Tomoko Masuzawa in *The Invention of World Religions* (Chicago: University of Chicago Press, 2005).

3. See, for instance, Mazuzawa, *Invention*, 46–64.

4. See, for instance, Julien Ries, "Idolatry" in *The Encyclopedia of Religion*, Vol. 7, edited by Mircea Eliade (New York: Macmillan, 1987), 72–82.

5. Ricci's treatment of the Daoists is the topic of Ronnie Littlejohn's chapter in this volume.

6. Stephen Batchelor, *The Awakening of the West: The Encounter of Buddhism and Western Culture* (Berkeley: Parallax Press, 1994), 227–249; Donald S. Lopez Jr., *Buddhism and Science: A Guide for the Perplexed* (Chicago: University of Chicago Press, 2008), 153–195; Donald Lopez, Jr., "Introduction to the Translation," Burnouf, *Introduction*, 1—27; and Masuzawa, *Invention*, 121–146.

7. See especially Lopez's works cited in note 6.

8. Burnouf, *Introduction*, 77–8; also see, for instance, his discussion of stupa worship, 338ff.

9. Gregory Schopen, "Archeology and Protestant Presuppositions in the Study of Indian Buddhism," in *Bones, Stones, and Buddhist Monks*, ed. Gregory Schopen (Honolulu: University of Hawai'i Press, 1997), 1–22. Academic studies of Buddhism not primarily based upon textual analysis are still few and far between. Even academic studies of ritual and practice tend to be text-based. Radicalism in the field is often a matter of studying different kinds of texts than most in the field. Indeed, Schopen himself, as one can see in the essay cited, substitutes a new kind of text-the inscription-for the usual old texts. On the other hand, Western converts to Buddhism and other amateur students have turned to living representatives for understanding, but it is noteworthy that many Asian teachers in the West have a positively Protestant need to anchor their teaching in old texts.

10. Burnouf, *Introduction*, 55–79. It is widely reported that Buddhism has died out in the Indian subcontinent. However, the Newar people of Nepal have continuously maintained the traditions and texts of Buddhism. I would like to thank Todd T. Lewis and Leonard van der Kuijp for drumming this point into my head in their NEH Summer Institute *Buddhist Traditions of Tibet and the Himalayas* in 2009. Hodgson received his manuscripts from this community.

11. Ibid.

12. Ibid., 83–113.

13. Ibid., the distinction is introduced 140ff.

14. Ibid., 51, see 14. One should consider not only the enormity of this claim, but the methodological presuppositions it seems to entail. It assumes Burnouf was able to read through all of the texts (he actually claimed that was fairly simple), analyze them all in terms of belief content, measure them against some standard of "simple" and "complex" and simultaneously, but independently, discovering their historical order. Burnouf gives no defense of this claim or his method in *Introduction*. One suspects it never occurred to him that he needed to, such was the hold this most Protestant of assumptions had on him. In fact in reading *Introduction*, one is struck over and over again by how little the texts he quotes support the notion of a simple and complex message or his picture of that simple message.

15. Ibid., 165. This claim is one of the most important leitmotivs of *Introduction* and found in one version or another throughout the work.

16. Ibid., 329.

17. This picture is deployed almost from the moment the distinction between "simple" and "complex" sutras is made (see 145ff.), but is implicit in the earlier discussion of the relation of Chinese, Mongol and Tibetan texts the Sanskrit and Pali ones, *Introduction*, 55–79.

18. Ibid., 411–478.

19. Ibid., 245–409.

20. Ibid., 188–209, the talking statues are found at 208. While it is not completely clear, Burnouf seems to take this sutra as an early, simple one.

21. Ibid., 329.

22. Ibid., 327–344.

23. Ibid., 161 where this leitmotiv begins.

24. Ibid., 68–70.

25. See Masuzawa's discussion of the importance to the West of the "universalism" of Buddhism. *Invention*, 131–46 and following.

26. For the history of the American version of Buddhism, see Rick Fields, *How the Swans Came to the Lake: A Narrative History of Buddhism in America*, 3rd ed. (Boston: Shambhala, 1992).

27. Masuzawa, *Invention*, 126.

28. Donald Lach, *Asia in the Making of Europe: The Century of Discovery* (Chicago: University of Chicago Press, 1965), v. 1, bk. 2, 742–94. Like Lach, I will use the 1853 and 1854 reprints of R. Parke's translation as edited by Sir George T. Staunton. Juan Gonzalez Mendoza, *The Historie of the Great and Mightie Kingdom of China, and the Situation Therof*, vols. 1 and 2, trans. R. Parke (London: Hakluyet Society Publications, Old Series, 1853–1854), vols. xiv and xv (Google Books). All references are to volume I, part 2, unless otherwise indicated.

29. Mendoza, *Historie*, 36.

30. Ibid., 39.

31. Ibid., 50–52.

32. Ibid., 39–44.

33. Ibid., 44–5. At several points in the travel narratives of the second volume, missionaries spit at the idols or otherwise abuse them without suffering the usual consequences. See for instance vol. 2, section 4, chapter 14.

34. Ibid., 46–47.

35. Ibid., 39.

36. Ibid., 36–39.

37. Ibid., 53.

38. In Chinese, "Shakyamuni" is rendered *Shih-chia-fo* or *Shih chia-mu-ni*. Lach, *Asia* v.1, bk. 2, 815, n. 448.

39. Ibid., 55–59. For funerals see also pages 59–61. For festivals, Vol. 1, book 3, chapter 18, 137–140.

40. For a brief overview see M. Howard Rienstra's "Introduction" to *Jesuit Letters from China 1583–84* (Minneapolis: University of Minnesota Press, 1986); and Donald F. Lach and Edwin J. Van Kley, *Asia in the Making of Europe: A Century of Advance*, Book 4: East Asia (Chicago: University of Chicago Press, 1993), 1983–1999.

41. *Jesuit Letters from China*, 24–5.

42. Lach, v.1, bk. 2, 802–3. In Latin, *De Christiana expedition apud Sinas*. See David E. Mungello, *Curious Land: Jesuit Accommodation and the Origins of Sinology* (Honolulu: University of Hawai'i Press, 1985), chapter 2. The English version is *China in the 16th Century: The Journals of Matthew Ricci, 1583–1610*, trans. Louis J. Gallagher, S.J. (New York: Random House, 1953). It is this version of Ricci-Trigault that I make use of in what follows.

43. Matteo Ricci, S.I., *Fonti Ricciane: Storia dell'Introduzione del Cristianesimo in Cina*, edited by Pasquale d'Elia, S.J., 3 vols. (Rome: La Libreria dello Stato, 1942–1949).

44. Gallagher, "Translator's Preface" to *China in the 16th Century*, xvii.

45. Ibid., 82–92.

46. Ibid., 104. Ricci-Trigault later notes that each cult actually subdivides numerous times, so that is actually more accurate to speak of 300, than 3.

47. Ibid., 94–98.

48. Ibid., 104–105.

49. Ibid., 105.

50. See Masuzawa, *Invention*, 62–63.

51. Ricci, *China in 16th Century*, 105.

52. This argument may not as bad as it seems—a simple denial of the possibility of multiple versions of true religion. As we shall see in a moment, Ricci believed the beliefs of the Literati in one way contradicted the beliefs of the followers of Sciequia for while the former believed in the True God, the latter did not. Thus both systems could not be true.

In his most important work in Chinese, *The True Meaning of the Lord of Heaven*, Ricci wrote of "the Religion of Three in One" and developed this argument in detail. See Ricci, *The True Meaning of the Lord of Heaven (T'ien-chu Shih-i)*, translated and edited by Douglas Lancashire and Peter Hu Kuo-chen, S.J. (St. Louis, MO: Institute of Jesuit Resouces and The Ricci Institute for Chinese Studies, 1985), 401–407 (paragraphs 508–520).

The True Meaning of the Lord of Heaven was originally published in Chinese in 1603, was widely disseminated in China and translated into many East Asian languages. However, beyond a Latin summary made by Ricci for Rome, the work was not translated into any European language before a French version in 1811. See "Translators' Introduction," *The True Meaning,* 19–21.

53. Ricci, *China in the 16th Century,* 98.

54. Ricci thus sought to "purify" Confucianism by unearthing its original essence through the reading of its old text and ignoring its living representatives. His methodology and assumptions are thus quite close to Burnouf's in the latter's "rescue" of Buddhism. This point should not be be overlooked by those who believe Ricci introduced Confucius and Confucianism to Europe.

55. Ibid., 448.

56. As we have seen, Ricci-Trigault also distinguished the cult of Sciequia from the cult of Lauzu. It has relatively little to say about the latter, most of it disparaging, much of it repeating what is said about the cult of Sciequia. However, it seems that whatever else its errors, it did not include the worship of idols. See ibid., 102–104. In *The True Meaning of the Lord of Heaven* Ricci groups the two cults together philosophically for advocating that the universe arose from nothing, see chapter 2.

57. Ibid., 105.

58. Ibid. To his Chinese audience Ricci allows that the idols can in fact be possessed of evil spirits and the Devil who are capable of deceiving and seducing men and leading them to Hell when God drops his protection. See *The True Meaning of the Lord of Heaven,* 401 (paragraphs 506 and 507).

59. It is impossible for one who has not read Ricci's original diaries to determine to what degree this hostility reflects Ricci's own final attitude, and to what degree it is a matter of Trigault's editorializing to appeal to his Christian audience. For instance, Jonathan Spence writes that Ricci and the Buddhist scholar Li Zhi had a cordial and even close relationship, and Ricci was quite saddened when Li Zhi chose suicide rather than disgrace. See *The Memory Palace of Matteo Ricci* (New York: Viking Penguin, 1985), 255–7. To complicate matters further, it is unclear to me whether this Li Zhi is the same individual as the anonymous man whose very similar suicide is reported in Ricci-Trigault without an iota of remorse, and in fact is said to be divinely sanctioned punishment for questioning Ricci's work (400–01).

60. Ibid., 98–99.

61. Ibid., 102-3.

62. Ibid., 100-101.

63. Ibid., 100-101.

64. Ibid., 101-102.

65. Ibid., 102.

66. Ibid., 95.

67. See chapter 4: "A Discussion on Spiritual Beings and the Soul of Man, and an Explanation as to Why the Phenomena of the World Cannot Be Described as Forming an Organic Unity" especially, 203–13 (paragraphs 206–218).

68. Contemporary "Process Theologians" and "Open and Relational Theologians" do not share this perspective. I thank my colleague Dr. Denny Clark for this information.

69. Ricci, *China,* 337–43. In contemporary transliteration this name is rendered "San Huai." In China, he is referred to as "one of the Sanhoi" but Spence treats "Sanhuai" as a name. See *The*

Memory Palace of Matteo Ricci, 254–5. His proper name was Han Huangen, as is declared in the "Translator's Introduction" to *True Meaning*, 9. As Spence notes, much of *The True Meaning of the Lord of Heaven* echoes this debate.

True Meaning, especially the already cited chapter 4, was also influenced by the criticism of Huang Hui, a devout Buddhist and member of the Royal College (see "Translator's Introduction," 17 and Spence, 254). Huang Hui had critically annotated a copy of *TMLH* that Ricci saw. Spence says Ricci decided to avoid an open conflict with an individual so powerful. Ricci-Trigault tells what appears to be a somewhat garbled version of this story in which the one who annotated *TMLH* is an unnamed member of the Royal College who had dropped out of the Literati, left his family and became a priest of the idolaters. His blasphemy in equating himself with God leads to denunciation by the authorities and ultimately his imprisonment and suicide. See Ricci, *China in the Sixteenth Century*, 399–401.

70. Batchelor, *Awakening of the West*, 171. This may be something of an exaggeration on Ricci's part. Spence for instance writes that Chinese sympathetic to the cult criticized him for not reading their scriptures *carefully*. See Spence, *Memory Palace*, 252–53. Nonetheless, Ricci certainly believed he had nothing to learn from the cult. See, for instance, Ricci, *China*, 402.

71. Ricci, *China*, 402.

72. Ibid., 339–41.

73. Ibid., 341–42. According to Ricci-Trigault (400), Haung Hi's views were similar to Sanhua's. Ricci's writings in Chinese added several arguments against the idolaters (and sometimes the followers of Lauzu). The philosophically most important is that neither the "nothingness" of Lauzu nor the "voidness" of the idolaters can function as the primary substratum and originating substance that underlies the existence of the universe and the things in it as they claim. (*True Meaning*, 103–107, paragraphs 71–76). Ricci glosses "voidness" as absolute nonexistence and thus fails to see the connection of this position of the idolaters with the notion of the equality of all things. Other interesting arguments of Ricci's include those against the rebirth of animals (253, paragraph 278) and the pointlessness of vegetarianism (255–61, paragraphs 280–88) since God gave only humans rational souls and created animals for our use. He also objected to chanting Amida's name, since it did not involve deeply felt repentance (391, 397–8, paragraphs 488–490 and 500–501). Presumably these were not included in Ricci-Trigault since it was unlikely Europeans would be tempted by these views.

74. Ibid., 341 and 342.

75. Ibid., 342.

76. This "empowerment" often referred to as "the eye opening ceremony" is most fully described and analyzed in Donald K. Swearer's *Becoming the Buddha: The Ritual of Image Consecration in Thailand* (Princeton, NJ: Princeton University Press, 2004).

77. Ibid.

78. Sharf, "The Scripture on the Production of Buddha Images" in *Religions of China in Practice*, ed. Donald S. Lopez (Princeton, NJ: Princeton University Press, 1996), 261–7.

79. See, for instance, Michael Willis, "Depicting the Buddha" and Todd T. Lewis, "The Worship of Relic Memorials" both in *Buddhism: The Illustrated Guide*, ed. Kevin Trainor (New York: Oxford University Press, 2001), 42–45 and 48, respectively. The connection of the two practices is that sculptures of the Buddha were technically referred to as "relics of indication of referral." Ibid., 48.

80. "Emptiness" is not a metaphysical concept according to many contemporary interpretations, though it is clear, as we have already noted that Ricci believed it was.

81. In fact, Ricci's major mistake in this regard quite likely was in believing there was any part of the traditional Chinese thinking had space for transcendence in his sense. See, for instance, Donald L. Hall and Roger T. Ames, *Thinking through Confucius* (Albany: State University of New York Press, 1987) which fleshes out the difference between traditional Western and Confucian ways of thinking from this "absence."

82. Tenzin Gyatso, the Fourteenth Dalai Lama, *Essence of the Heart Sutra* (Boston: Wisdom Publications, 2002), 18.

83. The notion that the ascription of idolatry to any religious practice must be based upon a misunderstanding of the role of images in that practice seems to begin in Europe in the late eighteenth century. See, for instance, Voltaire's discussion of idolatry in his *Philosophical Dictionary*, ed. and trans. Theodore Besterman (New York: Penguin Books, 1972), 238–251.

84. Radical environmentalists, those, for instance, who embrace the Gaia ideology, are a notable exception to this attitude.

Bibliography

Adorno, Theodor. *Aesthetic Theory*. Translated by Robert Hullot-Kentor. Minneapolis: University of Minnesota Press, 1997.

Alliston, April. *Virtue's Faults: Correspondences in Eighteenth-Century English and French Women's Fiction*. Stanford, CA: Stanford University Press, 1996.

"An Excellent Treatise of the Kingdome of China and of the Estate and Government Thereof." In Richard Hakluyt, ed., *The Principal Navigations, Voyages, Traffiques and Discoveries of the English Nation*. London: J. M. Dent, 1927.

Anon. *Yu Jiao Li*. Beijing: Huaxia chubanshe, 1995.

Anon. *Hao qiu zhuan*. Beijing: Huaxia chubanshe, 1995.

Anon. *Jin Yun Qiao zhuan*. Beijing: Huaxia chubanshe, 1995.

Anderson, Benedict. *Imagined Communities: Reflections on the Origin and Spread of Nationalism*. Rev. ed. London: Verso, 1991.

Armstrong, Nancy. *Desire and Domestic Fiction: A Political History of the Novel*. New York: Oxford University Press, 1987.

Auerbach, Erich. *Mimesis: The Representation of Reality in Western Literature*. Translated by Willard R. Trask. Princeton, NJ: Princeton University Press, 1968.

Avity, Pierre d', sieur de Montmartin. *The Estates, Empires, and Principallities of the World Represented by ye Description of Countries, Maners of Inhabitants, Riches of Prouinces, Forces, Gouernment, Religion; and the Princes That Haue Gouerned in Euery Estate*. With the beginning of all militarie and religious orders. Translated out of French by Edward Grimstone. London, 1615.

Bairoch, Paul. *Economics and World History: Myths and Paradoxes*. Hemel Hempstead: Harvester, 1993.

Ballaster, Ros. *Fabulous Orients: Fictions of the East in England 1662–1785*. New York: Oxford University Press, 2005.

Ban, Zhao 班 昭. Nujie 《女 誡》 (*Precepts for Women*). *Images of Women in Chinese Thought and Culture*, edited by Robin Wang, 177–88. Indianapolis: Hackett Publishing, 2003.

Banerjee, Pompa. *Burning Women: Widows, Witches, and Early Modern European Travelers in India*. New York: Palgrave, 2003.

Barbour, Richmond. *Before Orientalism: London's Theatre of the East, 1576–1626*. Cambridge: Cambridge University Press, 2003.

Barker-Benfield, G. J. *The Culture of Sensibility: Sex and Society in Eighteenth-Century Britain*. Chicago: University of Chicago Press, 1992.

Barnhart, Richard. *Painters of the Great Mind: The Imperial Court and the Zhe School*. Dallas: Dallas Museum of Art, 1993.

Barrett, T. H. "Chinese Religion in English Guise: The History of an Illusion." *Modern Asian Studies* 39 (2005): 509–33.

Batchelor, Stephen. *The Awakening of the West: The Encounter of Buddhism and Western Culture*. Berkeley, CA: Parallax Press, 1994.

Bayliss, Robert. "What *Don Quixote* Means (Today)." *Comparative Literature Studies* 43, no. 4 (2006): 382–97.

Bennett, Josephine Waters. *The Rediscovery of Sir John Mandeville*. New York: MLA, 1954.

Berling, Judith. "Taoism in Ming Culture." In *Cambridge History of China*. Vol. 8. *The Ming Dynasty*, edited by Denis Twitchett, 953–85. Cambridge: Cambridge University Press, 2005.

Bernadine of Escalante. *A Discourse of the Navigation which the Portugales Doe Make to the Realms and Provinces of the East Partes of the World and of the Knowledge that Growes by Them of the Great Thinges, which Are in the Dominions of China*. Trans. John Frampton. London, 1579.

Botero, Giovanni. *Relations of the Most Famous Kingdoms and Common-wealths Thorowout the World Discoursing of Their Situations, Religions, Languages, Manners, Customes, Strengths, Greatnesse and Policies*. London, 1630.

Boxer, C. R., ed. *South China in the Sixteenth Century: Being the Narratives of Galeote Pereira, Fr Gaspar Cruz, Fr. Martin de Rada*. London: Hakluyt Society, 1953. Pereira's and Cruz's narratives were included in *Hakluytus Posthumus, or Purchas His Pilgrimes: Containing a History of the World in Sea Voyages and Lande Travells by Englishmen and Others* (1625; London: Glasgow: James MacLehose, 1906), Vol. 11.

Brathwaite, Richard. "The English Gentlewoman." In *Daughters, Wives, and Widows: Writings by Men about Women and Marriage in England, 1500–1640*, edited by Joan Larsen Klein, 235–56. Urbana: University of Illinois Press, 1992.

Brockey, Liam Matthew. *Journey to the East: The Jesuit Mission to China, 1579–1724*. Cambridge, MA: Harvard University Press, 2008.

Brook, Timothy. *The Confusions of Pleasure: Commerce and Culture in Ming China*. Berkeley: University of California Press, 1998.

Burnouf, Eugene. *Introduction to the History of Indian Buddhism*, trans. Katia Buffetrille and Donald S. Lopez Jr. Chicago: University of Chicago Press, 2010.

Burton, Robert. *The Anatomy of Melancholy*. Edited by Thomas C. Faulkner, Nicholas K. Kiessling, and Rhonda L Blair. Oxford: Clarendon Press, 1989.

Campany, Rob. "Demons, Gods, and Pilgrims: The Demonology of the Hsi-Yu Chi." *Chinese Literature: Essays, Articles, Reviews* 7, no. 1/2 (1985): 95–115.

Carey, Daniel, ed. *Asian Travel in the Renaissance*. London: Wiley-Blackwell, 2004.

Cervantes, Miguel de. *Don Quixote De La Mancha*. Translated by Samuel Putnam. New York: Modern Library, 1998.

Chan, Albert, S. J. "Late Ming Society and the Jesuit Missionaries." In *East Meets West: The Jesuits in China, 1582–1773*, edited by Charles E. Ronan, S. J. and Bonnie B. C. Oh, 153–72. Chicago: Loyola University Press, 1988.

Chaudhuri, K. N. *Asia before Europe: Economy and Civilization of the Indian Ocean from the Rise of Islam to 1750*. Cambridge: Cambridge University Press, 1990.

Chen, Bing 陳兵. "Ming-Qing Daojiao." In *Daojiao tonglun*. Edited by Mou Zhongjian. Jinan, Shandong: Wenlu Press, 1991.

Ch'ien, Chung-shu. "China in the English Literature of the Seventeenth-Century." *Quarterly Bulletin of Chinese Bibliography* 1 (1940): 351–84.

Clarke, J. J. *The Tao of the West: Western Transformations of Taoist Thought*. London: Routledge, 2000.

Coates, Timothy J. *Convicts and Orphans: Forced and State-Sponsored Colonizers in the Portuguese Empire, 1550–1755*. Stanford, CA: Stanford University Press, 2001.

Cocks, Richard. Letter to Lord Salisbury. December 10, 1614. *Calendar of Japan Papers* 1614. Reprinted in *Letters Written by the English Residents in Japan 1611–1623*, edited by N. Murakami and K. Murakawa, 149–51. Tokyo: Sankūsha, 1900.

Cook, Daniel, and Henry Rosemont, eds. *G.W. Leibniz: Writings on China*. La Salle, IL: Open Court, 1994.

Cormack, Lesley B. "Britannia Rules The Waves?: Images of Empire in Elizabethan England." *Early Modern Literary Studies* 4.2; Special Issue 3 (1998): 10.1–20.

Critchley, John. *Marco Polo's Book*. Aldershot: Variorum, 1992.

Crump, J. I. *Song-Poems from Xanadu*. Ann Arbor: University of Michigan Center for Chinese Studies, 1993.

Cummins, J. S. *A Question of Rites: Friar Domingo Nararrete and the Jesuits in China*. Cambridge, England: Scolar Press, 1993.

DeBruyn, Pierre-Henry. "Daoism in the Ming." In *Daoism Handbook*, edited by Livia Kohn, 594–622. Boston, MA: Brill, 2004.

Dehergne, Joseph. "Les Hisotiens Jesuites du Taoisme." In *Actes du Collque International de Sinologie. La Mission Francaise de Pekin aux XVII et XVIII siecles*, 59–67. History of Christianity Collection. The Beijing Center for Chinese Studies, 1976.

Despeux, Catherine. "Talismans and Diagrams." In *Daoism Handbook*, edited by Livia Kohn, 498–540. Boston, MA: Brill, 2004.

Du Halde, Jean-Baptiste. *The General History of China*. Translated by Richard Brookes. London: John Watts, 1736. Accessible through Gale CENGAGE Learning.com "Eighteenth Century Collections Online," http://infotrac.thomsonlearning.com/.

Duara, Prasanjit. "Superscribing Symbols: The Myth of Guandi, Chinese God of War." *Journal of Asian Studies* 47 (1988): 778–95.

Dudbridge, Glen. *Books, Tales and Vernacular Culture*. Leiden: Brill, 2005.

———. *The Hsi-Yu Chi: A Study of Antecedents to the Sixteenth-Century Chinese Novel*. Cambridge: Cambridge University Press, 1970.

Dunne, George H. *Generation of Giants: The Story of the Jesuits in China in the Last Decades of the Ming Dynasty*. Notre Dame, IN: University of Notre Dame Press, 1982.

Ebrey, Patricia. "Gender and Sinology: Shifting Western Interpretations of Foot-binding 1300–1890." *Late Imperial China* 20 (1999): 1–34.

———. *Women and the Family in Chinese History*. London: Routledge, 2003.

Eckermann, Johann Peter. *Conversations of Goethe*. Translated by John Oxenford. New York: Da Capo Press, 1998.

————. *Conversations with Goethe.* Translated by Gisela C. O'Brien. New York: Frederick Ungar Publishing, 1964.

Esposito, Monica. "Daoism in the Qing (1644–1911)." In *Daoism Handbook,* edited by Livia Kohn, 623–58. Boston, MA: Brill, 2004.

Fields, Rick. *How the Swans Came to the Lake: A Narrative History of Buddhism in America,* 3rd ed. Boston: Shambhala, 1992.

Fletcher, Joseph. "Integrative History: Parallels and Interconnections in the Early Modern Period, 1500–1800" [1973]. In *Studies on Chinese Islamic Inner Asia,* edited by Beatrice Forbes Manz, part 10. Aldershot, England: Variorum Press, 1995.

Frank, Andre G. *ReOrient: Global Economy in the Asian Age.* Berkeley: University of California Press, 1998.

————. *World Accumulation, 1492–1789.* New York: Monthly Review Press and Macmillan Press, 1978.

Fuller, Mary. "Making Something of It: Questions of Value in the Early English Travel Collection." *Journal of Early Modern History* 10 (2006): 11–38.

Gabbard, D. Christopher. "Gender Stereotyping in Early Modern Travel Writing on Holland." *Studies in English Literature 1500–1900* 43 (2003): 83–100.

Gavitt, Philip. *Charity and Children in Renaissance Florence: The Ospedale Degli Innocenti, 1410–1536.* Ann Arbor: University of Michigan Press, 1990.

Girardot, Norman J. 'Finding the Way': James Legge and the Victorian Invention of Taoism." *Religion* 29 (1999): 107–21.

————. *The Victorian Translation of China: James Legge's Oriental Pilgrimage.* Berkeley: University of California Press, 2002.

Goethe, Johann Wolfgang von. "Translations." In *The Translation Studies Reader,* edited by Lawrence Venuti, 64–66. New York: Routledge, 2004.

Goossaert, Vincent. "The Quanzhen Clergy, 1750–1950." In *Religion and Chinese Society.* Vol. 2, edited by John Lagerwey, 699–771. Hong Kong: Chinese University Press, 2004.

Gowing, Laura. *Domestic Dangers: Women, Words, and Sex in Early Modern London.* Oxford: Clarendon Press, 1996.

Gu, Wenbi 顧文璧. "Mingdai wudang shan de xingsheng han Suzhou ren de da guimo Wudang jinxiang luxing." *Jianghan kaogu* (1989): 71–75.

Gyatso, Tenzin (the Fourteenth Dalai Lama). *Essence of the Heart Sutra.* Boston: Wisdom Publications, 2002.

Hall, David L., and Roger T. Ames. *Thinking through Confucius.* Albany: State University of New York Press, 1987.

Hauf, Kandice J. "The Community Covenant in Sixteenth Century Ji'an Prefecture, Jiangxi." *Late Imperial China* 17, 2 (1996): 1–50.

Hayot, Eric, Haun Saussy, and Steven G. Yao, eds. *Sinographies: Writing China.* Minneapolis: University of Minnesota Press, 2008.

Hegel, G. W. F. *Lectures on the History of Philosophy.* Vol. 1, translated by E. S. Haldane and Frederick C. Beiser. Lincoln: University of Nebraska Press, 1995.

Henderson, Katherine Usher, and Barbara McManus, eds. *Half Humankind: Contexts and Texts of the Controversy about Women in England, 1540–1640.* Urbana: University of Illinois Press, 1985.

Hessney, Richard. "Beautiful, Talented and Brave: Seventeenth-Century Chinese Scholar-Beauty Romances." PhD diss., Columbia University, 1979.

Heylyn, Peter. *Cosmographie in Four Bookes: Containing the Chorographie and Historie of the Whole Vvorld, and all the Principall Kingdomes, Provinces, Seas and Isles Thereof.* London: Henry Seile, 1652.

"Hic Mulier." In *Half Humankind: Contexts and Texts of the Controversy about Women in England, 1540–1640,* edited by Katherine Usher Henderson and Barbara McManus, 264–77. Urbana: University of Illinois Press, 1985.

"An Homily of the State of Matrimony." In *Daughters, Wives, and Widows,* 13–25.

How to Read Chinese Poetry. Edited by Zong-qi Cai. New York: Columbia University Press, 2008.

Hsia, Adrian, ed. *The Vision of China in the English Literature of the Seventeenth and Eighteenth Centuries.* Hong Kong: Chinese University Press, 1998.

Hsia, C. T. *The Classic Chinese Novel: A Critical Introduction.* New York: Columbia University Press, 1968.

Hsiung, Ping-Chen. *A Tender Voyage: Children and Childhood in Late Imperial China.* Stanford, CA: Stanford University Press, 2005.

Huang, Martin Weizong. "Dehistoricization and Intertextualization: The Anxiety of Precedents in the Evolution of the Traditional Chinese Novel." *Chinese Literature: Essays, Articles, Reviews* 12 (1990): 45–68.

———. *Desire and Fictional Narrative in Late Imperial China.* Cambridge, MA: Harvard University Press, 2001.

Huang, Ray. *1587, A Year of No Significance: The Ming Dynasty in Decline.* New Haven, CT: Yale University Press, 1981.

Hull, Suzanne. *Chaste, Silent and Obedient, English Books for Women 1475–1640.* San Marino, CA: Huntington Publications, 1988.

———. *Women According to Men: The World of Tudor-Stuart Women.* Walnut Creek, CA: AltaMira Press, 1996.

Humboldt, Wilhelm von. "From the Introduction to His Translation of *Agamemnon.*" In *Theories of Translation: An Anthology of Essays from Dryden to Derrida,* edited by Rainer Schulte and John Biguenet, 55–59. Chicago: University of Chicago Press, 1992.

Jing, Wang. *The Story of Stone.* Durham, NC: Duke University Press, 1992.

Jones, David Martin. *The Image of China in Western Social and Political Thought.* New York: Palgrave, 2001.

Jost, Francis. *Introduction to Comparative Literature.* New York: Pegasus, 1974.

Kahn, Joseph. "Waking Dragon." Review of *When China Rules the World: The End of the Western World and the Birth of a New Global Order,* by Martin Jacques. *New York Times,* December 31, 2009, Sunday Book Review. http://www.nytimes.com/2010/01/03/books/review/Kahn-t.html.

Katz, Paul. "Enlightened Alchemist or Immoral Immortal? The Growth of Lu Dongbin's Cult in Late Imperial China." In *Unruly Gods: Divinity and Society in China,* edited by Meir Shahar and Robert Weller. 70–104. Honolulu: University of Hawai'i Press, 1996.

Kim, Eui-Yeong, *Thoreau's Orientalism: A Study of Confucian and Taoist Elements in Thoreau's Reading and Writing.* PhD diss., University of Illinois at Urbana-Champaign, 1990. ProQuest (AAT 9124441).

Kinney, Anne Behnke. *Representations of Childhood and Youth in Early China.* Stanford, CA: Stanford University Press, 2004.

Klein, Joan Larsen, ed. *Daughters, Wives, and Widows: Writings by Men about Women and Marriage in England, 1500–1640*. Urbana: University of Illinois Press, 1992.

Ko, Dorothy. *Teachers of the Inner Chambers: Women and Culture in Seventeenth-Century China*. Stanford, CA: Stanford University Press, 1994.

Kohn, Livia. "The Taoist Adoption of the City God." *Ming Qing yanjiu* 5 (1996): 69–108.

———, ed. *Daoism Handbook*. Boston: Brill, 2004.

Lach, Donald, and Edwin Van Kley. *Asia in the Making of Europe*. 3 vols. Chicago: University of Chicago Press, 1965.

Lagerwey, John. "The Pilgrimage to Wu-tang Shan." In *Pilgrims and Sacred Sites in China*, edited by Susan Naquin and Chun-fang Yu, 293–332. Berkeley: University of California Press, 1992.

Legge, James. *The Notions of the Chinese Concerning God and Spirits*. Hong Kong: Hong Kong Register Office, 1852.

———. *The Religions of China: Confucianism and Taoism Described and Compared with Christianity*. London: Hodder and Stoughton, 1880.

Lewis, Todd T. "The Worship of Relic Memorials." In *Buddhism: The Illustrated Guide*, edited by Kevin Trainor, 48. New York: Oxford University Press, 2001.

Li, Qiancheng. *Fictions of Enlightenment*. Honolulu: University of Hawai'i Press, 2004.

Li, Qingjun 李庆军. "Of Golden Lilies and Gentlewomen: Women's World in Early Modern Literature and Travel Narratives." Paper presented at the National Conference of ASIANetwork, Emory University Conference Center, Atlanta, Georgia, April 2010.

Linschoten, John. *The Voyage of John Huyghen Van Linschoten to the East Indies*. Edited by Arthur Coke Burnell. Vol. 1. London: Hakluyt Society, 1880.

Little, Stephen. 2004. "Daoist Art." In *Daoism Handbook*, edited by Livia Kohn, 709–46. Boston: Brill, 2004.

Littlejohn, Ronnie. "The Daogu 道姑 of *The Peony Pavilion*." Paper presented at the National ASIANetwork/ASDP Conference, Whittier, CA, April 2005.

Liu I-ming[Yiming]. "How to Read the *Original Intent of the Journey to the West*." In *How to Read the Chinese Novel*, edited by David L. Rolston, 299–315. Princeton, NJ: Princeton University Press, 1990.

Lodge, Thomas. *Rosalind*. London: Cassell & Company, Ltd., 1887.

Longobard, Niccolo. "A Generall Collection and Historical Representation of the Jesuites Entrance into Japon and China, until Their Admission in the Royall Citie of Nanquin." In Samuel Purchas, *Hakluytus Posthumus, or Purchas His Pilgrimes*. Vol. 12, 314–331.

Loomba, Ania. *Colonialism/Postcolonialism*. 2nd ed. London: Routledge, 2005.

Lopez, Donald S. *Buddhism and Science: A Guide for the Perplexed*. Chicago: University of Chicago Press, 2008.

Lu, Hsiao-Peng. "The Fictional Discourse of *Pien-Wen*: The Relation of Chinese Fiction to Historiography." *Chinese Literature: Essays, Articles, Reviews* 9, no. 1/2 (1987): 49–70.

Lu Xun. *Lu Xun Quanji*. 18 vols. Beijing: Renmin Wenxue Chubanshe, 2005.

Ma, Ning. "When Robinson Crusoe Meets Ximen Qing: Material Egoism in the First Chinese and English Novels." *Comparative Literature Studies* 46.3 (2009): 443–66.

Mackerras, Colin. *Western Images of China*. New York: Oxford University Press, 1989.

Major, John, Sarah Queen, Andrew Meyer, and Harold Roth, trans. *The Huainanzi: A Guide to the Theory and Practice of Government in Early Han China*. New York: Columbia University Press, 2010.

Mann, Susan. *Precious Records: Women in China's Long Eighteenth Century*. Stanford, CA: Stanford University Press, 1997.

Markley, Robert. *The Far East and the English Imagination, 1600–1730*. Cambridge: Cambridge University Press, 2006.

Masuzawa, Tomoko. *The Invention of World Religions*. Chicago and London: University of Chicago Press, 2005.

Mazzola, Elizabeth, and Corinne Abate. "Indistinguished Space." In *Privacy, Domesticity, and Women in Early Modern England*, edited by Corinne Abate. Burlington, VT: Ashgate Publishing, 2003.

McCants, Anne M. C. *Civic Charity in a Golden Age: Orphan Care in Early Modern Amsterdam*. Urbana: University of Illinois Press, 1997.

McDaniel, Kathryn Noble. "Foreign Bodies: Reflections of Self and Others in English Travel Literature, 1650–1750." PhD diss., Vanderbilt University, 2000. Proquest (AAT 9996211).

McKeon, Michael. *Origins of the English Novel*. Baltimore: Johns Hopkins University Press, 1987.

McMahon, Keith. *Misers, Shrews, and Polygamists: Sexuality and Male-Female Relationships in Eighteenth-Century Chinese Fiction*. Durham, NC: Duke University Press, 1995.

Mendoza, Juan Gonzalez. *The Historie of the Great and Mightie Kingdom of China, and the Situation Therof*, vols. 1 and 2, trans. R. Parke. London: Hakluyt Society Publications, Old Series, vols. 14 and 15 (Google Books), 1853 and 1854.

Milhouse, Virginia H., Molefi Kete Asante, and Peter O. Nwosu, eds. *Transcultural Realities: Interdisciplinary Perspectives on Cross-Cultural Relations*. Thousand Oaks, CA: Sage, 2001.

Miller, Timothy S. "The Early History of Orphanages: From Constantinople to Venice." In *Home Away from Home: The Forgotten History of Orphanages*, edited by Richard B. McKenzie, 23–42. New York: Encounter Books, 2009.

Mohanty, Chandra Talpade. "Under Western Eyes: Feminist Scholarship and Colonial Discourses." *Colonial Discourse and Post-Colonial Theory*, edited by Patrick Williams and Laura Chrisman, 196–221. New York: Columbia University Press, 1994.

Moseley, C. W. R. D., ed. *The Travels of Sir John Mandeville*. Harmondsworth: Penguin Books, 1983.

Moule, A. C., and Paul Pelliot, trans. *Marco Polo, the Description of the World*, 2 vols. London: George Routledge and Sons, 1938.

Mungello, David E. *Curious Land: Jesuit Accommodation and the Origins of Sinology*. Honolulu: University of Hawai'i Press, 1989.

———. *Drowning Girls in China: Female Infanticide in China*. New York: Rowman and Littlefield, 2008.

———. *The Great Encounter of China and the West, 1500–1800*. 3rd ed. Lanham, MD: Rowman and Littlefield, 2009.

Naquin, Susan. "The Peking Pilgrimage to Miao-feng Shan: Religious Organizations and Sacred Site." In *Pilgrims and Sacred Sites in China*, edited by Susan Naquin and Chun-fang Yu, 333–77. Berkeley: University of California Press, 1992.

Navarette, Domingo. *The Travels and Controversies of Friar Domingo Navarette, 1618–1686*. Edited by J. S. Cummins. Cambridge, U.K.: Hakluyt Society, 1962.

Nieuhoff, Johannes. *An Embassy from the East-India Company of the United Provinces, to the Grand Tartar Cham Emperor of China*, translated by John Ogilby. London: White-Friers, 1673.

Nuerjing 《女兒經》 (*Classic for Girls*). In *Images of Women in Chinese Thought and Culture*, edited by Robin Wang, 437–46. Indianapolis: Hackett Publishing, 2003.

Odell, Dawn Virginia. "'The Soul of Transactions': Illustrated Travels and Representations of China in the Seventeenth Century." PhD diss., University of Chicago, 2003. Proquest (AAT 3097146).

Odoric of Pordenone. "The Travels of Friar Odoric of Pordenone." In *Cathay and the Way Thither*. Edited by Sir Henry Yule. London: Hakluyt Society, 1913.

Overmyer, Daniel L. "Protestant Christianity in China: Perspectives from the History of Chinese Religions and Early Christianity in the Roman World." *China Review* 9 (2009): 41–61.

Pagden, Anthony. "The Immobility of China: Orientalism and Occidentalism in the Enlightenment." In *The Anthropology of the Enlightenment*, edited by Larry Wolff and Marco Cipolloni, 57–78. Stanford, CA: Stanford University Press, 2007.

Pantoia, Diego de. "A Letter of father Diego De Pantoia, one of the Company of Jesus, to Father Luys de Guzman, Provinciall in the Province of Toledo; written in Paquin, which is the Court of the King of China, the ninth of March, the yeare 1602." In Purchas, *Purchas his Pilgrimes*, vol. 12, 331–410.

Paper, Jordan. *The Spirits are Drunk: Comparative Approaches to Chinese Religion*. Albany: State University of New York Press, 1995.

Pearson, M. N. "Objects Ridiculous and August: Early Modern European Perceptions of Asia." *Journal of Modern History* 68 (1996): 382–97.

Penny, Benjamin. "Meeting the Celestial Master" *East Asian History* 15/16 (1998): 53–66.

Pinto, Fernão Mendez. *The Travels of Mendes Pinto*. Edited by Rebecca D. Catz. Chicago: University of Chicago Press, 1989. Excerpts from Pinto appeared as "Observation of China, Tartaria and other Easterne parts of the World," in *Purchas his Pilgrimes*, vol. 12, 59–141.

Plaks, Andrew H. "Full-Length *Hsiao-Shuo* and the Western Novel: A Generic Reappraisal." *New Asia Academic Bulletin* 1 (1978): 163–76.

———. *The Four Masterworks of the Ming Novel: Ssu Ta Ch'i-Shu.* Princeton, NJ: Princeton University Press, 1987.

Polo, Marco. *The Description of the World.* Edited by A. C. Moule and Paul Pelliot. London: George Routledge, 1938.

———. *Marco Polo: The Travels.* Translated by Ronald Latham. Baltimore: Penguin Books, 1958.

Pomeranz, Kenneth. *The Great Divergence: China, Europe, and the Making of the Modern World Economy.* Princeton, NJ: Princeton University Press, 2000.

Porter, David. *Ideographia: The Chinese Cipher in Early Modern Europe.* Stanford, CA: Stanford University Press, 2001.

———. "Sinicizing Early Modernity: The Imperatives of Historical Cosmopolitanism." *Eighteenth-Century Studies* 43, no. 3 (2010): 299–306.

Průšek, Jaroslav "Urban Centers: The Cradle of Popular Fiction." In *Studies in Chinese Literary Genres,* edited by Cyril Birch, 259–98. Berkeley: University of California Press, 1974.

Ptak, Roderich. "*Hsi-Yang Chi:* An Interpretation and Some Comparisons with *Hsi-Yu Chi.*" *Chinese Literature: Essays, Articles, Reviews* 7, no. 1/2 (1985): 117–41.

Qian, Zhongshu. "Thomas Percy and His Chinese Studies." In *Vision of China in the English Literature of the 17th and 18th Centuries,* edited by Adrian Hsia, 301–25. Hong Kong: The Chinese University Press, 1998.

Ricci, Matthew (and Nicola Trigault, S. J.) *China in the Sixteenth Century: The Journals of Matthew Ricci 1583–1610.* Translated by Louis J. Gallagher, S.J. New York: Random House, 1953. Abbreviated as "A discourse of the Kingdome of China," in *Purchas his Pilgrimes,* Vol. 12, 411–69.

Ricci, Matteo S. I., *Fonti Ricciane: Storia dell'Introduzione del Cristianesimo in Cina,* edited by Pasquale d'Elia, S.J., 3 vols. Rome: La Libreria dello Stato, 1942–1949.

———. *The True Meaning of the Lord of Heaven (T'ien-chu Shih-i).* Translated and edited by Douglas Lancashire and Peter Hu Kuo-chen, S.J.

St. Louis, MO: Institute of Jesuit Resources and The Ricci Institute for Chinese Studies, 1985.

Richardson, Samuel. *Clarissa, or the History of a Young Lady* [1747-8]. Harmondsworth: Penguin Books, 1985.

———. *Pamela: Or, Virtue Rewarded* [1741]. London: Oxford University Press, 2001.

Rienstra, M. Howard, ed. and trans. *Jesuit Letters from China, 1583–84*. Minneapolis: University of Minnesota Press, 1986.

Ries, Julien. "Idolatry," trans. Kristine Anderson, in *The Encyclopedia of Religion*, Vol. 7, ed. Mircea Eliade, 72–82. New York: Macmillan, 1987.

Robbins, Bruce. "Race, Gender, Class, Postcolonialism: Toward a New Humanistic Paradigm?" In *A Companion to Postcolonial Studies*, edited by Henry Schwarz and Sangeeta Ray, 556–68. London: Blackwell, 2000.

Rolston, David L. *Traditional Chinese Fiction and Fiction Commentary: Reading and Writing between the Lines*. Stanford, CA: Stanford University Press, 1997.

Rubiés, Joan-Pau. *Travel and Ethnology in the Renaissance: South India through European Eyes, 1250–1625*. Cambridge: Cambridge University Press, 2000.

Ruggieri, Michele, et al. *Jesuit Letters from China 1583–84*, edited and translated by M. Howard Rienstra. Minneapolis: University of Minnesota Press, 1986.

Sachdev, Rachana. "Contextualizing Female Infanticide: Ming China in Early Modern European Travelogues." *ASIANetwork Exchange* (18, 1): 24–39.

Schipper, Kristofer, and Franciscus Verellen. eds. *The Taoist Canon: A Historical Companion to the Daozang*, 2 vols. Chicago: University of Chicago Press, 2004.

Schleiermacher, Friedrich. "On the Different Methods of Translating." In *The Translation Studies Reader*, edited by Lawrence Venuti, 43–63. New York: Routledge, 2004.

"The Schoolhouse of Women." In *Half Humankind*, 137–55.

Schopen, Gregory. "Archeology and Protestant Presuppositions in the Study of Indian Buddhism." In *Bones, Stones, and Buddhist*

Monks, edited by Gregory Schopen, 1–22. Honolulu: University of Hawai'i Press, 1997.

Scott-Warren, Jason. *Early Modern English Literature*. Cambridge: Polity, 2005.

Sebes, Joseph, S.J. "The Precursors of Ricci." In *East Meets West: The Jesuits in China, 1582–1773*, edited by Charles E. Ronan, S.J. and Bonnie B. C. Oh, 19–61. Chicago: Loyola University Press, 1988.

Semedo, Alvarez. *The History of that Great and Renowned Monarchy of China*. London: E. Tyler. E Books and Internet Archive. American Libraries, 1655, http://www.archive.org/stream/history ofthatgre00seme#page/n1/mode/2up.

Sharf, Robert H. "The Scripture of the Production of Buddha Images." *Religions of China in Practice*, edited by Donald S. Lopez, 261–67. Princeton, NJ: Princeton University Press, 1996.

Shen Jiji. "Ren the Fox Fairy." In *Selected Chinese Short Stories of the Tang and Song Dynasties*, 7–22. Beijing: Foreign Languages Press, 2001.

Shaw, Peter. *The Reflector: Representing Human Affairs, as They Are: and May Be Improved*. London: T. Longman, 1750.

Shoemaker, Robert. *Gender in English Society, 1650–1850*. London: Longman, 1998.

Sieber, Patricia. *Theaters of Desire: Authors, Readers, and the Reproduction of Early Chinese Song-Drama, 1300–2000*. New York: Palgrave Macmillan, 2003.

Silk, Jonathan. "The Victorian Creation of Buddhism." *Journal of Indian Philosophy* 22 (1994): 171–96.

Slingerland, Edward. *Effortless Action: Wu-wei as Conceptual Metaphor and Spiritual Ideal in Early China*. Oxford: Oxford University Press, 2003.

Smith, Adam. *An Inquiry into the Nature and Causes of the Wealth of Nations*. 2 vols., edited by Salvio M. Soares. MetaLibri Digital Library, 2007, http://www.ibiblio.org/ml/libri/s/SmithA_WealthNations_p.pdf.

———. *The Wealth of Nations* [1776]. New York: Random House, 1937.

Smith, Joanna Handlin. *The Art of Doing Good: Charity in Late Ming China*. Berkeley: University of California Press, 2009.

Smith, Richard. "Ritual in Ch'ing Culture." In *Orthodoxy in Late Imperial China*, edited by Liu Kwang-Ching, 281–310. Berkeley: University of California Press, 1990.

Sowernam, Esther. "Esther Hath Hanged Haman." In *Half Humankind*, 217–43.

Spence, Jonathan. *The Chan's Great Continent: China in Western Minds.* New York: W.W. Norton, 1998.

———. *The Memory Palace of Matteo Ricci.* New York: Viking Penguin, 1984.

———. *The Search for Modern China.* New York: Norton, 1990.

Struve, Lynn A., ed. and trans. *Voices from the Ming-Qing Cataclysm: China in Tigers' Jaws.* New Haven, CT: Yale University Press, 1993.

Sun, Anna Xiaodong. *Confusions over Confucianism: Controversies over the Religious Nature of Confucianism, 1870–2007,* PhD diss., Princeton University, 2008. ProQuest (AAT 3305310).

Swearer, Donald K. *Becoming the Buddha: The Ritual of Image Consecration in Thailand.* Princeton, NJ: Princeton University Press, 2004.

Swetnam, Joseph. "The Arraignment of Lewd, Idle, Froward, and Unconstant Women." In *Half Humankind*, 189–217.

Tang Xianzu. *The Peony Pavilion (Mudan ting)* 《牡丹亭》. Translated by Cyril Birch. Bloomington: Indiana University Press, 2002.

Tarocco, Francesca. *The Cultural Practices of Modern Chinese Buddhism: Attuning the Dharma.* London: Routledge, 2008.

Teltscher, Kate. "India/Calcutta: City of Palaces and Dreadful Night." In *The Cambridge Companion to Travel Writing*, edited by Peter Hulme and Tim Youngs, 191–206. Cambridge: Cambridge University Press, 2002.

Terpstra, Nicholas. *Abandoned Children of the Italian Renaissance: Orphan Care in Florence and Bologna.* Baltimore: Johns Hopkins University Press, 2005.

"The Jesuits in the Far East." In Samuel Purchas. *Purchas His Pilgrimes*, Vol. 12, 239–331.

T'ien Ju-Kang. *Male Anxiety and Female Chastity: A Comparative Study of Chinese Ethical Values in Ming-Ch'ing Times.* New York: E. J. Brill, 1988.

Tikoff, Valentina. "'Not All the Orphans Really Are': The Diversity of Seville's Juvenile Charity Wards during the Long Eighteenth Century." In *Raising an Empire: Children in Early Modern Iberia and Colonial Latin America*, edited by Ondina E. González and Bianca Premo, 41–74. Albuquerque: University of New Mexico Press, 2007.

Trexler, Richard. "The Foundlings of Florence, 1395–1455." *History of Childhood Quarterly* 2 (1975): 259–84.

Tsien, Tsuen-Hsuin. *Paper and Printing.* Edited by Joseph Needham. Vol. 5.1, Science and Civilisation in China. Cambridge: Cambridge University Press, 1985.

Twitchett, Denis, and Frederick W. Mote, eds. *The Cambridge History of China.* Vol. 8, Part 2. Cambridge: Cambridge University Press, 1998.

Van der Sprenkel, Otto. "Western Sources." In *Essays on the Sources for Chinese History,* edited by Donald Leslie, Colin Mackerras, and Wang Gungwu. Canberra: Australian National University Press, 1973.

Viazzo, Pier Paolo, Maria Bortolotto, and Andrea Zanotto, "Five Centuries of Foundling History in Florence: Changing Patterns of Abandonment, Care and Mortality." In *Abandoned Children,* edited by Catherine Panter-Brick and Malcolm T. Smith, 70–91. Cambridge, U.K.: Cambridge University Press, 2000.

Voltaire. *Philosophical Dictionary.* Edited and translated by Theodore Besterman. New York: Penguin Books, 1972.

Von Glahn, Richard. "Myth and Reality of China's Seventeenth-Century Monetary Crisis." *The Journal of Economic History* 56.2 (1996): 429–54.

Von Glasenapp, Helmuth. *Kant und die Religiomen des Osten (Kant and the Religions of the East).* Kitzingen-Main: Holzner Verlag Press, 1954.

Waltner, Ann. "Infanticide and Dowry in Ming and Early Qing China." In *Chinese Views of Childhood,* edited by Anne Behnke Kinney, 193–217. Honolulu: University of Hawai'i Press, 1995.

Ward, Adrienne. "China in 17th and 18th century Italy: Travel Literature, Scholarly/Reformist Writings, Theater." PhD diss., University of Wisconsin-Madison, 1998. Proquest (AAT 9839388).

Watson, Burton, trans. *The Complete Works of Chuang-tzu.* New York, Columbia University Press, 1968.

Watt, Ian. *The Rise of the Novel: Studies in Defoe, Richardson and Fielding.* Berkeley: University of California Press, 1957.

Webb, John. *An Historical Essay Endeavoring a Probability that the Language of the Empire of China Is the Primitive Language.* London: Nath Brook, 1669.

Wiesner, Merry. *Women and Gender in Early Modern Europe.* Cambridge: Cambridge University Press, 1993.

Willis, Michael. "Art and Architecture: Depicting the Buddha." In *Buddhism: The Illustrated Guide,* edited by Kevin Trainor, 42–45. New York: Oxford University Press, 2001.

Winston, Kenneth, and Mary Jo Bane. "Reflections on the Jesuit Mission to China." Faculty Working Paper Series. RWP10-004. Cambridge, MA: Harvard Kennedy School, 2010.

Wong, R. Bin. *China Transformed: Historical Change and the Limits of European Experience.* Ithaca, NY: Cornell University Press, 1997.

Wood, Frances. *Did Marco Polo Go to China?* London: Westview Press, 1995.

Wu, Ch'eng-en. *The Journey to the West,* translated by Anthony C. Yu, 4 Volumes. Chicago: University of Chicago Press, 1980–84.

Xuanzang. *Da Tang Xiyu Ji.* Shanghai: Shanghai Renmin Chubanshe, 1977.

Yang, Chi-ming. "Forging the Orient: Virtue and Exoticism in Eighteenth-Century England, 1660–1760." PhD diss., Cornell University, 2003. Proquest (AAT 3104430).

Yen, Alsace. "A Technique of Chinese Fiction: Adaptation in the 'Hsi-Yu Chi' with Focus on Chapter Nine." *Chinese Literature: Essays, Articles, Reviews* 1, no. 2 (1979): 197–213.

Yoshinobu, Sakade. "Divination as Daoist Practice." In *Daoism Handbook,* edited by Livia Kohn, 541–86. Boston: Brill, 2004.

Yu, Anthony C. "History, Fiction and the Reading of Chinese Narrative." *Chinese Literature: Essays, Articles, Reviews* 10, no. 1/2 (1988): 1–19.

———. *Journey to the West.* 4 vols. Chicago: University of Chicago Press, 1977–83.

Zhao, Henry Y. H. *The Uneasy Narrator: Chinese Fiction from the Traditional to the Modern.* Oxford: Oxford University Press, 1995.

Index

217

About the Contributors

daniel dooghan is Assistant Professor of World Literature in the English and Writing Department at The University of Tampa. His current project, "Literary Cartographies: Lu Xun and the Production of World Literature," is a methodological inquiry into the effects of translation on cultural exchange between China and the West through a case study of the prominent modern Chinese author Lu Xun. He is also researching the effects of Anglophone and minority Chinese writers on the representation of China to a Western readership, and the role of world literature in reinscribing hegemonic identities.

qingjun li is Assistant Professor of Asian Studies and Chinese Language at Belmont University. She holds her Ph.D. in English from Middle Tennessee State University (MTSU). She is also Associate Professor of English at Zhengzhou University, Peoples Republic of China, where she has been twice recognized as the Teacher of Excellence. She is author of three books and numerous articles, including her recent essay, "Pound's Poetic Mirror and the China Cantos: The Healing of the West," *Southeast Review of Asian Studies*, 30 (2008). Her research interests are in Chinese American literature, women's literature, and comparative literature.

ronnie littlejohn is Chair of Philosophy and Director of Asian Studies at Belmont University. He is author of four books, including introductions to Confucianism and Daoism in the I.B. Tauris Academic Studies of Religions Series, as well as over fifty articles. He has edited two collections, *Riding the Wind with Liezi: New Essays on a Daoist Classic* (SUNY Press) and *Polishing the Chinese Mirror*. His field research is with Daoshi lineages in Fujian province. He was the one American scholar chosen to give a Keynote Presentation at the *First International Forum on Laozi and Daoist Culture* sponsored by the Ministry of Education, P.R. China. In November 2009, he made one of the dedicatory addresses for the *Laozi and Daoist Culture Center*, at the birthplace of Laozi in Luyi County, Zhoukou City, Henan Province, China.

ning ma is an Assistant Professor of Chinese at Tufts University. Her research interests include late imperial Chinese fiction, the rise of the novel, material culture, and world history. She is currently working on a book manuscript that traces similar changes in Chinese and European narrative works during the early modern period, with the argument that these parallel shifts are related to the rise of a global network of capital flow and commodity exchange.

terry logan mazurak is Bernie McCain Professor of Philosophy and Religion, Emeritus at The College of Idaho where he taught for twenty-seven years. He is a graduate of Carleton College and the University of Washington. His current research interests include early Mahayana Buddhism, the phenomenology of Edmund Husserl and Buddhist Modernism. He and his wife Kristina live in Caldwell, Idaho.

rachana sachdev is Associate Professor of English and Coordinator of Asian Studies at Susquehanna University. She has published several articles on early modern gynecological discourses; the most recent, "Of Paps and Dugs: Nursing Breasts in Shakespeare's England," appeared in *English Language Notes* 47, 2 (Fall/Winter 2009). Her current research project focuses on representations of infanticide and position of children in Asia in the European travel writing from the early modern era. A brief section of the chapter on Ming China, "Contextualizing Female Infanticide: Ming China in Early Modern European Travelogues" was recently published in *ASIANetwork Exchange* (Fall 2010).